Derbyshire Hearth Tax Assessments

1662-1670

Derbyshire

Hearth Tax

Assessments
1662-70

Edited by David G. Edwards
with an Introduction
incorporating material by the late
C.A.F. Meekings

Derbyshire Record Society

Volume VII, 1982

Published by the Derbyshire Record Society
18 Mill Lane, Wingerworth, Chesterfield, Derbyshire

First published 1982

ISBN 0 9505940 9 1

The hearth-tax assessments for the hundreds of High Peak,
Morleston & Litchurch, Scarsdale and Wirksworth are published
by courtesy of the Derbyshire County Librarian

The photographs of Hartshorne Old Manor House, Melbourne Hall
and Snitterton Hall are reproduced by kind permission of the
Derbyshire County Planning Officer

Printed by H. Charlesworth & Co Ltd, 254 Deighton Road, Huddersfield

CONTENTS

LIST OF TABLES AND ILLUSTRATIONS

Tables

Plates

Figures

FOREWORD AND ACKNOWLEDGEMENTS

In 1947 the Derbyshire Archaeological Society embarked on a plan to publish the county's hearth-tax assessments in a series of instalments, and accordingly approached the Public Record Office to ascertain the nature of the relevant documents there which would supplement the assessments held at Derby Public Library. The society found itself unable to proceed with the project, but meanwhile Mr Cecil Meekings of the PRO, who had made a special study of hearth-tax records, took it upon himself not only to sort out the Derbyshire material, which was in need of some rearrangement, but also to draft an extensive introduction to the assessments and returns and prepare a series of tables showing the total numbers of hearths and entries recorded for each place in the county at different dates. After Mr Meekings's untimely death in 1977, Dr David Crook of the PRO brought this work to the attention of Miss Joan Sinar, the county archivist, happily just at the time when the Derbyshire Record Society, at my own suggestion, decided to include the hearth-tax assessments in its publishing programme.

Mr Meekings's text and figures have made my own task much easier; indeed, I could not have hoped to write anything so full about the administration of the tax in the county or to compile such a comparative table of totals. The introduction which follows has therefore been a joint effort, and it is only fair to indicate the division of responsibility. Section 1 is largely my own work but incorporates certain phrases from Mr Meekings's transcript. Section 2 (including Table 1) is a joint effort. Section 3 represents the bulk of Mr Meekings's text, subject only to minor editing and a little additional material. Sections 4 to 6 and the appendix are practically entirely mine. Table 2 is based on Mr Meekings's tabulation, but I have checked all the figures relating to the assessments published here, and I have made a few amendments to the remainder on the basis of other evidence. I alone am responsible for Tables 3 and 4. In section 4 I have attempted some analysis of the assessments, but with the object only of indicating topics which I hope others will study more deeply. I welcome constructive comments from readers.

The choice of assessments for publication is dealt with in section 2 of the introduction. The houses illustrated in the photographs are not intended to be fully representative of those which survive in the county from the period of the assessments, but have been chosen as good examples of the more modest gentry dwellings still plentiful in Derbyshire, especially the north.

It remains to acknowledge my indebtedness not only to the late Cecil Meekings but also to the following people in addition to those mentioned on p.iv and in the list of references (section 6 of the introduction): Dr David Crook, Assistant Keeper, Public Record Office, for supplying and permitting the use of Mr Meekings's manuscript material and notes, and for other assistance and encouragement; Mrs Anne Mellors, Local Studies Librarian, Derby Public Library, for the loan of photocopies of the assessments held at Derby; Mr Philip Riden, secretary of the Derbyshire Record Society, for transcribing the assessments for Borrowash, Spondon, Coton, Rosliston, Repton, Walton on Trent and Winshill from the relevant documents at the Public Record Office, and for arranging the supply of microfilm copies of the assessments for the remainder of the hundreds of Appletree and Repton & Gresley from the PRO; Mr Frank Fisher of Ashleyhay for lending me his own transcript of the assessments held at Derby, which has served as a useful check on my own; Mr Anthony Fletcher and Dr David Hey of the University of Sheffield, as well as Mr Philip Riden, for critically reading the introduction in draft and suggesting points for improvement; the president and other committee members of the Derbyshire Record Society, for assistance and encouragement; Mrs Jeanne Barthorpe of Wingerworth, for drawing the final versions of Figures 1 and 2; Carol Bretman for typing much of the final camera-ready copy of the book; and lastly, my family, for tolerating - good-humouredly for the most part - my activity in this project.

If I may be allowed a personal note in conclusion, it seems appropriate that, having a professional qualification in fuel technology and employment in that field, I should take it upon myself to deal with the records of a tax on fireplaces, coincidental though such a fusion of interests may be.

David Edwards
Wingerworth, 1982

INTRODUCTION

1. The hearth tax : its nature and general history

The Hearth Tax, or Chimney Money as it was popularly called, a type of levy entirely new to England, was introduced in 1662 and withdrawn in 1689. It was at the rate of two shillings per annum for each hearth or stove assessed. Although the idea of such a tax may seem quaint to present-day readers, it has to be remembered that the period from the Restoration to the reign of Queen Anne was one of experiment in the field of national and business finance. Among other things, it saw the founding of the Bank of England in 1694 and Parliament's attainment of a much greater degree of control over the supply of revenue to the sovereign. It was the period of final transition from medieval to modern in public finance.

The hearth tax, granted to Charles II and his heirs in perpetuity by the Act of 1662 (14 Charles II, c.10)[1], was intended to be part of the 'ordinary' revenue of the king, that is, the finance necessary to conduct the normal business of government for the whole of his reign. The Convention Parliament, which sat from April to December 1660, failed to grant Charles an adequate ordinary revenue. A committee appointed by the Commons reported in September 1660 that an annual sum of £1,200,000 would be sufficient. However, it was soon apparent that income from the existing sources would fall seriously short of this, and by mid-1661 it had become clear that the deficiency was in the region of 25 per cent. A number of reasons combined to make Parliament reluctant to fulfil its financial obligation to the king completely, and a number of proposals fell by the wayside before, on 1 March 1662 and apparently in response to further pressure from Charles, a bill was brought in suddenly for a levy on fire hearths. This bill became law on 19 May. The new tax did not completely answer requirements for a long time; in fact the intended total annual yield of £1,200,000 for the ordinary revenue was never achieved in the first twenty years after the Restoration, and the initial yield of the hearth tax itself was far short of £300,000.

The exact authorship of the idea for this tax is uncertain, as also is the amount of support and opposition it received in the Commons between the introduction and passing of the bill. In view of the unpopularity of the tax in the country at large throughout the period of its imposition, it is not surprising that nobody wished to claim credit for the proposal. However, there are grounds for supposing that Sir William Petty - the foremost economic thinker of the time[2] - was concerned in its germination, though the idea would not have been an original one, as a similar tax was in operation in France and the United Provinces at the same period. It seems more than a coincidence that Petty's Treatise of Taxes and Contributions[3], which sought to justify such a tax, was written early in 1662.

Between 1662 and 1688 the hearth tax formed one of the three principal branches of the nation's ordinary revenue, with a reasonable yield after a shaky start which was due as much as anything to defects in administration. The other two main branches were the Customs and the Excise, the remainder of the ordinary revenue coming from Crown lands and a host of lesser sources. The customs dues were of long standing, but excise duties dated only from 1643 (introduced by the Parliamentary regime) and were continued at the Restoration partly as compensation to Charles for the loss of the proceeds of the Court of Wards and other feudal dues which had effectively been abolished in 1646 and which Charles agreed not to resume. It was traditional that ordinary revenue should be raised by indirect taxation such as the customs and excise, and that direct taxes such as the Subsidy should be reserved for 'extraordinary' revenue, i.e. to finance war and meet other unusual expenses. However, this principle had been violated during the Interregnum by the use of the Monthly Assessment (a form of land tax). It may seem that the hearth tax violated it too, as being a direct levy on persons, but in fact it was looked on by the government and others - notably Sir William Petty - as a form of excise: the number of hearths that a person had in his house could be regarded as a reflection of his purchasing power. This may have been very well in theory, but by those on whom it fell, the tax had the appearance of a direct levy like the Poll Tax and, worse than that tax, it was permanent.

There is plenty of evidence of the unpopularity of the hearth tax[4]. Hostility was especially marked after the revising Act of 1663 (15 Charles II, c.13) empowered constables to enter houses to check the accuracy of the assessments (a power reinforced by the second revising Act of 1664, 16 Charles II, c.3), during the periods when the tax was farmed out to private individuals and at times of national crisis. In Derbyshire, disaffection does not seem to have reached the level of homicide as in Dorset, where a chimney officer was killed in riot at Bridport, but Cox noted in the county records one case of grievous assault on a collector[5]. The justification for such opposition cannot be discussed here, but it should be mentioned that the Commons were generally hostile to the tax from about 1666 to 1681 and that the traditional Whig historical view of it as an oppression - best exemplified by Macaulay's account - evidently needs some correction. It was the Revolution of 1688 which put an end to the tax: William III ordered its abolition the following year as a political move to win popular support (1 William & Mary, c.10). Ironically this action occurred just when the tax was realising, under efficient administration, its full potential value, and only a few years later it was found necessary to introduce the almost equally odious Window Tax.

The actual tax, as laid down by the 1662 Act, was to be paid in two equal instalments at Ladyday (25 March) and Michaelmas (29 September). Payment was to be made by the occupier of the premises or, if they were vacant, by the owner. There were of course some exemptions: people who were too poor to be liable for the usual taxes and the church and poor rates, and those who - upon certification by the parish officers and the minister each year - occupied premises worth not more than 20s per annum or possessed real or personal property worth not more than £10. However, under the second revising Act, no person with more than two hearths was to be exempt. Also exempt were hearths and stoves in hospitals or almshouses endowed with no more than £100 per annum, private ovens within houses, and 'any blowing house and stamp furnace or kiln'. This last category of exemption gave rise to much dispute and was of particular concern in Hallamshire and the adjoining district of north Derbyshire as well as other areas of the country. The conflict arose from the interpretation of the words 'blowing house and stamp furnace or kiln' in relation to the hearths or forges of smiths. Official judgement on this point was pronounced more than once, sometimes clearly, sometimes rather ambiguously (at least to the modern reader). It seems that the government and the legal profession decided that smiths' hearths by no means fell into the category of blowing houses, 'because there is that which is properly and usually called a blowing house and that is a place used for melting of iron or lead ore which was the only thing meant by the Act to be excepted under the word blowing-house'[6]. This interpretation of the letter of the law was no doubt correct, but in the country it was contended that such a judgement was contrary to the spirit of the Act: the justices, in Yorkshire at least, insisted that it was their prerogative to be the arbiters on such matters and ordered payments and distresses exacted on smiths' forges to be reimbursed, since in their opinion such forges were included in the concept of blowing houses[7].

It is significant that in the hearth-tax assessments for 1672 both in the West Riding[8] and in Scarsdale hundred[9] the numbers of forges were specified separately from personal hearths against each person. Although it is doubtful whether the argument was ever properly settled, the Hallamshire smiths were eventually relieved of tax demands on their forges, according to Sir John Reresby, so the Yorkshire justices implicity won their point. The above quotation incidentally makes it clear that there seems no justification for one modern writer's implied statement that lead-smelting furnaces were liable for the tax[10].

For more details of the general history of the hearth tax the reader must be referred to the sources already quoted (especially L.M. Marshall and the Calendar of Treasury Books - though the figures quoted for the receipts of the tax by W.A. Shaw in his introduction to the latter are often erroneous) and, for by far the best modern discussion of its administration, to the work of C.D. Chandaman[11]. A recent general history of the period also provides a useful less-detailed background[12]. Reference may also be made to published hearth-tax records for other counties[13].

2. The surviving records and their selection for the present collection

The main importance of the hearth tax for the modern student lies in its essential by-product: lists of inhabitants for every place in England together with some indication (in the number of hearths in their occupation) of their social standing. Unfortunately, the records which contain these lists were legally returnable to local and central government (that is, to the quarter sessions and the King's Remembrancer's Office of the Exchequer) only during certain of the administrations which managed the tax. There were similar records at other periods, but they seem to be practically all lost and those few that remain are nearly all in private custody. Hence, in the Public Record Office or other public collections we can find such records for only three administrative periods, namely: (1) 1662 Michaelmas - 1664 Ladyday (sheriffs); (2) 1664 Michaelmas - 1665 Ladyday, and in a few cases 1666 Ladyday also (receivers); (3) 1669 Michaelmas - 1674 Ladyday (receivers). The periods for which there are generally no records are those in which the tax was farmed out (1666-9 and 1674-84) and in which direct collection was finally reverted to, under a commission (1684-8).

Table 1 summarizes the documents which survive for Derbyshire, in the Public Record Office(class E179) and in Derby Public Library (Derbyshire Collection). It had been hoped to reproduce the lists for 1664, supplemented where necessary by those of 1662, as providing the most coherent if not quite the most comprehensive set of names. However, it proved too expensive to procure photocopies of all the appropriate documents from the Public Record Office. The Society has therefore been obliged to take the second-best course of publishing the lists of names and hearths for 1670 Michaelmas preserved at Derby for the hundreds of High Peak, Morleston & Litchurch, Scarsdale and Wirksworth, together with the 1662 or 1664 lists for Appletree and Repton & Gresley. Although this course leaves something to be desired, it has been possible to supplement the lists by Table 2 (p.lviii) showing the totals of names and hearths recorded at 1662 and 1664 as well as 1670, which should go some way towards satisfying the social or economic historian.

The lists are records produced by the various administrators of a tax for their own purposes and not for those of the modern genealogist or historian. Consequently some remarks on the administrations which produced them are essential to full understanding of the records themselves; these remarks, together with details of the documents, form Section 3 following.

TABLE 1. THE PRINCIPAL SURVIVING HEARTH-TAX RECORDS FOR DERBYSHIRE

Hundred	Appletree	High Peak	Morleston & Litchurch	Repton & Gresley	Scarsdale	Wirksworth
<u>1662</u>						
E 179/94/378	D	G	G(1)	F	D	G
E 179/245/7	D(2)	D(2)	D(2)	*D(2)	D(2)	D(2)
E 179/245/8	G	-	-	-	-	-
<u>1664</u>(3)						
E 179/94/400	-	-	-	-	G(4)	-
E 179/94/401	-	-	G(5)	-	-	-
E 179/94/402	-	-	-	-	-	G(6)
E 179/94/403	-	G(7)	-	-	-	-
E 179/94/404	-	-	?	-	-	-
E 179/94/405	*G(8)	-	-	-	-	-
E 179/245/10	-	-	-	D	-	-
<u>1670</u>						
DC 9953	-	-	-	-	-	G
DC 9954	-	-	-	-	G	-
DC 9955	-	G(9)	-	-	-	-
DC 9956	-	-	G	-	-	-
<u>1672</u>						
E 179/94/394	-	-	-	-	D(10)	-
E 179/245/9	D(11)	D(12)	-	-	-	D(13)

Indication of completeness and/or legibility:
D = defective F = fair G = good

* Microfilm copy at Derby Reference Library

Footnotes:

1. Derby is largely missing
2. See p.xx.
3. 'Not chargeable' hearths or persons are included.
4. Possibly one membrane missing; no separate assessment for some places which are identifiable at other dates.
5. Markeaton missing.
6. Bonsall and Newton Grange missing.
7. Some 80 entries illegible.
8. Borrowash and Spondon missing; Shottle and Postern largely illegible.
9. The individual townships in the constablewicks of Hathersage and Tideswell (thirteen in all) are not identified, nor are two townships in other constablewicks.
10. Six constablewicks missing.
11. Two membranes missing out of twenty-four; parts illegible.
12. Three membranes missing out of thirty-six; parts illegible.
13. One membrane missing out of twenty-one.

Further documents available:

- E 179/370/17 - arrears schedule ('desperate') for county
- E 179/326/7 - exemption certificates for county, 1670-1 (but not adding any names to DC 9953-6)
- E 179/326/8 - ditto, 1673-4

3. The administration of the tax in Derbyshire

3.1 Under the sheriffs, 1662-4

Three Derbyshire sheriffs - Sir William Boothby of Broadlowash, Sir Thomas Gresley of Drakelow, and George Vernon of Sudbury[14] - were the local heads of the administration during the four collections from Michaelmas 1662 to Ladyday 1664, when the tax was managed by the local government in the counties. During this period two assessments were made: one in the summer of 1662, on which the instalments due at Michaelmas 1662 and Ladyday and Michaelmas 1663 were collected, and the other in the winter of 1663-4 on which the Ladyday 1664 instalment was collected. In all, according to these assessments the Derbyshire sheriffs should have collected £4064 3s for the four collections. In fact they collected £3914 17s 3d, of which the Exchequer received (between 12 February 1663 and 7 December 1664) £3800 14s 8d, the balance, £114 2s 7d, being retained locally as the poundages to which the sheriffs, high and petty constables and clerk of the peace were statutorily entitled for their work. £149 5s 9d was not collected, and of this total a very small amount was lost in certificates exempting from payment persons already included in the assessment, which certificates the Exchequer auditors allowed, whilst rather more was lost in certificates and returns claiming exemption which the parish officials submitted but the auditors disallowed. The two items, 'certified exempt' and 'desperate arrears' as they were called, accounted for £25 15s of the uncollected money. The other arrears were classed by the auditors as 'recoverable': £118 4s from constables and £5 7s from individual persons. There was a small book-keeping surplus of 3d. In short, the Derbyshire sheriffs collected about 98 per cent of what they should have done: a very high percentage, since for the whole of England and Wales the amount collected only slightly exceeded 80 per cent of the amount assessed. So far, therefore, as collection on the persons and their hearths listed in the enrolled assessments is concerned, Derbyshire was well above the average. Nearly everyone listed paid, and paid for the full total of hearths at which they were assessed.

We may now briefly examine the administration and records of each of the three sheriffs, beginning our remarks on each with an abstract of the account which the sheriff had to have audited and declared in the Exchequer before he could be discharged from his connection with the tax.

DERBYSHIRE	Account of William Boothby, Bt, late sheriff, for half a year ending 1662 Mich.		
Charge	On 20,964 hearths* in the county less the duty on 5370 which was received by his successor		£779 14s 0d
Discharge	Poundages**	£21 15s 2d	
	Payments to Exchequer***	£724 18s 0d	
			£746 13s 2d
		Remains	£33 0s 10d
Arrears,	on constables, recoverable		£20 17s 0d
	on persons, recoverable		£3 4s 0d
	on persons, desperate		£9 0s 0d
		Surplus	2d

Sworn: 7 Nov. 1664 Declared: 10 Dec. 1664

*Detailed, viz: Derby 1479; Scarsdale 5523; Repton & Gresley 1995; Morleston & Litchurch 2374; Wirksworth 2411; High Peak 4217; Appletree 2965

**Sheriff 3d; clerk of the peace 1d; high constables 1d; petty constables 2d

***Detailed, viz: £500, 12 Feb. 1663; £218 16s 7d, 11 May 1663; £6 1s 5d, 7 Dec. 1664

Four sorts of records go to the making of this account. The Exchequer duplicate of assessment is summarized as the 'charge'; the returns and the tallies, showing what was and was not collected and how much was paid to the Exchequer, are summarized in the 'discharge'; and the arrears schedules, showing what was still owing (after the auditors had gone through the returns), are summarized in the 'remains'. All tallies of this date are lost, but their details are recoverable elsewhere. The other records, which all comprise lists of names, have all been preserved, so we may now say a word about each of them.

E 179/94/378. Exchequer duplicate of assessment for Michaelmas 1662 (63 mm.). This is a parchment roll, defective and incomplete. The first membrane is a heading, signed by three justices and the clerk of the peace, describing the assessment as enrolled at the general quarter sessions beginning on 17 July 1662. The following membranes bear contemporary numbers. The Derby lists come first, but of these m.1 is a small fragment, m.2 is lost and mm. 3 and 4 are very imperfect. Scarsdale hundred occupies mm. 5-21, being generally defective and illegible. Repton & Gresley hundred fills mm. 22-27; some of these membranes have lost their heads, so a few names are lost for several places: Bretby, Castle Gresley, Chilcote, Coton, Ingleby, Measham, Melbourne & King's Newton, Normanton, Repton, Stanton by Bridge and Walton on Trent. Morleston & Litchurch hundred occupies mm. 28-37, Wirksworth hundred mm. 37-46 and High Peak hundred mm. 47-58; these are generally complete and in good condition. Appletree hundred fills mm. 59-63, one or two membranes being wanting at the end. These can be recovered from the item next described. Throughout the roll the lists are written in two or three columns on the face of the membranes only.

E 179/245/8. Exchequer duplicate of assessment, Michaelmas 1662 (copy) (52ff.). This is a copy of the above enrolment made by the clerks in the Exchequer auditor's office for issue to the receiver newly appointed at Michaelmas 1664 (the date it bears), but covers Appletree hundred only[15]. It supplies details of places now wanting from the previous item. The lists are written on each side of the folios, in single columns.

This was the first assessment to be made, and had been delivered to the Exchequer by 21 September 1662. It was rapidly made and, as was generally the case with these first assessments, speedily enrolled and sent up to London by the clerk of the peace. The county copy, enrolled for the sheriff, is now lost.

We have seen from his account that Boothby received money from only about four-fifths of the county. This is a common feature of this first collection. In October and November the constables and sheriff went out of office, but the original Act had not made it clear whether incoming or outgoing sheriff was to manage the collection. We can assume that the old petty constables made the collection and handed the money over to the high constables in the early autumn. By that time the old sheriff would be on the point of retiring. An impasse frequently arose, neither incoming nor outgoing sheriff being willing to complete the collection. Elsewhere this difficulty not only caused great delay: it led to the loss of money collected and to some unrest. Whatever difficulties there may have been between Boothby and his successor Thomas Gresley, they were soon composed. Boothby paid his last instalment to the Exchequer in May 1663 and Gresley paid in the Michaelmas money which he had received at the same time as he made his first payment of Ladyday money, in July.

E 179/245/7. Particulars of account and arrears schedules, Michaelmas 1662 (211 ff. and 3mm.). This consists of:

(i) A check list, giving the names of the petty constables in 1662 arranged by hundreds, within which the constables appear to be arranged in alphabetical order of the parishes and constablewicks.

(ii) Returns for each of the six hundreds. Each batch is preceded by the high constable's return for the hundred as a whole, an example of which is given later. It shows which petty constables had submitted returns and which had not. It thus acts as a table of contents for each hundred and enables one to discover at a glance whether the return for a particular place exists.

(iii) The three arrears schedules, namely of arrears depending on constables, on persons recoverable and on persons desperate.

The outstanding point about the returns is that they were made out not, as we should suppose, in the autumn of 1662 but in October 1664. The explanation of this is simple. The original Act had failed to make clear the manner in which the sheriffs should account for the tax, and by the summer of 1664 the sheriffs had been replaced as local administrators by receivers and rules had been laid down on the way in which they were to account. Treasury letters were sent out with instructions to the sheriffs, and Boothby, on receiving the Treasury letter, ordered the high constables then in office to obtain, from the petty constables who had made the 1662 collections, complete lists showing who had and had not paid. The high constables delivered these lists to the sheriff on 8 October 1664, together with their own return showing what petty constables had neglected to obey the order and the arrears, if any, owing from them. An example of these high constables' returns, for Repton & Gresley hundred, is transcribed on p.112 of this volume. From it we see that there are no returns for Coton & Rosliston, Repton, Winshill or Walton on Trent, but all the returns for the other twenty-five constablewicks follow.

The following summary gives the numbers of constables in the other hundreds who did or did not submit returns, with a note of the places which were in arrears where no returns had been submitted. The total number for High Peak is small because most constablewicks comprised several places.

Hundred	Returns submitted	No returns
Appletree	20	27
High Peak	9	5
Morleston & Litchurch	35*	12**
Scarsdale	27	4
Wirksworth	9	14

Appletree: Chaddesden 11s, Ednaston 18s (noted as since paid); the rest were quit

High Peak: Chelmorton £3 3s, Hathersage 1s; Bakewell, Bowden Chapel and Eyam were quit

Morleston & Litchurch: Heanor 7s, Ilkeston 2s, Ripley 1s, four constables in Derby 20s; Barrow, Crich, Darley, Littleover and Long Eaton were quit

Scarsdale: Eckington £4 16s, Dronfield 7s, Dore & Totley 10s; Morton was quit

Wirksworth: Hopton & Carsington £3 6s, Hognaston £2 10s, Middleton & Cromford 4s, Matlock 3s (noted as since paid); Bonsall, Callow & Ible, Dethick Tansley & Lea, Fenny Bentley, Hartington, Kirk Ireton, Mapleton & Thorpe, Middleton & Smerrill, Parwich and Wensley & Snitterton were quit

*includes two constables in Derby

**includes four constables in Derby

If the response to Boothby's order was rather poor in Appletree and Wirksworth hundreds, the general state of affairs was quite satisfactory; only a few petty constables had seriously failed.

The returns themselves contain much of interest. Some are clearly the original paper assessments which the petty constables made in 1662 (or else an exact copy of it) and sent to the clerk of the peace for him to enrol. After enrolment they seem to have been returned to the petty constables, who now made use of them once more as a return. The Bolsover return is particularly interesting, for it is written in an engrossing hand and the names are arranged in alphabetical order. There are a number of others, including one for Pleasley and Langwith where the total is given as 'Fower Skoare & Five' but where the writing and arrangement are neat. Most of the returns however were specially written in the autumn of 1664. All are countersigned by the high constable of the hundred to the effect that this and no other return was received from the petty constable for 1662. They also give some information about the collections. The constables of Allestree and Weston Underwood, for example, paid their moneys to the high constable in 1662 on 7 and 21 November respectively; the constable of Alvaston & Boulton also paid in on 21 November. Details on these and other returns show that the high constables gave written acquittances to the petty constables for what they received. It is therefore reasonable to assume that when Boothby made his first payment to the Exchequer in February 1663 he was merely remitting a lump sum out of receipts that were still coming in, but that his payment in May represented the balance of all he had collected.

The arrears schedules, which are each quite short, list defaulters with the amount due from them as summarized at the foot of the account. The desperate-arrears schedule contained defaulters with one or two hearths only. It was a voucher which discharged the sheriff for the total contained in it; no attempt was made to recover such arrears - whence the name. The amounts owing were: Appletree 11s; Scarsdale 114s; Repton & Gresley 7s; Wirksworth 48s. The schedule of recoverable arrears depending on persons contained defaulters who had three or more hearths. Both this and the schedule of arrears depending on constables were issued to the receiver (who replaced the sheriffs) for him to attempt to recover the moneys. It really concerns only three places: Heanor, where the parsonage of three hearths was in arrears; the vicarage and five other houses in Dronfield (31 hearths); and ten persons with three hearths apiece in Eckington. The arrears depending on constables may be summarised thus: in Scarsdale and Wirksworth hundreds, £7 each; in High Peak £5 14s; in Morleston and Litchurch £1 3s. Eckington appears as the largest place where the petty constable really neglected his duty, since apart from the 30s owing from persons there was 66s of desperate arrears and the constable himself was charged with £4 19s. Nothing had been collected in Hopton & Carsington (66 hearths) and Chelmorton (63 hearths). These three places thus account for about half the arrears owing from the whole county, the balance being made up by varying amounts from some twenty different places.

On the whole, few people whose names were enrolled in 1662 obtained certificates exempting them from paying that autumn: wariness and evasion came later. Among these returns there are however some examples of certificates, though they were made out in the autumn of 1664 and not in 1662. To an Exchequer auditor, none of them was sufficient. He required the countersignature of a justice of the peace against the signatures of incumbent, churchwardens, overseers, constable and parish clerk. None of these exemption certificates had such a justice's signature; hence there is no item for exemptions in Boothby's account. The auditor's rule in these cases was to disregard the certificate and make the petty constable himself responsible for the moneys collected. For example, in the constablewick of Bowden Middlecale forty persons, each with a single hearth, are included in a certificate; for Wirksworth there is a similar list of forty persons whose wealth was declared to be 'not sofishant' for them to pay the tax. In the constables' arrears schedules the constables for both these places are charged with £2. Throughout 1663 the tendency grew for persons to obtain exemption certificates. The language of the following example can be paralleled from many places in other counties. There is always the insistence that the first assessment was too strict and included many with grounds for exemption.

> Returns of those that did not pay for theire harths att Michaelmas 1662 and are exempt by the Act.
> Wee the Minister and Churchwardens & other Inhabitants within Tadington & Presley doe humbly Certiffye the Right Worshipffull Justices of the peace & all other whome it may concerne:
> That wee beleeve the Late Headborrowes of Taddington and Prestcliffe were to strict in puting in the Fire Harths within Taddington and Prestcliffe Foruppon our view of the said harths wee Find it to bee thus.
> George Eaton hath a little Cottage, neare to his dwelling house that hath no harth the Chymney is Covered with Clods, neither hath there been any Fire in the said Cottage for six yeares Last past: the house is now a stable or beast house.
> Humphrey Dakin & his Chilldren Live by Almes among their Neighbors & pay not any assessments or Lownes either to King or Church.
> John Kirke Left his Cottage about August Last & took anothere tenement with a Fire harth and now dwells in the same & pays For it.
> Ellice Rowork is put in For one Chymney which never had hearth nor Fire

Kindled in it since the house was built.
Richard Willshaw is put in For a Chymney which hath no hearth belonging to it, the Chymney is walled up in the inside & hath had noe Fire Kindled in it above 12 yeares last past.
Robert Dakin, Isaack Wibbersley & Hugh Wibbersley of Prestcliffe & Henry Gould senior And Edward Rowland of Taddington are put in for Chimneyes of very small Coates which have noe hearths belonging unto them, nor any thing els, unlesse it bee a little Furnace & imployed to no other use but bakeweinge theire houshold bread in; all which persons above named pay honestly & willingly For the Fire harths in the houses wherein they dwell

(signed) Anthony Mellor — Minnestr' of Taddington
Geo: Bagshaw &)
Isaak Wibbersley) Church Wardens
(endorsed) Wormhill

In studying the arrears schedules above, we dealt with Boothby's completed account. It may be noted that the final payment he made to the Exchequer just before his account was declared represents money collected - about £6 5s - as a result of the stirring-up of the constables in the autumn of 1664. In High Peak hundred for example, £1 18s was owing from Hope constablewick just before the returns were sent in, but this was paid up on 8 October.

We may now study the next account, which is as follows.

DERBYSHIRE	Account of Thomas Gresley, Knight, late sheriff, for a year ending 1663 Michaelmas		
Charge	On 20,964 hearths in the county for the year	£2096 8s	
	On 5370 hearths for 1662 Mich.	£268 10s	£2364 18s
Discharge	Exemptions, detailed*		£2 1s
	Poundages	£65 11s 4d	
	Payments to Exchequer**	£2183 6s 8d	£2248 18s
		Remains	£113 19s
Arrears,	on constables	£97 7s	
	on persons, recoverable	£2 3s	
	on persons, desperate	£14 9s	
		Even	
Sworn: 12 Aug. 1664	Declared: 20 Aug. 1664		

*In Ashbourne 38 hearths and in Coton 3; the names are given.
**Detailed, viz: £901 15s 8d (for Ladyday) and £260 7s 2d (for Michaelmas 1662), 17 July 1663; £1000, 20 May 1664; £21 3s 10d, 10 Aug. 1664

There was no new assessment, the one already described serving for both half-years, as elsewhere in the country. The 'returns' are lost. Considerable interest attaches to this particular account, since it was the first to be audited and declared according to certain Treasury regulations of July 1664 which provided, among other things, for three distinct arrears schedules instead of the single composite schedule prepared hitherto. It also laid down that each account should be signed by the Exchequer auditor responsible for it. It was the first of over a hundred hearth-tax accounts to be laid out in this manner and only the eighth (out of some 170) of the sheriffs' accounts of the tax to be declared.

The Michaelmas 1662 collection was a fairly good one, but receipts from it came only slowly to the Exchequer. The Ladyday 1663 collection was much poorer and its receipts came in even more slowly. During the current session of Parliament therefore, Charles II's ministers, through the Treasury secretary Sir Philip Warwick and others who sat in the Commons and Lord Ashley the Chancellor of the Exchequer, attempted to get the first revising Act passed, which would remedy existing defects and ensure that the revenue collected equalled the assessed value of some £170,000 less costs of collection. Early in their session the Commons examined all the Exchequer duplicates of assessment and found little wrong with them, confirming the total by a vote on 4 June 1663. They were in an intractable mood however, and it was not until Charles II announced his intention of proroguing them within a week that they got down to the business of passing the Act desired by the ministerial members. It was rushed through in so short a time that final touches were still being added on the day the session ended. It is not at all surprising therefore that it did not wholly remedy the existing defects, especially those in the machinery of collection, which was what was really at fault. It did however attempt to simplify the existing provisions about exemption, provisions which had been added to the original bill, rather clumsily, during debate. A new assessment was to be made, to include everyone occupying a house or chambers. Those who ought to pay were to be included in a 'chargeable' section and those who were entitled to exemption were to be included in a 'not chargeable' section.

In most places this new assessment was made in the winter of 1663-4 (i.e. much later than the government had intended) and in nearly all places the collection at Ladyday 1664 was based on it. The government had hoped that it might be prepared in time for the collection at Michaelmas 1663. The Treasury tried to supplement the revising Act by letters addressed to the justices of the peace at both autumn and winter sessions, suggesting means of improving the collection including the appointment of some one person to 'solicit' or look after it. Where such appointments were made, the clerk of the peace was usually the person so selected by the justices. These had little effect: the decline in receipts continued. So, when the Commons reassembled in the early spring of 1664 they were told bluntly by Charles II that, though he asked no extraordinary supply of them he expected them to make sure that he got what they had granted. They were in a better humour now and passed the second revising Act, which discharged the sheriffs and local officials from administering the tax, allowed the king to create his own machinery of administration, and clarified the code of exemptions. At the time this was done only a very few of the 1664 Ladyday duplicates had reached the Exchequer, so the Treasury did not know what results the first revising Act had had on them. Had it known, it would have been even more anxious to replace the sheriffs by a more efficient administration. For there was everywhere a decline, amounting in the country as a whole to some 200,000 hearths: a loss of some 12 per cent or £20,000 a year in tax. Derbyshire, as we can see from the following abstract, suffered a decline by about the average percentage.

DERBYSHIRE	Account of George Vernon Esq., late sheriff, by Benjamin Edbury, gent.[16], his deputy, for half a year ending Ladyday 1664		
Charge	On 18,148 enrolled hearths*	£907 8s	
	and on 243 hearths not enrolled but on which the duty was collected	£12 3s	£919 11s
Discharge	Poundages	£26 16s 1d	
	Payments to Exchequer**	£892 10s	£919 6s 1d
	Remains		4s 11d
Arrears, on persons, desperate			5s
	Surplus		1d

Sworn: 15 Dec. 1664 Declared: 22 Dec. 1664

*Detailed, viz: Morleston & Litchurch (inc. Derby) 3409; Appletree 2350; Scarsdale 4852; Wirksworth 1971; High Peak 3767; Repton & Gresley 1799. These are of course totals of 'chargeable' hearths only.

**Detailed, viz: £760, 24. Sep. 1664; £132 10s, 7 Dec. 1664

Apart from the decline in assessment we may compare the amount which the Exchequer received from Derbyshire for this collection with that received from the 1662 Michaelmas collection up to July 1663, which was £979 3s 9d (i.e. excluding the small amount which Boothby collected by prompting the constables in October 1664). In other words, in less than two years there had been a decline of £90 in the real value of the tax in the county. Plainly both assessment and collection at Ladyday 1664 show how great was the need for a more efficient administration.

Moreover Derbyshire, in respect of both the smallness of the arrears and the speed with which its sheriffs passed their accounts, was considerably better than most counties. This point may be emphasised. At the end of December 1664 all three Derbyshire sheriffs (Boothby being the nineteenth and Vernon the thirtieth) had had their accounts declared. In no other county were all the sheriffs quit. There were still outstanding fifty accounts for 1662 Michaelmas and sixty for 1663, and for Ladyday 1664 only two others had been declared at all. Not until February 1665 was Derbyshire joined by Staffordshire and a few other counties in having all its accounts declared. In spite of all Ashley's efforts, nearly half the counties still had one or more accounts to be declared when the plague in London put a stop to all business in July. On the whole therefore, the two Derbyshire sheriffs or their men of business, and Benjamin Edbury, appear as rather better administrators than most of their brethren.

The returns for this collection are lost, but the small arrears schedule (E 179/370/17; 1m.) and nearly all the Exchequer duplicate of assessment survive. The latter is particularly important. At first this may seem paradoxical, since the total of hearths at 1664 Ladyday is so much lower than in 1662. These however are chargeable hearths only. If we add the total of not-chargeable hearths we get a grand total which usually greatly exceeds the total hearths recorded in 1662. This is found wherever we can compare the two assessments, as the following figures from neighbouring counties show.

Hearths	1664			1662
	Chargeable	Not chargeable	Total	
Lancashire	34,995	12,256	47,251	43,488
Leicestershire	20,120	4,427	24,547	21,934
Staffordshire	26,830	7,441	34,271	29,134
Warwickshire	21,457	5,530	26,967	23,815
Chester City	2,861	494	3,355	3,004

We are however concerned more with the number of persons than of hearths, and here (with a small number of exceptions) it is true of the whole country that, wherever the assessments have survived to enable us to make a comparison, the 1664 Ladyday assessment contains more names than any other. Table 2 shows how far this is true for Derbyshire. We may illustrate the point here by a few Cheshire examples, as follows.

Persons	1664			1662
	Chargeable	Not chargeable	Total	
Chester	900	459	1359	925
Nantwich	322	326	648	272
Congleton	235	197	432	195
Sandbach	105	47	152	110
Middlewich	80	60	140	81
Audlem	60	76	136	61
Northwich	46	82	128	55
Witton	45	51	96	49

There are exceptions of course, sometimes important ones. In our own county for example, whereas the 1670 assessment gives 611 names for Derby there are only 504 names at Ladyday 1664. Of these, 478 are 'chargeable', so the reason for the exception is plain: the 'not chargeable' section has been scamped. The position in three other towns is more typical:

Total persons	1662	1664	1670
Chesterfield	-	315	211
Wirksworth	236	449	239
Ashbourne	189	229	126

There is no mystery about this. The 'not chargeable' section invited people to get themselves enrolled in it. They might and did wall up their hearths and they got exemption certificates when their qualifications for them were slight if any. But that did not affect their general willingness to have themselves enrolled in a section which they thought (and on this point there is plenty of evidence) would ensure permanent exemption. They were to be grievously mistaken, for the displacement of the sheriffs from office led to new assessments being made at the following Michaelmas. At the time however they fondly imagined that they had secured permanent exemption for themselves, and the modern local historian and genealogist benefit from this misplaced hope. We may see the general influence at work in those returns for Michaelmas 1662 already described, which were made up, it will be remembered, in the autumn of 1664, i.e. several months after the 'chargeable' and 'not chargeable' assessments for Ladyday 1664 had been submitted. We will take a single example from many. In 'Chester, Eaton and Quornden' 42 persons were listed in 1662. The return lists them correctly, but then goes on to give a further list of 19 'not leyable' who had not appeared at all in 1662! But they did appear in the 1664 Ladyday 'not chargeable' section.

The sections of this Ladyday 1664 assessment will now be described briefly. At an unknown date the Exchequer duplicate was split up, so the section for each hundred now has its own reference number. All sections have the same form, being written in columns of 'chargeable' and 'not chargeable' side by side, usually on both sides of the membranes.

E 179/94/401. Derby town and Morleston & Litchurch hundred (13 mm., complete). The face of m.1 and the dorse of m.13,having served as outer covers for the roll, have become rubbed so that on each some twenty entries are illegible; otherwise perfect.

E 179/94/405. Appletree hundred (11 mm., complete). The dorse of m.11 and the tails of mm. 3 and 4 (protruding beyond the rest) have become rubbed; otherwise perfect.

E 179/94/400. Scarsdale hundred (17 mm., probably complete). The tails of mm.9-11 protrude beyond the rest and are slightly damaged, and a few entries on the face of m.13 are illegible; otherwise perfect. The total of hearths comes to some 150 less than the total as given in the account, so it is possible (but by no means certain) that, although the dorse of m.17 is blank, a single membrane may be missing.

E 179/94/402. Wirksworth hundred (9 mm., complete). In excellent condition throughout.

E 179/94/403. High Peak hundred (17 mm., complete). Some eighty entries in all, on parts of mm. 13, 14, 16 and 17, are illegible; otherwise perfect.

E 179/245/10. Repton & Gresley hundred (5 mm., incomplete). Four of the membranes are illegible in parts, and an unknown number of membranes have been lost.

3.2 Under the first receivers, 1664-5

In June 1667 the newly appointed Treasury commissioners were overhauling revenue business with great energy. Among a number of ex-receivers of hearth tax who were brought up by a Treasury serjeant-at-arms, because they had not accounted, was William Allestrey of Derbyshire. He was possibly the 'Mr Wm Allestrey' entered for thirteen hearths under Derby All Saints in 1670. On taking up his post he had had to deposit bonds in £1100 on his own account and three others in £1000. He told the commissioners that he had lost most of his papers, including the new assessment made for Michaelmas 1664. This prepares us for the complete absence of any surviving records of current administration supplementary to the account and also, since Allestrey desired 'to Accompt by the Great Roll', for the use of the old 1662 Michaelmas Exchequer duplicate for the 'charge'.[17]

DERBYSHIRE	Account of William Allestrey Esq., appointed receiver by patent of 23 August 1664, for a year and a half ending Michaelmas 1665		
Charge	Sheriffs' arrears:		
	1662 Mich. account	£24 1s	
	1663 Mich. account	£99 10s	£123 11s
	On 20,964 hearths		£3144 12s
	Total		£3268 3s
Discharge	Poundages*	£182 2s	
	Payments to Exchequer and the London Chamber, detailed**	£2962 12s	£3144 14s
	Remains		£123 9s
Arrears,	on persons recoverable 1663 Mich., not recoverable through lapse of time		£5 7s
	still outstanding on constables from the sheriffs' time, detailed		£118 2s
	Even		

Sworn: 23 July 1667 Declared: 3 Oct. 1667

*Receiver 1s.; petty constables 2d.

**£600, 5 Dec. 1664; £250, 16 June 1665; £56 5s, 8 May 1667; £1772 10s, 9 May 1667 (this sum represents payments made to the City Chamber two years earlier, for which a fictitious tally was now struck in the Exchequer); £202 10s 2d (the same applies) and £81 6s 10d, 17 July 1667

Apart from the surviving book for Appletree hundred, already described (E 179/245/8), which does not appear to have ever been issued to Allestrey, the only surviving record of this account is:

E 179/6193. Commission for the recovery of sheriffs' arrears (8 mm., complete). Commissions, dated 23 June 1665 and 3 March 1666; one copy of the articles of enquiry; and copies of the arrears schedules on constables for 1662 Mich. and 1663 Mich. and on persons for 1662 Mich. and 1663 Mich. Returned to Exchequer: 1 August 1666.

Elsewhere a varying measure of success attended the efforts of the receivers charged with collecting arrears due in the sheriffs' time. Allestrey noted briefly on the dorse of his commission: 'All the persons... refuse to make any payment except two (viz) William Kenderdine Constable of Riply and Mathew Fox Constable of Stensby who hath paid each of them one shilling'. As that was the only result of the enquiry in Derbyshire, we need not trouble further about the instructions laid down in the articles. As for his administration of the current revenue, Allestrey's account shows that he collected roughly £150 more than the first two sheriffs on the same assessment but, as the poundages came to 1s and 2d instead of 7d, the government benefited only to the extent of some £50. This gain was more apparent than real, for as the details of payments show, the money came into the Exchequer and City Chamber much more slowly than under the sheriffs. Moreover, the latter had accounted very promptly, whereas Allestrey, like many of his brethren, did not do so until arrested. The receivers' administration did not bring about the expected improvement, partly because many of the men chosen as receivers were selected rather for past loyalty or present interest than for any business ability, but principally because England, already suffering from that marked economic depression which had been a contributory cause of the sheriffs' failure, entered a protracted and expensive war in the middle of which the plague, first striking at London, gradually spread to parts of the provinces. It is a profound pity that we have no assessment for 1665 for Eyam to place beside the other three we have for that village.

3.3. Under the second receivers, 1669-74

The first receivers had been replaced in the spring of 1666 by the agents of the first hearth-tax farm. The farm was surrendered at the beginning of 1669, with effect from the Michaelmas collection that year. Although the Treasury had had adequate warning of the impending surrender, they had no plan ready for the administration of the tax. Eventually they called on two experts - Col. William Webb, who had been auditor to the late farmers, and Richard Sherwyn, a Treasury clerk of great experience - who were asked to study the business and to draw up a report showing how the revenue might best be managed. This was ready on paper by February 1670, but Ladyday 1670 had passed before it was working in practice. Once more it was to be administration by receivers, but with the defects of that system remedied in the light of the experience of the past five years. Administrative areas were made more uniform in acreage and reduced to thirty-five. Instead of the flat scale of a shilling poundage for all areas, a carefully graduated scale was provided, ranging from 3s in Anglesey to 1s 6d for the London area and Surrey. For Derbyshire, like Cheshire, Lancashire, Nottinghamshire and Staffordshire, the rate was 1s 10s; in the West Riding it was 2s and in Leicestershire 1s 8d. A manual of instruction, a set printed form for exemption certificates and the terms of the commissions of receivership were drawn up by Sherwyn and Webb.

Finally, by Treasury order, Sherwyn and Webb, to whom others were later added, were constituted agents for the tax, with an office and establishment. This removed from the Treasury the burden of day-to-day administrative supervision, leaving it with decisions of policy and of account. The experience since 1662 had shown that the Treasury board was not the best or most efficient instrument for day-to-day departmental business. The agents (whose work was soon extended to deal with all the extraordinary taxation of the last Dutch war) did not concern themselves with the details of receipt, which continued to be the business of the Exchequer, or with audit, which remained the responsibility of the Exchequer auditors. They controlled the receivers' work and kept the Treasury in touch with the state of affairs in each area. Receivers were ordered to account by appointed dates and were suspended from continuing collection until their accounts had been satisfactorily stated; unsatisfactory receivers were dismissed and process set in motion against them, to recover any arrears depending on them.

For assessment the old system of Exchequer duplicates was revived, and sometimes the first series, prepared about Michaelmas 1670, included the names of those exempted by certificate as well as of chargeable persons, but thereafter details of exempt were usually omitted. There was a special place in the printed forms in which the justices filled in the number of the persons listed in the certificate, and the later assessments usually give the number of 'exempt by certificate' without listing the names. It would have been a great waste of money and labour to have included the names of those non-taxpayers on the parchment enrolments when they were all included in the certificates which accompanied the Exchequer duplicate to London.

We may now fit those Derbyshire records which survive into the general picture for this period. They are rather meagre. The local background may be quickly sketched. Gervase Bennet Esq. of Snelston[18], who had been receiver of aids for the county during the Dutch war, was appointed receiver in February 1670[19]. We can assume that he built up his staff of collectors during the spring and summer of that year and that they collected at Michaelmas the year-and-a-half's duty then owing. By the autumn he had died and John Vernon, brother of Sir Henry Vernon, with two partners, Slye and Cleake (whose precise identity is uncertain), applied for the receivership[20]. However, they did not get it, though Vernon obtained the Derbyshire excise subfarm. Thomas Milward was appointed receiver in March 1671[21] and he remained in office until Treasurer Danby brought the administration by receivers to an end with the 1674 Ladyday collection. This may have been the Thomas Milward of Eaton Dovedale who appears in the 1664 assessment under Doveridge, or the man of that name of Chesterfield who died in 1687 with goods valued at £700. Bennet's account, for a year and a half ending Michaelmas 1670, is wanting, but Milward's three accounts survive. The first two, for a year ending Michaelmas 1671 and a year ending Michaelmas 1672, were both sworn on 21 June 1673 and declared on 8 July 1673. The last, for a year and a half ending Ladyday 1674, was both sworn and declared on 4 March 1674/5. They may be summarised as follows.

<u>Charge</u>	Arrears for 1670 Mich.	£46 10s	
	Duty, 1671 Ladyday - 1674 Ladyday	£8060 6s	£8106 16s
<u>Discharge</u>	Exemptions*	£25 12s	
	Allowances for newly built and demolished hearths**	£49 16s	£75 8s
	Auditors' poundage***		£29 12s 10d
	Poundages on collections+		£829 3s 4d
	Payments to Exchequer (25 in all, 18 Aug. 1671 to 2 March 1674/5)		£7102 7s 10d
		<u>Remains</u>	£70 4s
<u>Arrears</u>, depending on smiths' hearths, empty houses and poor persons++			£70 4s

*This represents alterations only, i.e. legal certificates granted to persons already enrolled.

**This also represents alterations.

***This is a refund; the receivers paid their auditors 1d poundage on the total money paid into the Exchequer for each account.

+Receiver 1s 10d, petty constables 2d (for giving help to the receiver's subcollectors in their work), clerk of the peace 1d (for enrolling Exchequer duplicate and county copy)

++These are detailed in each account.

In short, Milward collected £7961 4s out of £8106 16s: rather more than 98 per cent of a 'charge' always substantially higher than that of 1662. The figures given in the 'charge' represent the gross unadjusted total of hearths in the Exchequer duplicates. At Ladyday 1671 it was 22,450; at Michaelmas it rose to 22,545 and in 1672 to 23,320. For the last three half years it was 22,952, but there was not really so large a decline, since the adjustments for the last account were substantially less than for previous ones. We may say that, in round figures, the net adjusted total rose from 22,400 hearths at Ladyday 1671 to nearly 22,900 at Ladyday 1674. In part this reflects improved administration, and the better payment which the receiver obtained for his work. The continuous decline in collections from Michaelmas 1662 was replaced by a small steady increase. This happened over the country as a whole. The net revenue received by the Exchequer for this tax was returned at about £140,000 a year by the agents in 1670; by the end of 1674 it had risen to £155,000.

The surviving supporting documents are few, as follows.

DC 9953-9956 (Derby Public Library, Derbyshire Collection). County copy of assessment, 1670. Covers High Peak, Morleston & Litchurch, Scarsdale and Wirksworth hundreds only. These are four paper books which were originally the collectors' records for these four hundreds. All four are complete and in good condition. The route by which they came to their present repository is in doubt. We also do not know why the corresponding books for Appletree and Repton & Gresley hundreds have apparently not survived.

DC 9953. Wirksworth hundred (50pp.) Collector John Wheeldon (see below, under DC 9955). No constables' names or hearth totals (except the grand total) are given. The pages bear contemporary numbering.

DC 9954. Scarsdale hundred (83pp.) Collector Hugh Wheeldon (see below, under DC 9955). The constables' names are not given. Frequently the figure for the total tax due from a place has been altered. Every tenth page bears contemporary numbering.

DC 9955. High Peak hundred (89pp.) Collectors Hugh and John Wheeldon. They may have taken over from Ed. Needham, described as 'late Collector' in the book. Hugh Wheeldon may have been the man of that name entered for two hearths in Chesterfield in 1670 and who is associated with the house which later became the Peacock Inn[22], or the Mr Wheeldon entered for five hearths in Hasland in 1670. A John Wheeldon appears under Chesterfield with one hearth the same year. The individual places in the constablewicks of Hathersage and Tideswell are not distinguished by headings. At the end of the list for each constablewick appears the name of the constable as well as the statement "Viewed by John Wheeldon & Hugh Wheeldon Collectors'. The pages bear contemporary numbering.

DC 9956. Morleston & Litchurch hundred (60pp). Collectors John Bancroft and Richard Riley. John Bancroft may have been the person of that name entered for three hearths in Derby All Saints in 1670, who appears to have been a baker[23]. A Richard Riley appears in the 1670 assessment under Ripley, with two hearths. The places are arranged in alphabetical order. Again the name of the constable (in one place - Littleover - a woman) is given at the end of the list in most cases. Some of the names in the lists are prefixed by 'f' (perhaps for freeholder) and a couple of others by 'P' (papist?). The pages were not originally numbered. Pages, not places, are totalled for hearths.

E 179/326/7. Exemption certificates, 1670-1. Eighty-four certificates (Derby 1-6 and 76; Appletree 60-64 and 79; High Peak 41-59; Morleston & Litchurch 25, 65-74, 77, 78, 80-84; Repton & Gresley 7-24, 26 and 27; Scarsdale 28-37; Wirksworth 38-40 and 75).

E 179/328/8. Exemption certificates, 1673-4. Forty-six certificates.

Only fifteen of the first batch of certificates are on printed forms, which were probably in short supply. Most of them were made out during the autumn of 1670, which suggests that it was about this time that Bennet's subcollectors prepared the assessment and collected the three half-years' duty. The Measham certificate is dated 14 June, and that for Coal Aston 29 July. There are eleven dated in August, ten in September, sixteen in October and eighteen in November. Thereafter there are only a few: four in December, three in January, five in February and three in March. The two latest are those for Youlgreave, 2 April 1671, and Darley, 17 April 1671. Three are dated in 1669: Coton 8 April, Stoney Middleton 7 June and Stapenhill 20 November. These presumably were made out whilst collection was suspended and made use of later. One is yet earlier: it was made out for three persons in Great Longstone and dated 1 December 1668; addressed to the 'Justices of the Peace...sitting at Tiddeswall', it was signed there next day by Robert Eyre and Robert Ashton. Few call for any comment; the only large one is that for fifty-nine persons in Derby St Peter's. The only certificate not for persons is one for an almshouse in West Hallam founded by John Scargill, a former rector. Most justices signed without comment, but Gervase Pole seems to have been cautious. Signing first on three Markeaton certificates he remarked 'I doe suppose this certificate is true', 'I doe beleeve this certificate may be true' and 'I suppose this certificate may be true'. Where he signed as second justice there is no comment.

These certificates were filed in the way normal to the period, by piercing a hole through the centre and stringing them together. In the course of time those on top, the last to be filed, have been lost, so those which remain are only a proportion of all there once were. In no case however do they add any names to those portions of the county copy of the assessment which survive, because the names of those exempt by certificate were entered in that assessment.

The certificates of the second batch, which appear to relate to the last account, are only the survivals of a greater number; the rest seem to have perished through damp. They are mainly on printed forms. Only two call for any comment. One, for a bakehouse hearth used by John Doe of 'Brampton in Morton', although dated 26 September 1671, was not countersigned by Clarke and Barker, the justices, until June 1673. The other is unusual in that it supplies supporting detail, rare at this date. It is for John Wright, of Stanton by Bridge, who is described as living in 'a poore smale house' belonging to the Earl of Huntingdon 'at the poole hed called Puddle dam, which house and a little Croft belonging to it is but five shillinges a yeare rent...John Marshall a baker lived in it & so by useing the harth much for his trade did pay, but this man...is a weaver and a poore man'.

That the authorities continued to keep a watch on the validity of such certificates is shown by a surviving letter from the JPs to Robert Fearne, high constable of Wirksworth hundred, in March 1674/5 (i.e. after the tax had again been put out to farm), ordering him to instruct the petty constables not only to make a return of the names of those lately certified as not chargeable with hearth money, but also to view the houses so certified. If the constables were to find any such houses with more than two chimneys, or otherwise outside the code of exemptions in respect of value of occupier's economic status, they were to bring before the justices the ministers and churchwardens who had signed the relevant certificates, to be proceeded against, as directed by the Privy Council[24].

Exchequer duplicate of assessment, 1672. This had in the course of time become split up into a number of jumbled items but has since been restored to something approaching its original order. All the membranes are in the same form, namely single columns on one side of the membrane, giving hearths and the duty payable for a full year. Membranes are totalled but places are not. The membranes for each hundred bear contemporary numbers, in a separate series.

E 179/94/394. Scarsdale hundred (36 mm., incomplete). This consists of mm.1 and 3-37. As the places are arranged alphabetically, it is certain that m.2 contained Barlow, Beauchief and Calow, whilst at the end came Tibshelf & Oxcroft, Walton and Wingerworth. The whole is otherwise complete and in good condition.

E 179/245/9. Appletree, High Peak and Wirksworth hundreds (75 mm. in three rolls, incomplete).

Appletree hundred (22 mm.). This document consisted originally of twenty-four membranes, but two of these (mm. 10 and 14) are now wanting. Most of the membranes have been added from unsorted miscellanea. Parts of the surviving membranes are illegible. Prefixed is the original first membrane of the whole roll, a fragment. The places are listed in alphabetical order.

High Peak hundred (33 mm.). Three of the original thirty-six membranes of which this document was composed are now wanting, namely mm. 3, 24 and 27. The rest have been restored to their original order from various items, namely E 179/54/399 and boxes of loose and fragmentary membranes. The constablewicks are arranged in alphabetical order, but places within them are in no particular order. Some membranes are illegible in parts.

Wirksworth hundred (20 mm.). Membranes 18 and 19 have been recovered from unsorted miscellanea. The original last membrane, probably m.21, is wanting. The places are listed in alphabetical order, running from Ashbourne to Wensley & Snitterton.

Arrears schedules. These, being schedules of recoverable arrears depending on persons, are included with each of the three accounts.

We may conclude this survey by noting three totals of hearths in the county at subsequent dates. At Michaelmas 1684 there were 35,824 and at Ladyday 1685 there were 36,329, including all exempt hearths. At the final collection, at Ladyday 1689, there were 36,901 hearths, again including exempt. According to one computation these were contained in 24,944 houses, but according to another and probably more accurate computation there were only 21,155 houses.[25] The difference between the two totals is due probably to the fact that the first represents entries, not all of which would correspond to individual houses. It is unfortunate that all these last and unquestionably more comprehensive surveys appear to be lost. We are however at least fortunate in possessing nearly the whole of the assessment for Ladyday 1664.

4. Analysis of the assessments

4.1 Geography

(a) The county as a whole

We merely note here the changes in the boundary of Derbyshire over the past century or so: changes which have affected the extreme north-west, north-east and south of the county; some of them can be seen on the map accompanying *The Place Names of Derbyshire*[26], whereas others are the result of later local government reorganisation. These changes mean that we must not expect to find in the hearth-tax assessments some places which are in the modern county; conversely, some places now in adjoining counties appear under Derbyshire in the seventeenth century. The main changes are shown below, the names referring to the modern civil parishes.

Now in Derbyshire but not in 1662-70

Whaley Bridge   Tintwistle   Netherseal   Overseal

In Derbyshire 1662-70 but not now (with present counties)

Ludworth	Cheshire	Oakthorpe & Donisthorpe	Leicestershire
Mellor	Cheshire	Chilcote	Leicestershire
Beauchief	South Yorkshire	Stretton en le Field	Leicestershire
Dore	South Yorkshire	Appleby	Leicestershire
Totley	South Yorkshire	Measham	Leicestershire
Norton	South Yorkshire	Willesley	Leicestershire
Winshill	Staffordshire	Packington	Leicestershire
Stapenhill	Staffordshire	Ravenstone	Leicestershire
Croxall	Staffordshire		
Edingale	Staffordshire		

The parishes now in Leicestershire were detached from the body of the county[27].

(b) The hundreds

As already indicated, Derbyshire was divided into six hundreds at the time of the hearth tax: Appletree, High Peak, Morleston & Litchurch, Repton & Gresley, Scarsdale, and Wirksworth. In the hearth-tax assessments Wirksworth is alternatively styled a wapentake, whereas the others are termed hundreds, and that continued to be true until at least 1817[28]. Three of the hundreds as revealed by the hearth tax differ slightly from those specified by Cameron[26]: the latter has Osmaston (by Derby) and Sinfin & Arleston in Morleston & Litchurch hundred, whereas the hearth-tax assessments have the former in Repton & Gresley and the latter in Appletree.

On the accompanying map, Fig. 1, the boundaries between the hundreds are drawn in accordance with Burdett's map of 1791. They can also be seen on Cameron's map already referred to (except for the error just mentioned), though there the exact correspondence with modern parish boundaries may be spurious in some parts. Our map shows that although High Peak, Repton & Gresley, Scarsdale and Wirksworth form relatively compact blocks of territory, Appletree has two detached portions lying within Morleston & Litchurch and the latter hundred has a small outlying part (the villages of Clifton and Compton) sandwiched between Appletree and Wirksworth next to the western boundary of the county. (The main boundary between Appletree and Morleston & Litchurch is considerably more irregular than is shown on our map). This intermixing of these two hundreds may perhaps be explicable in terms of medieval seigniories, but here it is enough to note it as a source of confusion and irritation to the local historian.

(c) Individual settlements

As will have been gathered from section 3, it was the petty constables who were made responsible at the most local level for assessment and collection of the hearth tax, as indeed they were for other national levies. Basically therefore, the assessment lists are arranged by constablewicks rather than by civil or ecclesiastical parishes, modern or ancient. The manorial origin of the office of constable was still evident in the seventeenth century, and this helps to explain many apparent anomalies in the geography of the hearth-tax assessments: constablewicks often by no means coincided with parishes. The Derbyshire situation is analogous to that in Dorset[29], where the tithings were the basic areas for the assessment. Appropriation of the ecclesiastical units for civil purposes, begun for poor-law administration in the Tudor period, had not proceeded far enough to make them taxation units.

The assessments printed in this volume do not consistently reveal the extents of the constablewicks however. The lists for Repton & Gresley hundred are the clearest in this respect, and those for High Peak and Morleston & Litchurch hundreds almost as good. In High Peak the constituent places of Hathersage and Tideswell constablewicks are not distinguished (they are noted in Table 3) and it is possible that a constable's name is missing after the Abney list. In Morleston & Litchurch no constable is recorded for Codnor & Loscoe, Darley Abbey, Hopwell, Kirk Hallam, Litchurch, Morley or Pentrich. No constables at all are recorded in the lists for Appletree, Scarsdale and Wirksworth hundreds; as external evidence for Scarsdale shows, it should not be assumed that each heading represents a separate constablewick (see below).

A common alternative to the word 'constablewick' in this period was 'township'. This particular meaning of township should not be confused with the later use of the word to denote places with separate census returns which were parts of ecclesiastical parishes but did not possess dependent chapels[30]. At least one seventeenth-century survey of Scarsdale hundred uses the word to mean 'constablewick', as in the description 'Wingerworth Tupton Swathwick Ounston & Bearchit make one intire Towneshippe'[31]. This example shows how a

FIG.1. DERBYSHIRE, SHOWING THE OLD COUNTY BOUNDARY, THE HUNDRED BOUNDARIES AND PRINCIPAL SETTLEMENTS IN EACH HUNDRED ACCORDING TO THE HEARTH TAX

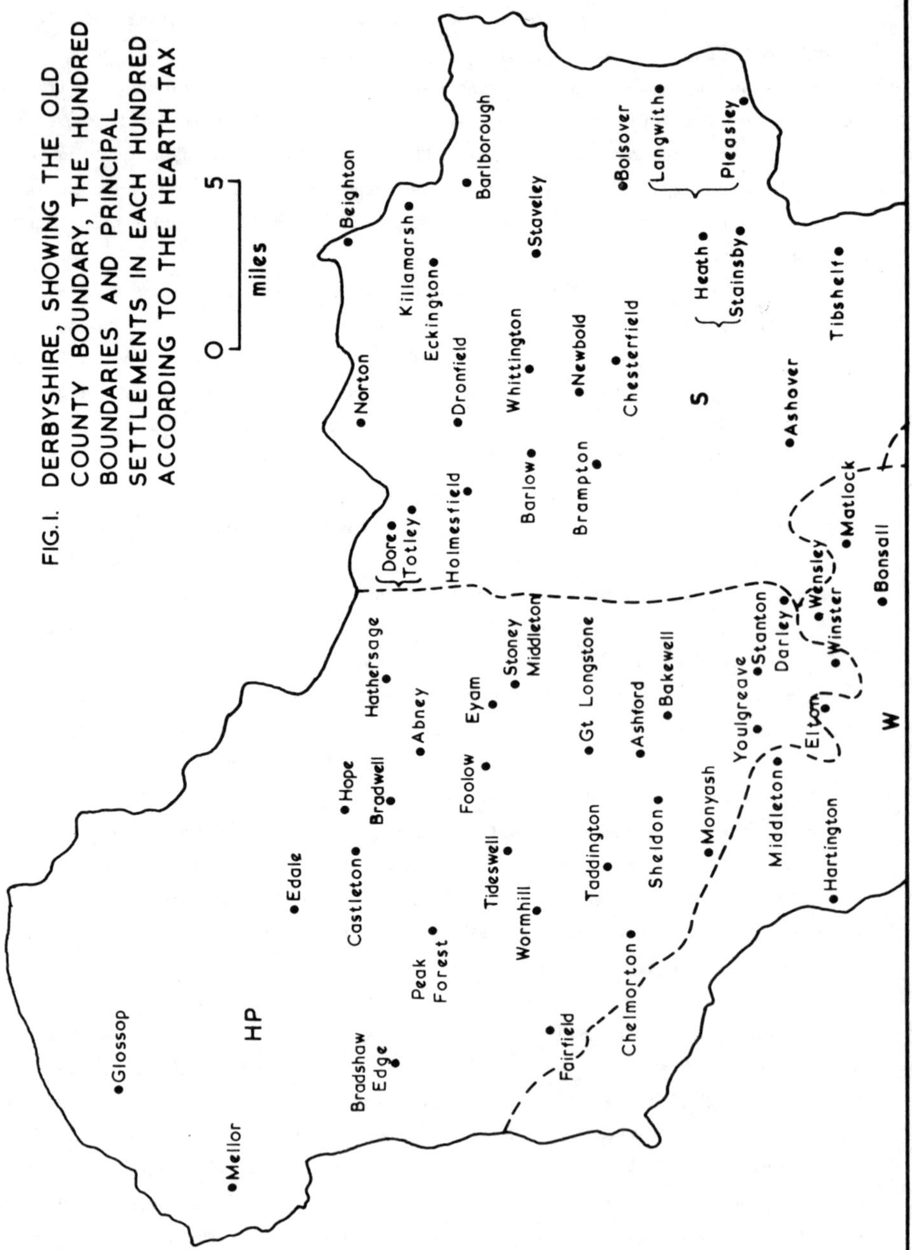

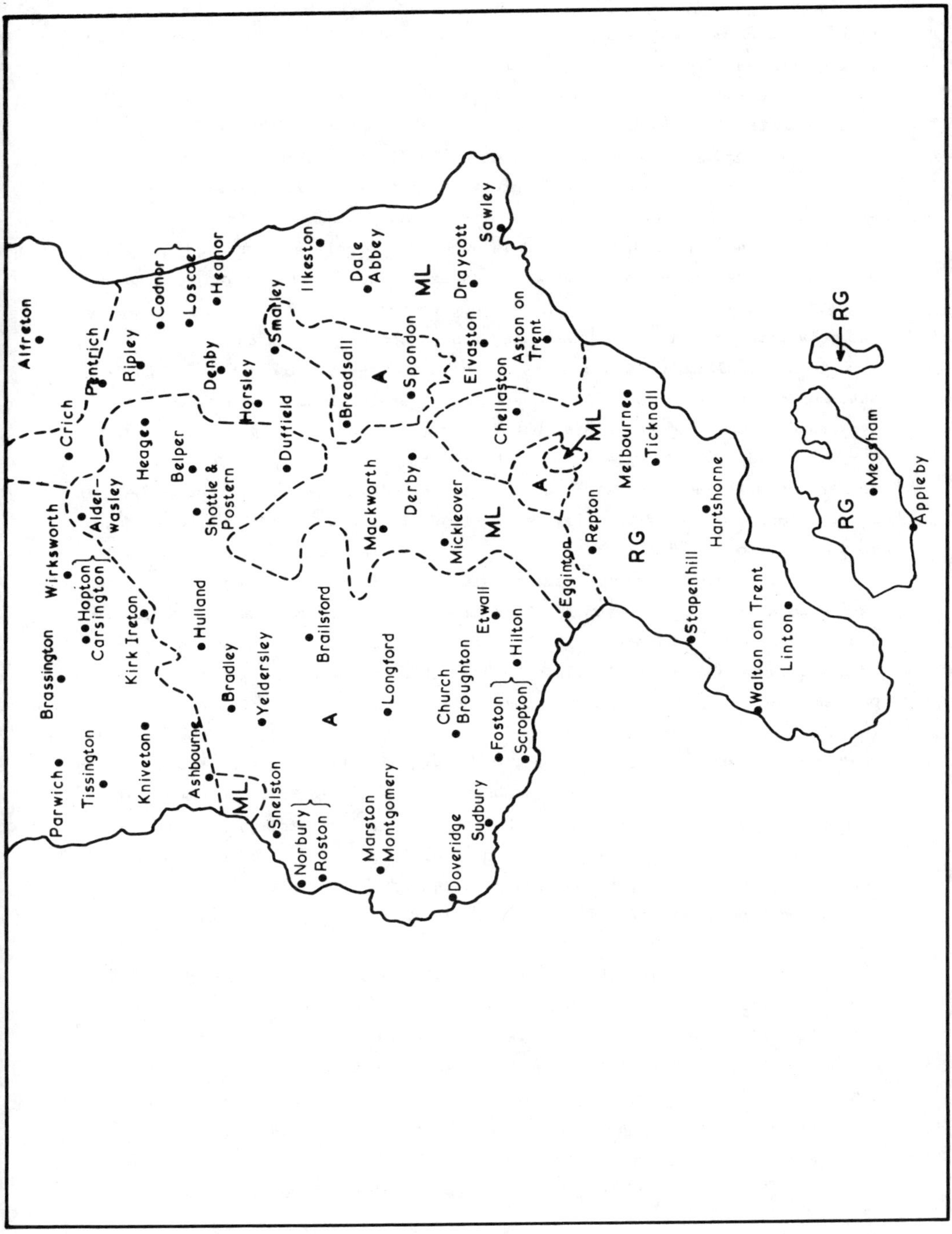
Alfreton
Pentrich
Ripley
Codnor
Loscoe
Heanor
Crich
Heage
Belper
Denby
Horsley
Smalley
Ilkeston
Dale Abbey
ML
Draycott
Sawley
Duffield
Breadsall
A
Spondon
Elvaston
Aston on Trent
Chellaston
ML
Melbourne
Ticknall
RG
Wirksworth
Hopton
Carsington
Alder-wasley
Shottle & Postern
Mackworth
Derby
Mickleover
ML
A
Repton
Hartshorne
Measham
RG
Appleby
Brassington
Kirk Ireton
Hulland
Brailsford
Etwall
Eggington
RG
Stapenhill
Walton on Trent
Linton
Parwich
Tissington
Kniveton
Ashbourne
Bradley
Yeldersley
A
Longford
Church Broughton
Hilton
Foston
Scropton
ML
Snelston
Norbury
Roston
Marston Montgomery
Doveridge
Sudbury

single constable could be responsible for geographically separate territories: Tupton and Swathwick adjoin Wingerworth, but Unstone and Birchitt are miles away and are themselves separated by Dronfield[32]. Here is one instance in which a manorial or feudal explanation seems appropriate: the Brailsford family were lords of the manor in Wingerworth (including presumably Tupton and Swathwick), Unstone and Birchitt - property which may have represented a single knight's fee, which is perhaps why it had a single constable.

Morton and Stretton, in Scarsdale hundred, provide another good example of incongruence between parishes and constablewicks. In the hearth-tax assessment the heading Stretton appears to apply to the manor of that name, covering not only Stretton itself but also Clay Lane, Woodthorpe, Egstow etc. (e.g. Archelaus Brelsford, of Egstow Hall, appears in the Stretton list)[33]. The heading Morton in 1670 also includes Pilsley, as is clear from at least the 1664 assessment; not only this, but the names of the rector of North Wingfield (Dr Berisford) and of contemporary inhabitants of Williamthorpe (e.g. Richard Ashmore of Williamthorpe Hall)[34] can be recognised in the Morton list. The manorial association of Pilsley, North Wingfield and Williamthorpe goes back to Domesday Book at least, but in 1086 Morton was associated with Ogston and Wessington, though it had the same tenant-in-chief, Walter de Aincurt. Walter also held a manor in Brampton and Wadshelf, and this is perhaps the origin of the name 'Brampton in Morton' in the hearth-tax assessments, referring principally though not exclusively to the Cutthorpe area (as suggested by the presence of Cornelius Clarke and George Heathcote, of the two Cutthorpe halls, in this list)[35]. The seventeenth-century survey of Scarsdale mentioned earlier confirms that Morton, Pilsley, North Wingfield and Williamthorpe, together with 'part of Brampton' formed a single township or constablewick. On the other hand, Stretton, Clay Lane, Woodthorpe and Egstow, as well as Pilsley, Williamthorpe and Tupton, lay within the ecclesiastical parish of North Wingfield, whereas Morton was another such parish which also included Brackenfield; furthermore, Wessington, though grouped with Brackenfield in the hearth tax, lay in the ecclesiastical parish of Crich.

In High Peak hundred there were similar incongruences between constablewicks and ecclesiastical parishes. For instance, in Tideswell constablewick only Tideswell itself, Litton, Miller's Dale and Wheston lay in Tideswell parish; Brushfield and Little Longstone were in Bakewell parish, and Grindlow, Hazlebadge and Great and Little Hucklow were in Hope parish. The ecclesiastical parish of Ashbourne provides yet another example: it included Clifton and part of Compton in the hundred of Morleston & Litchurch; Hulland, Sturston, the other part of Compton and Yeldersley in Appletree; and Ashbourne town, Alsop en le Dale, Hognaston, Parwich, Offcote & Underwood and Newton Grange in Wirksworth. Hulland poses another problem not yet completely resolved. The relatively large number of households recorded under this heading in the hearth-tax lists (113 in 1664) suggests that places other than just the district of that name are included, and indeed the first entry in the 1664 list is 'Alton Hall', presumably referring to the house of that name east of Kirk Ireton. One may therefore suppose that the list comprises not only Hulland itself but also Alton, Biggin (with which Alton formed a joint constablewick in later times)[36], Idridgehay and perhaps Ireton Wood, Turnditch and Windley as well as Hulland Ward and Hulland Ward Intakes; none of these names appears elsewhere in the assessment. This may yet be confirmed from other sources, but it is significant that all these places were in Appletree hundred[37].

Close examination of the hearth-tax lists shows that there are cases in which individual houses expected to be entered for a particular place appear in the lists under a neighbouring place. One example appears to be Park Hall in Barlborough, the home of the Pole family. In the 1670 assessment there is nobody of this name under Barlborough; instead, we find under Eckington both 'Mrs Poole' with ten hearths and 'Mr Frances Poole' with seven. It seems therefore that Park Hall was taken in with Spinkhill, which was in the parish and constablewick of Eckington. Francis Pole of Park Hall died in 1679 and his probate inventory mentions Nether Hall at Spinkhill. Mrs Pole's ten hearths presumably refer to the latter house and maybe also cover the Jesuit college. Another example is perhaps Carr House at Edale End, which some decades later at least was the home of the Champion family[38] and is just within the modern parish of Edale. There are no Champions listed under Edale in the 1670 assessment, but under Hope Woodlands there is an entry 'Tho. & Edw. Eyre for Carr house' which could refer to the Edale house.

A third example, the appearance of Wilne Hall under Draycott, not Wilne & Shardlow, in the 1670 assessment, is presumably explained by the fact that Church Wilne was associated parochially with Draycott and only Great Wilne with Shardlow. Against these three examples (and more might be detected) we can set that of Stanley Grange, a famous papist establishment lying only just inside the modern parish of Dale Abbey: in the 1670 assessment 'Mr Powtherill' (Powtrell) of that house does in fact appear with nine hearths at the head of the Dale Abbey list, not under Stanley. Had it been included under Stanley, it would have been in a different hundred - Appletree instead of Morleston & Litchurch - and it is interesting to note that an earlier document does indeed describe it as being in Appletree, perhaps as a result of a belief that it was in Stanley parish[39].

In the 1670 assessment at least, the lists for Alfreton and Ashover are divided into four parts by spaces between names, without any subheadings. The first division under Alfreton presumably refers to the town itself; from the correspondence between certain names and those in other sources[40], the others are perhaps Swanwick, Somercotes and Riddings in that order. The Ashover divisions presumably represent the four Quarters of that parish, and it may tentatively be suggested that these are, in order of appearance: Ashover (or Town), Upperend, Alton and Milltown quarters (again from identification of certain names with particular houses, e.g. the Lady Hunlocke with Stubben Edge Hall)[41]. Belper in 1662, Peak Forest in 1664 and Staveley in 1670 are similarly divided into two parts without subheadings.

Another large parish which was divided into quarters was Eckington, but in the 1670 assessment there are no divisions of the list; in 1664 however, the Eckington, Spinkhill, Ridgeway and Mosbrough quarters are presented separately. Even in the case of Derby, with its five parishes, the subheadings seem to have been inserted in the 1670 list as an afterthought, and we have the 'certified' in a single group for the whole borough. To add to what was said above on ecclesiastical parishes, it may be mentioned that three of those centred on Derby churches extended beyond the borough: St Alkmund's over Little Eaton, Quarndon, Darley Abbey and Little Chester; St Michael's over Alvaston; and St Peter's over Boulton, Normanton, Osmaston and Litchurch (Normanton and Osmaston being in Repton & Gresley hundred, not Morleston & Litchurch like the rest).

There is no space here for a full treatment of these problems, but enough has been said to provide a warning against taking the place-name headings in the hearth-tax assessments entirely at their face value. The list for any given place should be considered in relation to those for neighbouring places. Some tentative guidance appears in Table 3. The uncertainties about the exact geographical coverage in some cases, and the known combinations of settlements in others, do of course make it more difficult to draw demographic, social and economic conclusions from the lists and figures with respect to individual settlements. It is often safer therefore to work at the regional level.

4.2 Population and economic status

It is risky to estimate population from records such as the hearth-tax assessments, and if we do so, we should beware of quoting a figure with too much appearance of exactness: rather, we should offer a range within which the true value is likely to fall. With the hearth tax, in the first place one can never be sure without supplementary evidence that the list for any particular place includes all households in that place, even for those assessments which give the names of those not liable for liable for the tax. An example - though perhaps an extreme one - of the possible discrepancy is provided by the city of Worcester in the 1670s: an exhaustive list of household heads in 1679/80 yields a total of 2250, whereas the hearth-tax assessment for 1674 gives only 1120 including those exempt[42]. It appears therefore that one has to be satisfied with presenting an estimate of the minimum population. Further uncertainty arises from the choice of multiplier representing the average number of persons per household. When it is realised that a change of 0.1 in this multiplier produces a difference of 2000 in the population figure based on 20,000 households (the order of magnitude for Derbyshire from the hearth tax) - and the range of suggested multipliers is a good deal more than 0.1 - the folly of quoting county populations to anything closer than the nearest 1000 is obvious.

To obtain the most optimistic total of households in Derbyshire from the hearth-tax records we can take for each place that assessment which gives the greatest number of entries (Table 2). For most places this is the 1664 assessment, but for others it is either 1662 or 1670. The total thus obtained is a little over 16,200, representing a population of about 69,000 if the currently recommended multiplier of 4.25 for seventeenth-century households is used. It therefore seems safe to talk of a minimum population of around 70,000 for the county in the 1660s, a decade during which it is unlikely that there was any marked growth[43].

The above figure of 69,000 was distributed among the six hundreds as follows (to the nearest 1000).

Appletree	9,000	
High Peak	17,000	
Morleston & Litchurch*	12,000	*including Derby
Repton & Gresley	5,000	
Scarsdale	17,000	
Wirksworth	9,000	

Unfortunately, comparable figures for all the other counties of England are not readily available, and to put Derbyshire in perspective we must rely for the moment on a comparison of total numbers of hearths assessed in 1662, which have been published[44]. This is perhaps more a comparison of economic status than of population, though at the same time perhaps the average ratio of hearths to households did not generally vary much among the counties. On this basis, Derbyshire came well down the list: thirtieth out of forty (excluding London, Westminster and Southwark), with just under 21,000 hearths. It was thus to be contrasted with counties such as Middlesex (95,000), Devon (78,000) and Norfolk (74,000) but fell into the same league as the counties of Nottingham, Durham, Hereford and Bedford (rather smaller) and those of Leicester, Chester, Buckingham and Worcester (rather larger). Of the remaining counties adjacent to Derbyshire, the West Riding (including York) had nearly 63,000 hearths and Staffordshire about 27,200.

The Derbyshire towns can similarly be compared with those in other counties. Thus Derby, by far the largest town in the county, with 1479 hearths in 1662, was comparable with Birmingham, Chatham, Ely, Gateshead, Leicester, Ludlow, Northampton, Southampton and Warwick, all of which were assessed at a figure between 1400 and 1600 hearths. But it was small by the side of cities like Bristol (6925), Newcastle upon Tyne (5967), Norwich (7302) and York (7294), and was exceeded in number of hearths by at least thirty other English towns. In the adjacent counties, Nottingham had 2190, Sheffield around 1000, Leeds 1798, Chester 3004, Lichfield 1207 and Leicester (already mentioned) 1548. The other towns worthy of the name in Derbyshire were much smaller, next in size to Derby being Chesterfield (685 hearths in 1662), followed by Wirksworth (382), Ashbourne (358) and Bakewell (224). In the case of Wirksworth and Bakewell it must be noted that the figures probably included a not negligible number of households outside the towns themselves. Chesterfield was roughly comparable with Mansfield, Uttoxeter and Nantwich, to take three examples from neighbouring counties; Wirksworth and Ashbourne were roughly the same size as Worksop, Burton on Trent and Macclesfield.

The Derbyshire towns and villages can of course also be compared in terms of the maximum number of households (entries) recorded at the three dates (Table 2). Derby naturally heads the list again, with 611 (in 1670, corresponding this time to 1915 hearths), but now Wirksworth comes second with 449 (in 1664 - including 217 not chargeable, and representing 595 hearths) and Chesterfield is third with 315 (again in 1664 but representing 676 hearths). Next come Matlock (256) and Ashbourne (229). The remaining places with 150 or more entries (i.e. at least a quarter of the size of Derby) are:

Eckington	214
Brampton	207
Dronfield	205
Tideswell	c.200
Hartington	195
Bakewell	194
Ashover	190
Melbourne	177
Alfreton	168
Eyam	160
Staveley	158
Norton	155

Notes: Brampton here includes 'Brampton in Morton'; the Tideswell figure is after deducting c.50 for Litton from the 1664 total; Melbourne includes King's Newton; and many of these figures represent multiple settlements (e.g. 'Alfreton' includes also Riddings, Somercotes and Swanwick).

Without needing to convert such figures into population estimates, we can calculate for each place a population density - or rather its reciprocal in acres per household. The results can then be plotted on a map such as that showing the parishes and chapelries of the county around 1800[45]. As may be gathered from the discussion in section 4.1, there are difficulties in allotting the appropriate number of acres to certain places, but these problems can be overcome reasonably satisfactorily by making the assumptions detailed in Table 3 (p.lxix) and by assuming that constablewick boundaries were determined by those of parishes and their constituent settlements. Though these assumptions may not all be correct, they are justifiable as long as we are interested merely in a general picture of the county. To simplify the picture, in Fig. 2 the range of population density has been divided into only three classes, with limits chosen so as to divide the total area of the county into upper and lower quartiles (i.e. quarters of highest and lowest density) and a central half of moderate density, into which most places fall. This arrangement shows that the most densely populated parts of the county were mainly in the leadmining area of the Peak, in the coalfield district and in the Derby region. Other isolated regions of high density included the Ashbourne area. Particular districts of low density were the north-western 'horseshoe' and the agricultural south-west, as expected. Refinement of this fairly crude presentation must be left to others, but it is instructive to compare Fig. 2 with a map[46] showing population density in 1563 (though the latter is necessarily based entirely on ecclesiastical parishes and thus conceals some of the detail).

The four most densely populated townships were in fact the four towns with the greatest number of hearths in 1662, but the order of places in terms of density by no means corresponds to the order as regards population. Indeed, Ashbourne, with its very restricted area (57 acres), comes out highest for density: only 1/4 acre per household, contrasted with e.g. 5 acres per household for the borough of Derby on average. At the other end of the scale we have several townships or districts with over 100 acres per household, such as Hope Woodlands (361), Edale (147) and Barton Blount (167), the first two of which contained large areas of uncultivated moorland and hence would be expected to be thinly populated.

The economic status or social structure of individual places and districts can also be roughly compared on the basis of the proportions of houses with different numbers of hearths. Various classifications of hearth numbers have been proposed; here we adopt the one proposed by Fieldhouse[47] with four classes:

No of Hearths	Social Status of Occupier
1	Husbandmen and the poorer sort
2-3	Most craftsmen, tradesmen, yeomen
4-7	Wealthier ditto, and merchants
8+	Gentry and nobility

This can be only a rough guide, since (for instance) many lesser gentry are to be found in houses with fewer than eight hearths.

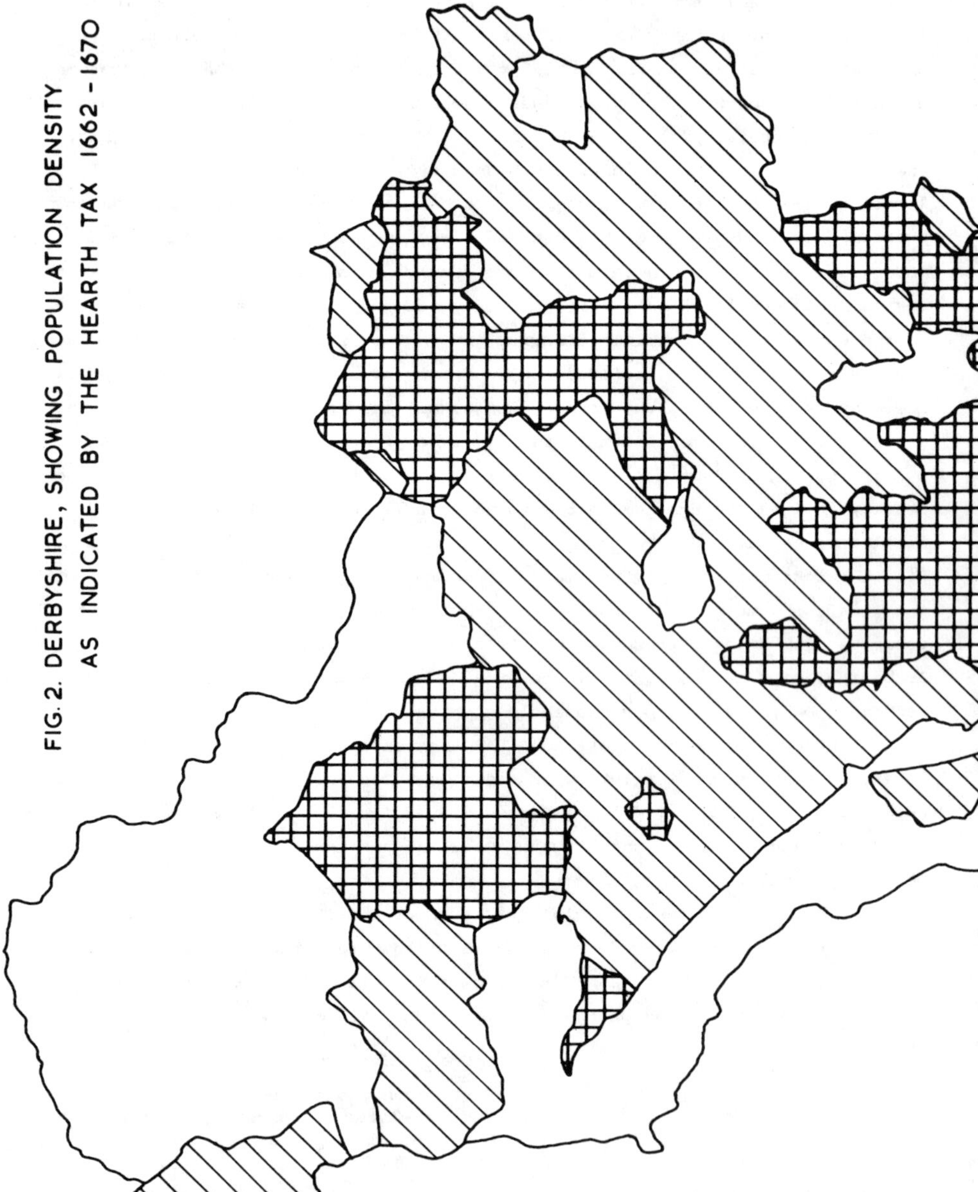

FIG. 2. DERBYSHIRE, SHOWING POPULATION DENSITY AS INDICATED BY THE HEARTH TAX 1662 - 1670

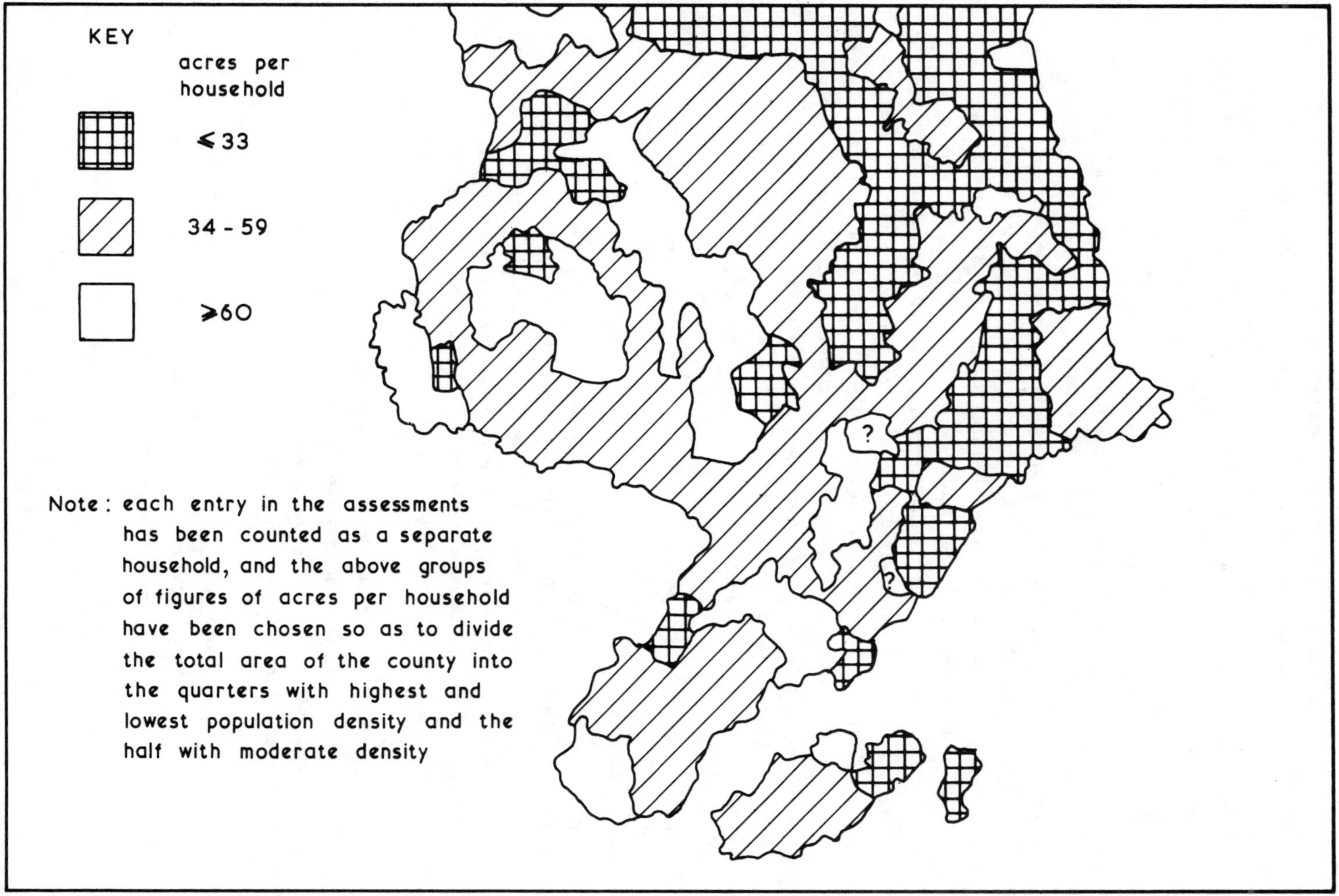
KEY
acres per household
≤33
34 - 59
≥60
Note: each entry in the assessments has been counted as a separate household, and the above groups of figures of acres per household have been chosen so as to divide the total area of the county into the quarters with highest and lowest population density and the half with moderate density
?
?

We leave the highest class to be discussed later, and concentrate on the first and third classes. For the hearth-tax documents transcribed here, and considering only the chargeable households, differences in the proportion of households with 4-7 hearths appear not only between individual places but also between the hundreds. In Scarsdale (excluding Chesterfield) almost 8 per cent of households fell into this class, whereas for High Peak the figure was only about 4.5 per cent; the other hundreds had intermediate figures (Wirksworth 7; Repton & Gresley 6.5; Morleston & Litchurch 6 excluding Derby; Appletree 5). Derby and Chesterfield had relatively high proportions, as might be expected: 25 and 33 per cent respectively. Correspondingly, single-hearth houses formed an appreciably higher proportion of the whole in High Peak than they did in Scarsdale, and amounted to less than a third of the total in Derby and only 12 per cent of the total in Chesterfield.

Similar comparisons can be made between individual places, and different types of settlement identified. Let us take for example the class of small-to-moderate villages: those with 25 to 100 households in the assessments. At one extreme there is a village like Wardlow near Tideswell, with twenty-nine households recorded in 1670, all but one of which were single-hearth, the exception having two hearths. Contrasted with this is Kirk Ireton, where eighteen out of the fifty-two households in 1670 had two or three hearths each and seven had between four and seven hearths apiece. Yet there was no really large house here either. Similar to size to Kirk Ireton in the 1670 assessment was Barlborough, with a similar distribution of households among our first three hearth-number classes but also having four in the category of large houses: two with eight hearths, one with twelve and the Hall with twenty-one. Barlborough therefore represented a well-balanced village in this respect. Such contrasts must of course be tempered by consideration of the exempt households, mainly single-hearth; whereas there were none of these in Wardlow according to the 1664 assessment, there were quite a few in Kirk Ireton and (if the figure shown in Table 2 be shared roughly equally with Whitwell) a considerable number in Barlborough.

It must be left to others to make a more detailed analysis, but a word of caution is necessary about places like Norton and Eckington in Scarsdale: the inclusion of smithy hearths in the assessments for 1670 no doubt gives a false impression of the size of certain houses.

4.3 Greater and lesser houses

Houses of eight or more hearths were classified in the previous section as the residences of gentry and nobility, but in view of the large number of

The Old Manor House, Hartshorne, near Swadlincote; not yet precisely identified in the hearth-tax return of 1662, but evidently one of the first four in the list (see p. 126)

Old Hall Farm, Youlgreave, built in 1630 and taxed on 6 hearths in 1670 (see p. 69: Henry Fox); ground-floor plan in M. W. Barley, *The English farmhouse and cottage* (1961), 170

Melbourne Hall (rear view), with 14 hearths taxed in 1662 (see pp. lxxiii and 125: Mr Fords)

The Hallowes, Dronfield (but formerly in Coal Aston constablewick), built in 1657 and taxed on 10 hearths in 1670 (see p. 154: Andrew Morewood)

Park Hall, Barlborough, with 7 hearths taxed in 1670 (see pp. xli, li and 144: Francis Pole)

Snitterton Hall, near Matlock, with 14 hearths taxed in 1670 (see pp. liii and 196: Henry Milward)

such houses throughout the county, only the very largest can be mentioned here. There were in fact twenty-four houses with twenty or more hearths recorded in the assessments transcribed (it is necessary to add this qualification, because an examination of other assessments shows that some houses were assessed at quite different totals at different dates). Eight of these were in Scarsdale, six in Repton & Gresley, three each in Appletree, High Peak and Morleston & Litchurch, and only one in Wirksworth hundred. In proportion to its area therefore, Repton & Gresley was the hundred most richly endowed with such houses.

Five great houses stand out from the rest. By far the largest in terms of hearths was Hardwick Hall, with 114 in 1670. Its owner, William, Earl of Devonshire, also had the second largest house: Chatsworth, with 79 hearths in 1670. Not far behind, with 68 hearths in 1662, was the seat of another aristocrat, Philip, Earl of Chesterfield: Bretby House. Derbyshire thus had three houses greater than any in Dorset at that time (to take an example from the published assessments for other counties); there, Sherborne Castle with 60 hearths headed the list. The other two of our five principal houses were both assessed at 48 hearths in 1670: Haddon Hall, seat of John, Earl of Rutland, and Oldcotes (Owlcotes), the house built by Bess of Hardwick to the north of Hardwick and then occupied by Henry Pierrepont Esq. (to whose family it had descended by marriage from the Cavendishes). Only two of those houses survive in more or less the same form today: Haddon and Hardwick. Oldcotes was demolished in the eighteenth century, while the Bretby and Chatsworth of that time have been replaced by new buildings.

Next in size came Bolsover Castle (36 hearths; another Cavendish residence, owned by William, Duke of Newcastle), Risley Hall (33), Durrant Hall (31) and Staveley Hall (30). Risley Hall was then occupied by Anchitell Grey, MP for Derby from 1665 to 1685 and in 1689-94 and famous for his record of the debates in the House of Commons; the house was in fact the property of his wife Anne Willoughby. Durrant Hall in Chesterfield was the residence in 1670 of the widow of George Taylor, lead merchant and benefactor to the town. Staveley Hall was the property of John Frechville, who had been created a baron in 1665. The remainder of the twenty-four largest houses were as follows.

Location	Occupier/Owner	No of Hearths (year)
Swarkestone	Sir John Harpur*	28 (1662)
Longford	Sir Edward Coke	27 (1664)
Sutton (Scarsdale)	Nicholas, Earl of Scarsdale	26 (1670)
Foremark	Sir Francis Burdett	24 (1662)
Calke	Sir John Harpur*	23 (1662)
Chesterfield	Mr Richard Clarke	23 (1670)
Drakelow	Sir Thomas Gresley	23 (1662)

Location	Occupier/Owner	No of Hearths (year)
Kedleston	Sir John Curzon	22 (1664)
Barlborough	Sir Francis Rodes	21 (1670)
Offcote	Sir Aston Cokaine	21 (1670)
Egginton	Sir Henry Every	20 (1670)
West Hallam	Mrs Powtrell	20 (1670)
Hassop	Rowland Eyre Esq.	20 (1670)
Osmaston (by Derby)	Nicholas Wilmot Esq.	20 (1662)
Radbourne	German Pole Esq.	20 (1664)

*these two were different persons.

There were a further ninety-five houses with between ten and nineteen hearths each. No less than twenty-two of these were in Derby (in 1670), including the residences of Sir John Shore, Sir Simon Degge and Mr William Allestrey (who, as mentioned earlier, may have been the same man as the county hearth-tax receiver for 1664-5). Scarsdale had twenty-six, only two of which were in Chesterfield. To take two examples from each of the hundreds, we may mention Bubnell Hall (Robert Bromhead) and Bradshaw Hall (Edward Ash) in High Peak; Beauchief Hall (Edward Pegge) and Wingerworth Hall (Sir Henry Hunloke) in Scarsdale; Elvaston Hall (Mr Stanhope) and Morley Hall (William Sacheverell: 'The first Whig') in Morleston & Litchurch; Chilcote Hall (William Milward Esq.) and Croxall Hall (Richard, Earl of Dorset) in Repton & Gresley; Etwall Hall (Sir Samuel Sleigh) and Sudbury Hall (George Vernon Esq.) in Appletree; and Hopton Hall (John Gell Esq.) and Tissington Hall (William Fitzherbert Esq.) in Wirksworth[48]. The number of eight-and nine-hearth houses was about one hundred, including twenty-seven in Derby. Especially in the towns, some of the houses with large numbers of hearths were undoubtedly inns, e.g. that of Richard Clarke in Chesterfield[49], and as this example and that of Durrant Hall (see page li) suggest, large hearth numbers may include fireplaces in ancillary buildings or other separate property.

It is among the houses of four to seven hearths, as well as those somewhat larger, that we find the sixteenth- and seventeenth-century small halls or manor houses which are so characteristic of the Derbyshire countryside today. For instance, Holme Hall near Bakewell, occupied in 1670 by William Eyre, had nine hearths, like Highlow Hall, the residence of his father Robert (entered at the head of the Eyam list). Aston Hall near Hope, built in 1578 and the residence of Thomas Balgay (Balguy), 'gent', had four hearths. These three houses are but a small proportion of the many in High Peak alone, and they have their equivalents in other parts of the county.

It is tempting to try to match the assessments for identifiable houses with contemporary probate inventories. However, from the few examples[49] studied by the present writer (DGE) it seems that it will often be impossible to equate the number of hearths liable for tax with the number of rooms in which a fireplace is indicated in the inventory. The reason for a discrepancy of this sort may lie in the assessment system or in a deficiency in the inventory. One example in which there is exact correspondence is the rectory at Barlborough, occupied by John Brocklehurst who died in 1682. His probate inventory mentions fire ranges in six of the rooms (living room, dining parlour, kitchen, far chamber, study chamber and green chamber) and the figure of 6 does in fact appear against 'mr Brocklehurst' in the 1670 assessment. The inventory of Francis Pole of Park Hall in the same parish, 1679, mentions only six fire ranges, whereas in 1670 he was assessed at seven hearths (see section 4.1(c)). George Milnes of Dunston Hall was assessed (under Newbold) at six hearths in 1670, but his inventory taken the following year includes seven ranges.

These discrepancies are minor, but much larger ones can be found. One case besides that of Richard Clarke mentioned above is that of Durrant Hall in Chesterfield, assessed in 1670 at thirty-one hearths - perhaps a suprisingly large number. The probate inventory of its owner Mrs Taylor however lists no more than about twenty rooms that could possibly have had a fireplace[50], so one suspects that the assessment is in error or that it covers some other property as well as the hall; unfortunately, the figure in the assessment for 1662 is illegible, and it remains to check the 1664 and 1672 figures. As pointed out in section 1, the idea that the figure of thirty-one includes lead-smelting hearths appears untenable[51]. Another large apparent discrepancy, though in the opposite direction, occurs with Bolsover Castle. This was assessed at thirty-six hearths in 1670. The seventeenth-century extensions to the castle had been completed by 1670, so the number of fireplaces which can be counted from the official guide should approach that figure[52]. In fact one can count at least fifty-four, and perhaps another eight. Possibly it was considered that some of these were not liable for tax, or that two or more discharging into a common chimneystack could be assessed as one. At any rate, an inventory of the castle in 1670 (referred to in the guidebook) and the assessment for 1672 should be checked, to try to resolve the problem.

4.4 Miscellaneous

One by-product of the index of personal names in this volume is an indication of the relative frequency of the various surnames in the county in the first decade after the Restoration. Table 4 gives the results of an examination of this index to discover the most common surnames. The picture is incomplete of course, as the assessments transcribed for the hundreds of High Peak, Morleston & Litchurch, Scarsdale and Wirksworth include only a few of the householders exempt from the tax. Another defect, less serious, is the difference in time between these assessments and those transcribed for the hundreds of Appletree and Repton & Gresley. The actual numbers of households recorded in Table 4 should not therefore be regarded as definitive. The number of index references for each surname (excluding the Introduction) has been rounded down to the nearest multiple of five, since a few persons - e.g. constables and owners of more than one property - are recorded more than once in the assessments. A lower limit of twenty-five has been chosen to restrict the length of the list.

Most of the more common surnames at that time were widely distributed over the county, but some were more localised, mainly in the hundreds of High Peak and Wirksworth. For instance, the Alsops (their name derived from the place) were concentrated in Wirksworth hundred, and it is interesting to observe how the Bagshaws and the Eyres, prominent families in the Peak District, overlapped geographically to only a limited extent at that time. Other fairly localised names were Buxton (in and around Chelmorton and from Wirksworth westward to the county boundary) and Kirke (in Chinley and Chapel en le Frith); most of the Clays were to be found in Scarsdale hundred. To put the numbers in Table 4 into perspective, it should be mentioned that the total number of entries in the assessments transcribed is well over 10,000.

Besides those who have been mentioned in section 4.3, there are a number of other persons in the assessments who have achieved some sort of fame, for instance John Flamsteed the first Astronomer Royal (under Ilkeston), Edward Manlove the writer on lead-mining (Ashbourne), John Gratton the Quaker preacher (Monyash), Leonard Wheatcroft the writer (Ashover), George Sitwell the Renishaw ironmaster (Eckington), Immanuel Halton the mathematician of Wingfield Manor, and Thomas Cotchett the builder of the Derby silk mill (or possibly his father; under Mickleover).

There are a number of people who almost certainly appear in the assessments under more than one place. Besides the definite example of the Earl of Devonshire at Chatsworth and Hardwick, one may cite Cornelius Clarke, Sheriff in 1670, under 'Brampton in Morton' (Cutthorpe Hall) and Norton (Norton Hall), Edward Ash under Tideswell and Bradshaw Edge (Bradshaw Hall), Edward Manlove under Ashbourne and Wirksworth, and Adrian Mundy, sheriff in 1671, under Quarndon, Duffield and Derby. Other cases may be found, but to be certain one must seek supporting evidence from other sources.

It is possible to link certain names in the assessments with practically contemporary events (and one or two cases can be identified in which published versions of such events, e.g. transfers of property, seem to conflict with the hearth-tax evidence). Two examples must suffice here. Under Wensley & Snitterton in 1670 the name of John Milward (the parliamentary diarist, of Snitterton Hall) was written first, but John has been crossed out and Henry substituted; in fact John died on 14 September that year and was succeeded by his second son Henry[53]. Under Beauchief, again in 1670, appears Edward Pegge, who had begun to build the present Hall shortly before; the lintel over the main door bears the date 1671 however, so it seems that his fourteen hearths are more likely to have referred to the old building[54].

Apart from indications of incumbents of churches, occupations are rarely stated (only sixteen times, plus one doubtful) in the assessments transcribed here: they are used merely to distinguish between persons of the same name when a place-name or an indication of seniority does not suffice. Thus the two John Wrights in Ashford are distinguished as tailor and shoemaker. Under Castleton we have three Thomas Halls, one without any distinguishing feature, one described as shoemaker and the third as 'son of James Hall', whereas the three John Halls (assuming 'Jo.' to stand for John) are differentiated as 'of goose hill', 'of the well' and 'de Pindall'.

Theoretically, the 1664 assessments, with their separate lists of chargeable and non-chargeable persons, should have given a greater number of entries for every place than the 1662 or 1670 documents. The fact that the 1662 or 1670 lists are fuller for certain places therefore needs some comment. In Appletree, Morleston & Litchurch, Scarsdale and Wirksworth hundreds the number of places apparently better catered-for in 1662 or 1670 is relatively small, while for Repton & Gresley the 1664 record is so defective that we must disregard it in this context. It is in High Peak hundred that an appreciable number of places are affected: two in Ashford constablewick, ten (all) in Bowden Middle Cale, three (all) in Bowden Chapel, six (all but one) in Chelmorton, three (all) in Darley, nine (all but two) in Glossop, three in Hope, one in Tideswell, and three in Wormhill. From this it will be seen that it is in the extreme north-west of the county that the 1664 assessment seems deficient. However, in such cases the differences are generally small and the number not chargeable is also usually small or nil, so most of the places concerned seem really to have had few persons qualifying for exemption.

In contrast, there are many places for which the inclusion of the exempt in 1664 means an appreciably greater total than in the other assessments. Examples (one from each hundred except Repton & Gresley) are Breadsall, Eyam, Horsley, Chesterfield and Matlock. It is for places like these that the presentation of the 1670 assessments for High Peak, Morleston & Litchurch, Scarsdale and Wirksworth in this volume instead of those of 1664 is the most unsatisfactory. On the other hand, Table 2 shows that the chargeable persons in some places in 1664 number less than the total in 1662 or 1670.

As regards the relative numbers chargeable and not chargeable in 1664, it is interesting that the latter exceeded the former in eighteen places (all in High Peak, Morleston & Litchurch and Scarsdale hundreds). Significantly the most spectacular differences in this direction were in four lead-mining village - Eyam, Great Hucklow, Little Hucklow and Stoney Middleton - pointing to the existence of relatively large numbers of poorly-off miners. Sheldon and Tideswell also fell into this group of places, but other lead-mining villages presented a quite different picture. Perhaps industrialisation can explain the existence of the same pattern in the other places of this group: Clifton & Compton, Draycott, Mackworth, Sawley, Wilne & Shardlow, Great Barlow, Clowne, Coal Aston, Dronfield, Hasland and Killamarsh. Any study of this should of course also take into account other places in which the number not chargeable equalled or approached the number chargeable.

5. Notes on style of transcript

1. The transcript preserves the order of appearance, though not necessarily the exact layout, of the material in the original documents.
2. Round (instead of the more usual square) brackets enclose:
   (a) editorial notes and membrane/folio numbers not appearing in the original, as well as the headings 'Chargeable' and 'Not Chargeable' where repeated in the transcript because of a change in layout;
   (b) words or parts of words which are illegible in the original, the identity of which can reasonably be deduced;
   (c) alternative readings of doubtful words;
   (d) letters added in expansion of abbreviations (see 9. below).
3. A question mark indicates a doubtful reading of (and only of) the immediately following word or figure.
4. Three dots (...) denote an illegible word, part of a word or figure, irrespective of length.
5. Underlining does not appear in the original.
6. Asterisks enclose matter deleted in the original but still legible or partly so.
7. The capitalisation of the original is preserved, though in many cases (especially with initial <u>d</u> and <u>w</u>) judgment has had to be subjective.
8. Initial <u>ff</u> is rendered as <u>F</u> and, where appropriate, initial <u>V</u> as <u>U</u>, medial <u>u</u> as <u>v</u> and <u>y</u> as <u>th</u>.
9. Abbreviations in the original are expanded (see 2(d) above) except for forenames, personal titles, indications of seniority and annotations such as 'Ret' against hearth numbers; in these cases, marks of abbreviation in the original are omitted for contractions (e.g. 'Wm') and are reduced to a simple full stop for suspensions (e.g. 'Widd.').
10. Marginal marks (e.g. crosses) in the original which are not readily intelligible are omitted.

6. References

1. *English Historical Documents VIII: 1660-1714* (ed. A. Browning) (1953), 307-308
2. E. Strauss, *Sir William Petty: portrait of a genius* (1954); Sir Irvine Masson and A.J. Youngson, 'Sir William Petty, F.R.S.', in Sir Harold Hartley (ed.), *The Royal Society: its origins and founders* (1960).
3. *The economic writings of Sir William Petty* (ed. C.H. Hull) (1899), I
4. L.M. Marshall, 'The levying of the hearth tax,1662-1688', *English Historical Review*, 51 (1936), 628-646; Public Record Office, *Calendar of Treasury books* (ed. W.A. Shaw) (I-VIII, 1904-24) (see indexes under the appropriate heading)
5. J.C. Cox, *Three centuries of Derbyshire annals* (1890), II, 124
6. Public Record Office, *Calendar of Treasury Books*, V, 160 (Lord Treasurer Danby to the Yorkshire JPs, 18 March 1675-6)
7. *Ibid.*, 137, 159, 417; *Memoirs of Sir John Reresby* (ed. A. Browning) (Glasgow 1936), 104-105, 125
8. D. Hey, *The rural metalworkers of the Sheffield region* (University of Leicester, Department of English Local History, Occasional Papers 2nd series, no 5, 1972) 12
9. Public Record Office, Exchequer, King's Remembrancer: Subsidy Rolls &c, E 179/94/394
10. S.C. Newton, 'The gentry of Derbyshire in the seventeenth century', *Derbyshire Archaeological Journal*, LXXXVI (1966), 1-30 (*sub* Cornelius Clarke and George Taylor, 16, 28)
11. C.D. Chandaman, *The English public revenue 1660-1688* (Oxford 1975), 77-109 & 316-323
12. J.R. Jones, *Country and court: England 1658-1714* (1978), 45-70
13. A list is given in J. West, *Village records* (1962), 134-135. The main ones are: *Dorset hearth tax assessments 1662-1664* (ed. C.A.F. Meekings) (Dorchester 1951); *Hearth tax returns, Oxfordshire, 1665* (ed. M.M.B. Weinstock) (Oxfordshire Record Society, XXI, 1940); *Surrey hearth tax, 1664* (ed. C.A.F. Meekings) (Surrey Record Society, XVII, 1940); 'Hearth tax returns' (ed. M. Walker), in *Warwickshire County Records*, I (1957)
14. Cox, 'Three centuries', I, 60. For Boothby, see e.g. S. Glover, *The history, gazetteer and directory of the county of Derby* (Derby 1829), II(1), 35, 42; and for Gresley and Vernon, see e.g. Newton, 'Gentry of Derbyshire', 23, 28
15. The piece number is given erroneously as E 179/94/405 in the Dorset volume cited in n.13.
16. Benjamin Edbury does not appear in any of the hearth-tax lists transcribed here; perhaps he was Vernon's steward.
17. Public Record Office, *Calendar of Treasury Books*, II, 9, 18, 23, 29, 136, 170, 208. Information on the bonds is from n.13 (Dorset)
18. Newton, 'Gentry of Derbyshire', 12
19. Public Record Office, *Calendar of Treasury Books*, III, 360, 532, 567, 589, 596
20. *Ibid.*, 503, 683, 731
21. Public Record Office, *Calendar of Treasury Books*, III, 799, 807
22. P. Borne *et al.*, 'The Peacock Inn, Chesterfield', *Derbys. Archaeol. Journ.*, XCVIII (1978) 31, 52
23. Ll. Jewitt, 'The traders' tokens of Derbyshire, described and illustrated, Part IV', *Reliquary*, IV (1863-4), 241-248

24. British Library, Add.MS. 6672, f.249. I am grateful to Mrs Miriam Wood of Matlock for bringing this to my attention.
25. Cox, *Three centuries*, II, 122, is the source of the first estimate; the origin of the second has not yet been identified.
26. K.C. Cameron, *The place-names of Derbyshire* (English Place Name Society, XXVII-XXIX, Cambridge 1959)
27. C. Castledine, 'The parish of Seal and the border areas of Leicestershire and Derbyshire', *Derbyshire Miscellany*, VII(6) (1976), 295-302
28. D. and S. Lysons, *Magna Britannia, V: Derbyshire* (1817), xi
29. *Dorset hearth tax assessments* (ed. Meekings)
30. E.g. Lysons, *Magna Britannia*, xxiii-xxxiv
31. Sheffield City Library, Beauchief Muniments, BM80 (untitled)
32. D.G. Edwards, 'Swathwick in Wingerworth: an exercise in historical geography', *Derbys. Miscell.*, VII(3) (1975), 111-115
33. G. Turbutt, 'Court rolls and other papers of the manor of Stretton', *Derbys. Archaeol. Journ.* XCV (1975), 12-36; M. Hetherington, 'Egstow Hall, Old Tupton', *Derbyshire Life and Countryside* (Jan. 1974), 30-33. (It is a little puzzling why Archelaus appears in the assessment and not his father Hercules, who was still alive in 1670).
34. Chesterfield Public Library Local map collection, 'Williamthorpe ... surveighed Anno Domini 1676'.
35. Chesterfield Rural District Council, *Official Guide* (3rd ed. 1966), 41. For Clarke, see also Newton, 'Gentry of Derbyshire', 15 (but note the error in the number of hearths quoted). I also acknowledge discussion with Mr Frank Slawson of Chesterfield on 'Brampton in Morton'.
36. Lysons, *Magna Britannia*, 301
37. Cameron, *Place-names of Derbyshire*
38. *The diary of James Clegg of Chapel en le Frith 1708-1755, Part 1* (ed. V.S. Doe) (Derbyshire Record Society, II, 1978), xix
39. Cox, *Three centuries*, I, 284, 286
40. R. Johnson, *A history of Alfreton* (Alfreton, nd, c.1970)
41. D.G. Edwards, *The Hunlokes of Wingerworth Hall* (Wingerworth, 2nd ed., 1976), 36
42. *Dorset hearth tax assessments* (ed. Meekings)
43. Information kindly provided by Mr Richard Clark of West Hallam and Mr Tom Arkell of Solihull regarding the recommended multiplier
44. *Dorset hearth tax assessments* (ed. Meekings)
45. Issued by the Derbyshire Record Office
46. Philip Riden, 'The population of Derbyshire in 1563', *Derbys. Archaeol. Journ.*, XCVIII (1978), 61-71
47. Roger Fieldhouse, 'The hearth tax and other records', in A. Rogers (ed.), *Group projects in local history* (Folkestone 1977)
48. For Grey, Frechville, Harpur (of Swarkestone),Gresley, Curzon, Every, Eyre, Wilmot, Degge, Ash, Pegge, Sacheverell, Sleigh, Vernon, Gell and Fitzherbert, see e.g. Newton, 'Gentry of Derbyshire'.
49. Rosemary Milward, 'Some seventeenth century Chesterfield inns and innkeepers', *Derbys. Miscell.*, IX (1) (1980), 25-40
50. Information kindly provided by Mrs Barbara Bestall of Sheffield
51. Newton, 'Gentry of Derbyshire', 28
52. Department of the Environment, *Bolsover Castle, Derbyshire* (by P.A. Faulkner) (1972)
53. *The diary of John Milward Esq., 1666 to 1668* (ed. C. Robbins) (Cambridge 1938)
54. R. Meredith, 'Beauchief Abbey and the Pegges', *Derbys. Archaeol. Journ.*, LXXXVII (1967), 99

TABLE 2. TOTALS OF HEARTHS AND ENTRIES, 1662, 1664 AND 1670

General note: The totals, except for those assessments printed in this volume, are the work of C.A.F. Meekings, with some minor amendments and additions based on an examination of the 1664 assessments by R. Clark of West Hallam. Absence of figures, except where commented on in the footnotes and Table 3, indicates a defective or missing assessment. H = hearths; E = entries; Ch. = chargeable; N. Ch. = not chargeable

1. APPLETREE HUNDRED: 1662 Mich. - E 179/94/378, mm.59-63, and E 179/245/8
1664 Ladyday - E 179/94/405

	1662		1664				
			Ch.		N. Ch.		Total
	H	E	H	E	H	E	E
Alderwasley**	91	68	70	50	14	14	64
Ashleyhay							
Alkmonton*	20	11	20	11		1	12
Arleston: see Sinfin							
Ash	16	5	16	5	nil		5
Ashleyhay: see Alderwasley							
Atlow*	24	23	22	22		4	26
Barton Blount	25	7	15	4	3	3	7
Belper	51 43	43 38	85	75	27	27	102
Borrowash***	9	6					
Boylestone**	39	29	26	20		5	25
Bradley	137	80	41	23	13	13	36
Sturston & Compton			42	29	18	18	47
Yeldersley			39	26	13	13	39
Brailsford**	88	45	66	37		8	45
Breadsall	68	49	62	48	23	23	71
Chaddesden*	61	46	35	28		18	46
Church Broughton***	34	26	28	22	12	12	34
Compton: see Bradley (and Clifton, in Morleston & Litchurch)							
Cubley	53	30	36	26	nil		26
Dalbury	46	21	36	20	12	11	31
Doveridge***	127	54	131	61	nil		61
Duffield**	138	71	129	72	50	50	122
Hazelwood	81	55					
Edlaston	36	24	37	23	10	10	33
Wyaston							
Ednaston	18	11	13	10	nil		10
Etwall**	80	35	70	36	12	12	48
Foston**	123	78	93	58	35	35	93
Scropton							
Hatton*	26	20	14	13		5	18
Hazelwood: see Duffield							

	1662		1664				
			Ch.		N.Ch.		Total
	H	E	H	E	H	E	E
Heage	83	54	60	47	8	8	55
Hilton	40	25	41	28	17	17	45
Holbrook	26	22	23	19	16	16	35
Hollington*	26	19	24	17		5	22
Hoon**			3		nil		
Hulland*	118	84	100	75		38	113
Ireton** Mercaston Mugginton***	79	57	78	53	13	13	66
Kedleston	37	13	36	12	5	5	17
Longford	85	36	84	37	nil		37
Mapperley: see Stanley							
Marston on Dove***	17	10	16	9	nil		9
Marston Montgomery	69	31	74	33	11	11	44
Mercaston Mugginton : see Ireton							
Norbury Roston	84	42	79	39	8	8	47
Osleston* Thurvaston	38	24	34	22		14	36
Osmaston (by Ashbourne)	40	23	28	15	9	9	24
Postern: see Shottle							
Radbourne	50	19	53	19	nil		19
Rodsley**	13	13	15	13	3	3	16
Roston: see Norbury							
Sapperton***			20	11	nil		11
Scropton: see Foston							
Shirley**	30	22	29	21	8	8	29
Yeaveley	35	23	21	20	3	3	23
Shottle Postern	113	102	c.99	c.92	37	37	c.129
Sinfin Arleston	16	6	16	5	2	2	7
Snelston	65	40	60	38	13	13	51
Somersal Herbert	36	16	31	14	7	7	21
Spondon**	114	58					
Stanley** Mapperley	36	28	14 12	14 10	17 nil	6	20 10
Stenson: see Twyford							
Sturston: see Bradley							
Stydd	11	5	7	4	4	4	8
Sudbury*	125	63	94	55		13	68
Sutton on the Hill	31	17	27	15	nil		15
Thurvaston: see Osleston							
Trusley	36	13	33	12	2	2	14
Twyford Stenson	37	18	32	18	12	12	30
West Broughton***	23	9					
Wyaston: see Edlaston							
Yeaveley: see Shirley							
Yeldersley: see Bradley							

2. HIGH PEAK HUNDRED: 1662 Mich. - E 179/94/378, mm. 47-58
1664 Ladyday - E 179/94/403
1670 Mich. - DC9955

	1662		1664					1670	
			Ch.		N. Ch.		Total		
	H	E	H	E	H	E	E	H	E
Abney	35	33	58	52	6	6	58	43	37
{ Alport***	} 33	14	32	13	1	1	14		
{ Great Rowsley									
Ashford	65	52	55	42	29	29	71	99	55
Aston	24	18	21	17	3	2	19	21	14
Bakewell***	224	106	226	103	91	91	194	220	91
Bamford***	30	27	19	19	11	11	30		
{ Baslow	48	35	43	34	12	12	46	} 179	70
{ Beeley***	119	32	129	32	2	2	34		
Beard**	25	15	22	12	nil		12	20	11
Beeley: see Baslow									
Birchover	45	32	45	32	7	7	39	39	29
Blackwell	20	19	18	17	nil		17		
Bowden Edge **	57	37	53	33	4	4	37	90	56
Bradshaw Edge	118	58	91	49	13	7	56	142	72
Bradwell	77	72	83	80	6	5	85	95	88
Brough	9	6	8	6	3	3	9	8	7
Brownside	11	7	12	8	nil		8	16	10
Brushfield***	9	9	9	9	nil		9		
Bubnell	33	16	33	16	3	3	19	35	17
Buxton**	38	17	33	13	nil		13	46	19
Buxworth	28	17	29	16	nil		16	34	16
Calver	20	19	21	19	19	19	38	21	18
{ Castleton	108	76	} 111	85	21	21	106 {	108	75
{ Losehill	16	15						17	15
Charlesworth	31	20	29	18	2	2	20	36	25
Chelmorton	53	51	36	25	17	17	42	51	37
Chinley	30	26	27	23	nil		23	31	26
Chisworth	22	18	23	19	nil		19	31	22
Chunal	9	7	9	7	nil		7	9	7
Combes Edge	67	41	53	34	3	3	37	74	40
Cowdale	8	5	8	5	nil		5	6	4
{ Curbar	} 35	30	33	28	23	23	51	34	28
{ Froggatt									
Darley Dale**	191	85	190	73	20	20	93	157	82
Derwent***	44	34	27	24	16	16	40		
Dinting	21	15	20	14	1	1	15	22	18
Edale	55	44	56	45	3	3	48	58	45
Edensor	50	35	43	31	14	13	44	46	31
Eyam***	89	56	84	59	101	101	160	110	76
Eyam Woodlands	35	26	67	42	19	19	61	37	25
Fairfield	51	43		40				63	54
Fernilee***								39	28
Flagg	33	23	28	18	nil		18	45	30
Foolow	54	43	41	34	19	19	53	51	38
Froggatt: see Curbar									
Glossop	77	47	74	44	3	3	47	86	49
Gratton	16	11	16	11	1	1	12	16	11

	1662		1664					1670	
			Ch.		N.Ch.		Total		
	H	E	H	E	H	E	E	H	E
Great Hamlet**	50	34	39	37	nil		27	71	38
Great Hucklow***	16	11	11	8	43	42	50		
Great Longstone	90	76	73	62	2	2	64	86	66
Great Rowsley: see Alport									
Grindlow***	18	14	14	12	5	5	17		
Hadfield	18	14	17	13	1	1	14	19	15
Hassop	34	11	34	11	nil		11	34	11
Hathersage***	59	47	50	45	10	10	55	163	130
Hazlebadge***	15	14	9	8	4	4	12		
Holme	12	6	12	6	nil		6	14	6
Hope	70	48	57	46	14	10	56	72	49
Hope Woodlands	71	38	67	42	19	19	61	66	32
Kinder	16	14	16	12	nil		12	23	17
Kingsterndale	10	9	10	9	nil		9	13	11
Little Hucklow***	24	15	18	10	28	28	38		
Little Longstone***	16	16	19	15	15	15	30		
Litton***	56	47							
Ludworth	45	38		37	nil		37	66	50
Mellor	69	51	63	48	nil		48	97	59
Miller's Dale: see Tideswell									
Monyash	52	44	51	45	38	38	83	56	42
Offerton	15	7	12	6	3	3	9	14	6
Ollersett**	20	12	20	13	nil		13	25	16
Outseats***	49	30	49	30	7	7	37		
Over Haddon**	35	30	31	26	4	4	30	122	47
Padfield	31	26	30	25	1	1	26	30	26
Peak Forest**	28	26	66	65	14	14	79	93	87
Phoside	35	28	21	17	nil		17	26	25
Pilsley (by Edensor)	24	21	23	20	5	5	25	19	16
Priestcliffe	36	28	28	25	8	8	33	29	22
Rowland	9	9	9	9	nil		9	10	9
Rowsley: see Alport									
Shatton	18	8	16	8	nil		8	18	9
Sheldon	54	45	29	26	27	27	53	38	28
Simmondley	22	13	21	12	1	1	13	25	17
Staden	11	6	10	6	nil		6	17	12
Stanton: see Youlgreave									
Stoney Middleton	62	42	69	49	70	70	119	86	56
Taddington	60	54	53	48	7	7	55	53	48
Thornhill	25	18	20	15	5	5	20	25	14
Thornsett	37	29	32	26	nil		26	39	29
Tideswell***	142	84	174	121	128	128	249	387	245
Miller's Dale			4	3	nil		3		
Wardlow	28	28	27	27	nil		27	30	29
Wheston***	28	19	27	19	5	5	24		
Whitfield	27	25	23	22	3	3	25	37	28
Whitle**	51	37	39	29	nil		29	46	32
Winster	118	93	107	85	15	15	100	106	84
Wormhill***	82	70		67	3	3	70	67	54
Youlgreave	213	81	130	80	17	17	97	123	71
Stanton in Peak		49	76	48	6	6	54	75	47

3. MORLESTON & LITCHURCH HUNDRED: 1662 Mich. - E 179/94/378, mm. 28-36
1664 Ladyday - E 179/94/401
1670 Mich. - DC 9956

	1662		1664					1670	
			Ch.		N.Ch.		Total		
	H	E	H	E	H	E	E	H	E
Allestree	44	30	38	26	12	12	38	53	33
Alvaston Boulton	54	45	44	36	10	10	46	62	47
Aston on Trent	68	45	59	38	24	24	62	62	35
Barrow on Trent	65	35	56	30	6	6	36	62	36
Boulton: see Alvaston									
Breaston	38	31	31	28	9	9	37	40	24
Clifton Compton	20 24	18 13	41	26	33	33	59	52	32
Codnor*** Loscoe	105	52	103	54	32	32	86	94	46
Codnor Castle & Park***			6	2	1	1	3	17	4
Compton: see Clifton (and Bradley in Appletree)									
Crich Fritchley	106	85	108	87	48	48	135	118	85
Dale Abbey	54	28	53	31	23	23	54	64	35
Darley Abbey***								8	2
Denby	58	38	61	41	22	22	63	67	36
Derby**	1479		1274	478	26	26	504	1915	611
Draycott	53	39	45	33	46	43	76	56	32
Egginton	72	36	71	34	20	20	54	70	32
Elvaston	78	41	54	36	34	34	70	68	38
Findern	38	26	31	21	7	7	28	47	26
Fritchley: see Crich									
Heanor	90	50	89	55	27	27	82	95	52
Hopwell	7	2	5	2	nil		2	7	2
Horsley***	96	70	94	70	43	43	113	103	70
Ilkeston	100	70	100	66	13	13	79	107	67
Kirk Hallam	16	11	11	11	5	5	16	17	10
Kirk Langley***	64	41	43	25	16	16	41	62	39
Litchurch	3	3	nil		3	3	3	3	3
Little Chester Little Eaton Quarndon	91	42	31 26 25	8 18 17	7 8 10	7 8 10	15 26 27	99	40
Littleover	33	19	41	27	6	6	33	50	29
Long Eaton	71	49	60	42	7	7	49	81	43
Loscoe: see Codnor									
Mackworth	47	37	31	24	26	26	50	40	28
Markeaton	37	23						42	26
Mickleover	96	60	75	48	24	24	72	99	55
Morley	52	31	46	25	10	10	35	50	28
Ockbrook***	61	49	53	44				62	43
Pentrich	75	61	71	60	29	29	89	64	48
Quarndon: see Little Chester									
Ripley	60	43	64	41	22	22	63	70	33
Risley	55	14	53	13	6	6	19	61	14
Sandiacre	33	22	31	19	16	16	35	40	20

	1662		1664					1670	
			Ch.		N.Ch.		Total		
	H	E	H	E	H	E	E	H	E
Sawley	42	30	43	28	30	29	57	53	26
Shardlow: see Wilne									
Snipley	42	29	44	30	5	5	35	46	29
Smalley	57	50	42	35	18	18	53	56	42
Stanton by Dale	46	28	47	31	14	14	45	49	25
West Hallam	64	25	64	24	15	15	39	67	25
Weston on Trent	44	31	46	29	13	13	42	55	28
Weston Underwood	29	19	26	19	3	3	22	33	18
Willington	29	22	30	24	nil		24	40	23
{ Wilne	39	19	33	16	26	26	42	44	19
{ Shardlow									
Wilsthorpe	10	6	10	10	nil		10	11	6

4. REPTON & GRESLEY HUNDRED:** 1662 Mich. - E 179/94/378, mm. 22-27 (A)
E 179/245/7, ff.115-146 (R)
1664 Ladyday - E 179/245/10

	1662A		1662R					1664				
			Ch.		N.Ch.		Total	Ch.		N.Ch		Total
	H	E	H	E	H	E	E	H	E	H	E	E
Appleby	47	10+	52	36	nil		36	46	36	8	8	44
Bretby	93	11+	92	17	4	4	21	86+	18	4	4	22
Calke: see Ticknall												
{ Castle Gresley**	8	4+	11	8								
{ Church Gresley***	56	12	50	11								
{ Donisthorpe***			13	8	31	31	86					
{ Oakthorpe	19	7+	19	15								
{ Swadlincote***	29	24	16	13								
Catton	22	6	22	6	nil		6	23	6	nil		6
Cauldwell**	36	20	35	19	nil		19	26	17	3	3	20
Chellaston	42	32	42	32	6	6	38	41	31	9	9	40
Chilcote**	58	26+	55	26	nil		26					
{ Coton	51	7+						41	32	9	9	41
{ Rosliston	38	28										
{ Croxall*	35	11	35	11		1	12	34	12	1	1	13
{ Edingale*												
Donisthorpe: see Castle Gresley												
Edingale: see Croxall												
Foremark	34	6	34	5	nil		5	34	5	3	3	8
Hartshorne	82	36+	87	41	14	13	54	80	42	11	11	53
Ingleby**	41	11+	41	21	2	2	23					
King's Newton: see Melbourne												
Linton	33	28	33	28	7	7	35	33	29	12	12	41
Lullington	49	21	50	22	7	7	29					
Measham	54	47	54	47	nil		47	48	41	69	69	110
{ Melbourne	188	112+	190	125	52	52	177	172	117	56	56	173
{ King's Newton												
Newhall: see Stanton Ward												
Newton Solney**	48	34	47	33	1	1	34					
Normanton *	46	4+	46	22		5	27					

	1662A		1662R					1664				
			Ch.		N.Ch.		Total	Ch.		N.Ch.		Total
	H	E	H	E	H	E	E	H	E	H	E	E
Oakthorpe: see Castle Gresley												
Osmaston			50	21	5	5	26					
Packington: see Willesley												
Ravenstone: see Willesley												
Repton	192	80+										
Rosliston: see Coton												
Smisby	39	22	39	22	13	13	35					
Stanton by Bridge*	45	17+	45	24		10	34	40	25	10	10	35
{ Stanton Ward	} 67	31	{ 13	9 }	12	12	43	{ 15	10	1	1	11
{ Newhall			{ 46	22 }				{ 34	21	14	14	35
Stapenhill	91	46	93	48	8	8	56					
Stretton en le Field: see Willesley												
Swadlincote: see Castle Gresley												
Swarkestone**	76	26	76	26	2	2	28					
{ Ticknall	73	48	69	48	nil		48					
{ Calke	45	9+	48	20	nil		20					
Walton on Trent	57	23+						57	29	12	12	41
{ Willesley*	23	7	23	7		3	10					
{ Packington*	18	11	18	11		11	22	14	11	11	10	21
{ Ravenstone*	32	15	32	15		8	23					
{ Stretton en le Field*	35	15	35	15		2	17					
Winshill	28	24										

5. SCARSDALE HUNDRED: 1662 Mich. - E 179/94/378, mm. 5-21
1664 Ladyday - E 179/94/400
1670 Mich. - DC 9954

	1662		1664					1670	
			Ch.		N.Ch.		Total		
	H	E	H	E	H	E	E	H	E
Alfreton**	160	104	158	101	67	67	168	192	121
Ashover**	238	142	211	132	59	58	190	249	139
{ Barlborough			} 227	100	94	93	193	{ 146	54
{ Whitwell								{ 128	66
Barlow (Great)			78	47	51	49	96	101	43
Barlow (Little)***								27	14
Beauchief	29	15	28	15	4	4	19	31	15
Beighton			89	63	17	17	80	110	66
Blackwell			52	34	18	18	52	61	35
Bolsover***			89	48	66	46	94	158	56
Bolsover Woodhouse***								32	16
{ Brackenfield { Wessington			} 60	39	nil		39	69	41
Brampton			186	111	68	63	174	229	112
'Brampton in Morton'	66	33	35	23	6	6	29	78	31
Brimington			60	33	16	14	47	69	32

	1662		1664					1670	
			Ch.		N.Ch.		Total		
	H	E	H	E	H	E	E	H	E
Calow	86	50	33	26	11	11	37	39	22
Walton			38	22	12	12	34	64	29
Chesterfield	685		575	214	101	101	315	777	211
Clowne			34	20	22	22	42	83	37
Coal Aston			56	27	35	34	61	66	32
Cowley***								20	13
Creswell: see Elmton									
Dore	107	76	71	47	36	32	79	104	63
Totley									
Dronfield***			198	102	105	103	205	161	61
Dronfield Woodhouse***								52	24
Stubley									
Duckmanton: see Sutton									
Dunston			18	16	5	5	21	28	19
Eckington			110	44	64	62	214	371	189
Mosbrough			57	37					
Ridgeway			88	56					
Spinkhill			27	15					
Elmton		25	32	30	16	16	46	39	32
Creswell									
Glapwell	35	28	33	26	11	11	37	36	26
Rowthorne***									
Hasland***			61	25	35	35	60	80	28
Heath: see Stainsby									
Higham: see Shirland									
Holmesfield	142	70	140	71	16	16	87	143	66
Killamarsh	81	54	63	44	53	52	96	78	48
Langwith: see Pleasley									
Morton	55	39	21	15	20	20	85	113	69
Pilsley***			72	50					
Mosbrough: see Eckington									
Newbold			76	46	35	35	81	89	45
Norton			290	122	34	33	155	333	118
Oakerthorpe: see South Wingfield									
Oxcroft: see Tibshelf									
Palterton: see Scarcliffe									
Pilsley: see Morton									
Pinxton: see South Normanton									
Pleasley***			83	64	41	41	105	87	60
Langwith									
Ridgeway: see Eckington									
Rowthorne: see Glapwell									
Scarcliffe			63	55	12	12	67	85	66
Palterton									
Shirland	45	30	69	47	15	15	62	86	52
Higham	38	24							
South Normanton	105	63	59	35	24	24	59	116	66
Pinxton			44	26	13	13	39		
South Wingfield	39	19	36	18	22	20	54	74	36
Oakerthorpe	32	19	27	16					
Spinkhill: see Eckington									

	1662 H	1662 E	1664 Ch. H	1664 Ch. E	1664 N.Ch. H	1664 N.Ch. E	1664 Total E	1670 H	1670 E
Stainsby***	288		273	77	71	71	148	174	68
Heath									
Staveley			185	114	45	44	158	217	116
Stretton***			104	86	8	8	94	115	86
Sutton Scarsdale**	120		50	14	19	19	76	122	59
Duckmanton			61	43					
Swathwick: see Wingerworth									
Temple Normanton			17	13	9	9	22	19	14
Tibshelf	56	43	61	46	46	46	92	68	45
Oxcroft									
Totley: see Dore									
Tupton: see Wingerworth									
Unstone: see Wingerworth									
Walton: see Calow									
Wessington: see Brackenfield									
Whaley***								23	13
Whittington			85	57	16	15	72	96	60
Whitwell: see Barlborough									
Wingerworth	42	39	56	42	36	34	122	112	65
Swathwick	27	20							
Tupton			20	10					
Unstone			67	36				89	44

6. WIRKSWORTH HUNDRED: 1662 Mich. - E 179/94/378, mm. 37-46
1664 Ladyday - E 179/94/402
1670 Mich. - DC 9953

	1662 H	1662 E	1664 Ch. H	1664 Ch. E	1664 N.Ch. H	1664 N.Ch. E	1664 Total E	1670 H	1670 E
Aldwark: see Brassington									
Alsop: see Cold Eaton									
Ashbourne***	358	189	290	146	84	83	229	295	126
Ballidon	27	25	25	23	2	2	25	25	21
Bonsall	122	99						146	103
Bradbourne	37	24	31	23	nil		23	31	21
Brassington	86	62	61	47	50	46	93	83	55
Aldwark									
Callow	19	9	28	20	13	13	33	36	22
Ible***	14	13							
Carsington: see Hopton									
Cold Eaton	32	13	27	14	1	1	15	29	12
Alsop									
Cromford: see Middleton									
Dethick***	72	53	59	43	21	21	64	71	41
Lea									
Tansley									
Elton			49	39	12	12	51	57	42
Fenny Bentley	34	20	30	19	7	7	26	39	19
Hartington**	230	164	201	161	34	34	195	255	187
Hognaston	34	27	27	24	9	9	33	40	28

	1662		1664					1670	
			Ch.		N.Ch.		Total		
	H	E	H	E	H	E	E	H	E
{ Hopton	91	51	82	43	40	40	83	86	40
{ Carsington									
Ible: see Callow									
Kirk Ireton	82	52	71	47	14	14	61	94	52
{ Kniveton	52	36						121	55
{ Offcote	80	37	54	21	19	19	40		
{ Underwood									
Lea: see Dethick, Tissington									
{ Mapleton	70	46	49	33	12	7	40	72	42
{ Thorpe**									
Matlock	177	116	231	156	100	100	256	206	120
{ Middleton	32	25	35	33	30	30	63	86	63
{ Cromford	33	30							
{ Middleton	46	39	46	39	14	14	53	55	39
{ Smerrill									
Newton Grange**								7	3
Offcote: see Kniveton									
Parwich	56	51	42	35	23	23	58	57	41
Smerrill: see Middleton									
Snitterton: see Wensley									
Tansley: see Dethick									
Thorpe: see Mapleton									
{ Tissington	81	41	62	35	5	5	40	80	42
{ Lea Hall									
Underwood: see Kniveton									
{ Wensley	92	51	93	52	28	28	80	106	47
{ Snitterton									
Wirksworth	382	236	378	232	217	217	449	439	239

*No hearth numbers are given in the assessments for persons not chargeable in 1662 (Repton & Gresley hundred) or 1664 (Appletree hundred). For Alkmonton and Hulland, see also Table 3.

**Alderwasley & Ashleyhay, Boylestone, Brailsford, Cauldwell, Chilcote, Duffield & Hazelwood, Etwall, Foston & Scropton, Ingleby, Ireton et al., Newton Solney, Rodsley, Shirley, Stanley, Swarkestone and Yeaveley: the totals (hearths and entries) for the Not Chargeable category in 1662 (Repton & Gresley hundred) or 1664 (Appletree hundred) exclude those persons who also appear in the Chargeable category, i.e. where not-chargeable hearths rather than not-chargeable persons are recorded. For Boylestone and Brailsford, the preceding footnote also applies. For Duffield and Etwall, see also Table 3.

Alfreton: the 1670 assessment is in four sections with hearths/entries 115/59, 28/20, 25/22 and 24/20 in that order (see p.xlii of the Introduction).

Ashover: the 1670 assessment is in four sections with hearth/entries 58/28, 58/35, 47/23 and 86/53 in that order (see p.xlii of the Introduction).

Beard: the 1664 assessment is headed 'Bowden Middlecale' (the name of the whole constablewick).

Bowden Edge: the 1670 assessment is headed 'Bowdon Chappell' (Bowden Chapel: the name of the constablewick comprising also Bradshaw Edge and Combes Edge and equivalent to Chapel en le Frith).

Buxton: the 1664 assessment is headed 'Chelmorton' (the name of the whole constablewick); Chelmorton township appears under the second heading of that name in the document.

Castle Gresley et al.: in the 1662 'returns', the nine persons listed as being not within the Act were originally entered with one hearth each and have been so counted here.
Darley Dale: the high figure for hearths in 1662 and 1664 appears to be due to the inclusion of Haddon Hall (listed under Over Haddon in 1670) (see Table 3)
Derby: the figures for 1670 are subdivided as follows; for 1664, see p.xxvi.

	H	E	
All Saints	922	229	
St Werburgh	326	102	
St Peter	258	93	
St Michael	131	42	
St Alkmund	188	65	(see also Table 3)
Certified (whole borough)	90	80	

Great Hamlet: the 1670 assessment is headed 'Boaden Midlecalles' (Bowden Middlecale, the name of the whole constablewick). Great Hamlet is equivalent to Hayfield township.
Hartington: the four Quarters are listed separately in 1662 and 1664; for 1664 the figures are 43, 32, 11, 11, 43 for Town Q., 53, 43, 8, 8, 51 for Middle Q., 46, 40, 15, 15, 55 for Upper Q., and 59, 46, nil, 46 for Nether Q. See also Table 3.
Hoon: no individuals are listed in 1664, only the total hearths for the township (see page 21); for 1662, see Table 3.
Newton Grange: note that Hanson Grange in this parish is listed under Mapleton & Thorpe in 1670 at least; see also Table 3.
Ollersett: the 1664 assessment is headed 'West Hamblett'.
Over Haddon: see the note on Darley Dale above, and Table 3.
Peak Forest: the 1662 assessment appears to be defective. The 1664 assessment is split into two parts with the numbers 47, 46, 5, 5, 51, and 19, 19, 9, 9, 28.
Repton & Gresley hundred: a plus sign indicates that the preceding figure is only part of the full total (which is unobtainable because of illegibility).
Spondon: the hearths total recorded in the assessment is four short of the true total given here; the 1664 assessment is missing.
Whitle: the 1670 assessment is headed 'White Hamlet'.

***See Table 3.

TABLE 3. KEY TO PLACES APPARENTLY INCLUDING OR INCLUDED UNDER OTHER PLACES IN THE HEARTH-TAX ASSESSMENTS

Place	Included under	Includes
Alkmonton		Hungry Bentley?
Alport	Over Haddon 1670	
Alton	Hulland	
Ashbourne		Newton Grange 1662?, 1664?
Ault Hucknall	Rowthorne, Stainsby	
Bakewell		Harthill?
Bamford	Hathersage 1670	
Barlow (Little)	Dronfield 1664?	
Barrowcote	Etwall?	
Beeley	Baslow 1670	Chatsworth
Biggin	Hulland?	
Bolsover		Bolsover Woodhouse 1664?, Whaley 1664?
Bolsover Woodhouse	Bolsover 1664?	
Borrowash	Ockbrook 1664?	
Brushfield	Tideswell 1670	
Burnaston	Etwall?	
Chapel en le Frith	=Bowden Edge, Bradshaw Edge and Combes Edge	
Chatsworth	Beeley	
Church Broughton		Sapperton 1662?
Church Gresley		Drakelow
Clay Lane	Stretton	
Codnor		Codnor Castle & Park 1662?
Codnor Castle & Park	Codnor 1662?	
Cowley	Dronfield 1664?	
Darley Abbey	Derby St Alkmund 1662? & 1664?	
Darley Dale		Nether Haddon 1662 & 1664
Derby Hills	?	
Derwent	Hathersage 1670	
Dethick		Holloway?
Donisthorpe	Swadlincote 1662?	
Doveridge		West Broughton 1664*
Drakelow	Church Gresley	
Draycott		Little (Church) Wilne
Dronfield		Little Barlow 1664? Cowley 1664?, Stubley 1664?, Dronfield Woodhouse 1664?
Dronfield Woodhouse	Dronfield 1664?	
Duffield		Turnditch?, Windley?
Earl Sterndale	Hartington Middle Q?	

Place	Included under	Includes
Egstow	Stretton	
Etwall		Barrowcote?, Burnaston?
Eyam		Highlow, Stoke?
Fernilee	Wormhill 1662?, 1664?	
Great Hucklow	Tideswell 1670	
Griffe Grange	Ible?	
Grindlow	Tideswell 1670	
Harthill	Bakewell?	
Hartington		Earl Sterndale?
Hasland		Tapton (1670 at least)
Hathersage		Bamford 1670, Derwent 1670, Outseats 1670, Nether Padley?
Hayfield	=Great Hamlet	
Hazlebadge	Tideswell 1670	
Highlow	Eyam	
Holloway	Dethick?	
Hoon	Marston on Dove 1662?	
Horsley		Horsley Woodhouse?, Kilburn?
Horsley Woodhouse	Horsley?	
Hulland		Alton, Biggin?, Hulland Ward, H.W. Intakes, Idridgehay?, Ireton Wood?, Turnditch?, Windley?
Hulland Ward	Hulland?	
Hulland Ward Intakes	Hulland?	
Hungry Bentley	Alkmonton?	
Ible		Griffe Grange?, Ivon-brook Grange?
Idridgehay	Hulland?	
Ireton Wood	Hulland?	
Ivonbrook Grange	Ible?	
Kilburn	Horsley?	
Kirk Langley		Meynell Langley?
Little Hucklow	Tideswell 1670	
Little Longstone	Tideswell 1670	
Litton	Tideswell 1664?, 1670	
Marston on Dove		Hoon 1662?
Meynell Langley	Kirk Langley?	
Miller's Dale	Tideswell 1662?	
Mugginton		Ravensdale Park?
Nether Haddon	Darley Dale 1662, 1664; Over Haddon 1670	
Nether Padley	Hathersage?	
Newton Grange	Ashbourne 1662?, 1664?	
North Wingfield	Pilsley (Scarsdale)	
Ockbrook		Borrowash 1664?
Outseats	Hathersage 1670	
Over Haddon		Alport 1670, Nether Haddon 1670, Rowsley 1670
Pilsley (Scarsdale)		North Wingfield
Pleasley		Shirebrook?

Place	Included under	Includes
Ravensdale Park	Mugginton?	
Rowsley	Over Haddon 1670	
Rowthorne		Ault Hucknall (part)
Sapperton	Church Broughton 1662?	
Shirebrook	Pleasley?	
Sinfin Moor	?	
Stainsby		Ault Hucknall (part)
Stoke	Eyam?	
Stretton		Clay Lane, Egstow, Woodthorpe
Stubley	Dronfield 1664?	
Swadlincote		Donisthorpe 1662?
Tapton	Hasland (1670 at least)	
Tideswell		Brushfield 1670, Great Hucklow 1670, Grindlow 1670, Hazlebadge 1670, Little Hucklow 1670, Little Longstone 1670, Litton 1664?, 1670 Miller's Dale 1662?, 1670, Wheston 1670
Turnditch	Duffield or Hulland?	
West Broughton	Doveridge 1664*	
Whaley	Bolsover 1664?	
Wheston	Tideswell 1670	
Wilne (Little or Church)	Draycott?	
Windley	Duffield or Hulland ?	
Woodthorpe	Stretton	
Wormhill		Fernilee 1662?, 1664?

*The last eight names in the Doveridge assessment for 1664 printed in this volume correspond to persons recorded for West Broughton in 1662.

TABLE 4. THE MOST COMMON SURNAMES IN DERBYSHIRE, 1662/1664/1670

Name	No. of households
Smith	175
Taylor Wright	105
Hall Jackson	95
Bennett Wilson	75
Buxton Harrison Turner Wood	70
Brown Walker Ward	65
Clarke Johnson Webster	60
Allen Eyre Fletcher Goodwin Hill Mellor Needham Newton Parker	55
Alsop Bagshaw Barker Booth Lowe Marshall White	50
Dakin Green Ragge Robinson Spencer Stone	45

Name	No. of households
Cooper Greaves Hadfield Hod(g)kinson Holmes Moore Morton Mosley Roberts	40
Burton Cooke Gregory Kirke Lee Smedley Stevenson Tomlinson	35
Adams Barber Bradshaw Clay Fox Frost Heathcote Hunt Middleton Storer Tompson Watson Wheeldon Wilde	30
Ashton Baker Bateman Beard Blackwell Bowden Eaton Elliott Furniss Hallam Hardy Hayward Lomas Mason Milward Pegge Redferne Rogers Shaw Sheldon Thorpe Toplis	25

APPENDIX: THE HOUSEHOLDERS OF MELBOURNE AND KING'S NEWTON IN 1662 AND 1695

As an offshoot of the present work, it is of interest to compare the householders of Melbourne and King's Newton assessed for and exempt from the tax in 1662 with those appearing in a published list[1] purporting to name all the inhabitants of those places in 1695, drawn up in accordance with the Act of Parliament 6 & 7 William & Mary c.6 for a tax on births, marriages, burials, bachelors and widowers. For the present purpose the published transcript has been taken as accurate; the original, which was in the hands of Viscount Hardinge at the time of publication, has not been sought. Each household is listed in turn, but in a few cases it is not absolutely clear where one household ends and another begins. Here the following combinations have been assumed to represent single households:

1. Henry, John and William Cooper + three servants
2. Anne and Isabel Chamberlin
3. Mary Brown, Thomas Cantril and Margaret Osborn + three servants
4. Anne and Mary Berrisford + two servants

The number of households on this basis is 186, which at a total of 651 people listed gives an average of 3.5 persons per household. Although, at the currently suggested countrywide average (for rural areas and smaller towns at least) of about 4.3 persons per household at that period, this low value is not outside the bounds of possibility for an individual parish, it does raise a suspicion that perhaps not absolutely all the inhabitants were included in the list, or that one should take more combinations than the above four as single households: for instance, there are apparently thirty-two single-person households and it may be that some of these persons really belonged to households immediately adjacent in the list (especially where the same surname is involved). However, an experimental comparison of population estimates yielded by the hearth-tax assessments and the 'Compton census' does allow agreement at a mean household size as low as 3.6 for Melbourne and King's Newton.

The total of 186 households in 1695 compares reasonably with 177 in 1662. At least two households - the most prominent ones - can be recognised at both dates: those at Melbourne Hall and King's Newton Hall. In 1695 the former was occupied by Thomas Coke esquire, as expected, but in 1662 a Mr Fords resided there. King's Newton Hall was the property of the Hardinge family; the occupier in 1662 was the Robert Hardinge who was knighted in 1674/5 and died in 1679, and in 1695 his son Robert was living there. Except for the incumbent - John Troughton was vicar in 1695 - no comparision of occupations can be made between the two dates, as the necessary information does not appear in the hearth-tax list.

The main object of this appendix is in fact a comparison of the surnames of the heads of the households in the two lists. The total number of surnames provided by the lists is 173, of which 62 appear in 1662 but not in 1695, and 48 in 1695 but not in 1662. Thus the community was less diverse in this respect at the later date, with 111 different surnames instead of 125 in 1662. Of the 63 surnames common to the two dates, twenty-one were represented by more households in 1695 than in 1662, and thirteen by a smaller number of households. For example, the Smiths advanced from two to five households, the Rolstons from one to four, the Berrisfords from two to six, and the Cartwrights/Cartricks from four to seven (these being the most marked examples). A complete list of the surnames would occupy an inordinate amount of space here, but a copy is available from the editor (DGE).

To complete the picture, we may look at the numbers of households represented by the various categories of surname, which are best shown in tabular form.

Surname category	No. of households in 1662	No. of households in 1695
A. 62 appearing in 1662 but not 1695	68	--
B. 48 appearing in 1695 but not 1662	--	57
C. 29 common to both dates, each with the same no. of households in 1662 and 1695	36	36
D. 21 common to both dates, each with a larger no. of households in 1695 than in 1662	39	76
E. 13 common to both dates, each with a smaller no. of households in 1695 than in 1662	34	17
TOTAL	177	186

The sum of the number of households in category C and the smaller of the two numbers in each of categories D and E is 92, or roughly half of the households in Melbourne and King's Newton at either date. This number can be looked upon as the core of households common to the two dates; the remainder represents to some degree the overall change that took place between1662 and 1695. Although this is a very rough indication - 33 years is sufficient for at least one change in generations, and the actual changes in house occupancy have not been investigated - it does seem to show tnat there was much movement in and out of the parish in the later seventeenth century, as could be gathered just from the comparison of the ranges of surnames. This evidence provides a further caution, if one were still needed, against the idea that there was little migration of ordinary people at that period.

Reference

1. R.E.C. Waters, 'A statutory list of the inhabitants of Melbourne, Derbyshire, in 1695', *Derbyshire Archaeological Journal* VII (1885), 1-30.

Derbyshire

HEARTH-TAX ASSESSMENTS/RETURNS

1662/1664/1670

APPLETREE HUNDRED

1662

Public Record Office, E 179/94/378

(60r.)

Spondon Constablery

Spondon Towne

Hen. Gilbert Esq.	10
Rich. Emery	6
Gilbt Drakelow	1
Joane Drakelow	1
Henry Gilbert for Taylors house	3
Fran. Bracknocke	3
Jo. Piggen	2
Tho. Stevenson	1
Jo. Johnson	2
Renald Johnson	2
John Carrington	3
Mary Widdowson	1
Fran. Brookes	1
Rich. Lockoe	1
Wm Bennett	1
Wm Lockoe	2
Mr Ja. Brecknocke Clarke	(blank)
Tho. Hall	2
Rich. Crosse gen	8
John Walker	1
Robt Soare	2
Jo. Tobb	1
Robt Lockoe	1

(61r.)

William Walker	1
Rich. Lockoe for Radford house	2
Tho. Wright	1
Wm Foxe	2
Jo. Lockoe at Colebrooke	1
Jo. Hudson sen.	1
Wm Dowman & his son William	2
Ralph Braddocke	2
Wm Hollingworth	5
Robt Smedley	2
Allexander Knight	2
Rich. Lockoe	1
Edw. Ollerenshawe	1
Jo. Antill	1
Robt Day for John Piggins house	1
Lawrence Fox	2
Jo. Hollingworth	4
Robt Knowles	1
Wm Knowles	1

Wm Bennitt	5
Tho. Bowes	1
Jo. Bowes	1
Joseph Price	1
Rich. Knowles	(3)
Edw. Knight	(1)
Griffith Dakaine	(1)
John Lockoe	(1)

(The above four hearth numbers have been taken from E 179/245/8, f.16r., as E 179/94/378 is torn.)

Wm Bagworth	1
Christopher Barton	1
Henry Ebb	4
Wm Coope	1
Jo. Morlidge	1
Wm Ollerenshawe	1
Jo. Hudson Jun.	2
Wm. Porter	1
	110

Borrowsash

Wm Statham	1
John Bainbridge	4
Michael Cooke	1
John Else	1
Fran. Adams	1
Tho. Pollard	1
	9

1664

Public Record Office, E 179/94/405

(1r.)

Appltree Hundred

duffeild

Persons Chargeable

Thomas Willett	?2
Wm Willett	4
Margarett Bradshawe	1
?Joh. Bloodworth Jun.	3
?Joh. Bloodworth sen.	1
Mrs Bradshawe widd.	1
Anthony Meller	1
John Wood	1
Humfry Holmes	1
John ?Matkin (?Mackin)	1
Nicholas Stevenson	1
Rich. Redfearne	1
widd. Mingas	2
Mr. Adryan Mundy	1
Francis Dudley	2
Rich. Orme	1
John Ball	1
Tho. Worrall	1
John Stables	1
Widd. Stables	1
Robt ?Matkyn (?Mackyn)	1
Tho. ?Robinson	1
Wm Ryley	1
Jo. Bache	2
Edmund webster	1
Ralph Rossington	2
Mr Willymot	10
Widd. ?Standley	1
Widd. Oldham	1
John Roberts	1
Mr Rich. Bateman	5
Peter Page sen.	1
Tho. ?Stalman	1
Rich. Palmer	1
Robt Clay	1
Mr Raynor	2

John Malyn	1
Mr Gervace Raynor	4
John ?Greene	1
Roger Statham	1
Francis Stewerdson	1
Wm sum(m)ers	1
John Saunders	1
John Wartopp	1
Mr Tho. Newton	7
Mr Wm ?Broadhurst	3
Roger Hodgkinson	3
Stephen Kirkland	1
Adam Malyn	1
Margery Pegge	1
... ...	2
widd. Roberts	1
Mr Buxton Vicar	?2
Wm Johnson	?2
Mr Henry Smith	1
Thomas Wetton	?1
Henry Parker	?1
Robt Orme	?2
Henry Orme	?2
Mr ?Vic. Bradshawe	4
Wm Fletcher	1
Wm Lees	2
Wm Bulloke	1
Widd. Swifte	1
Tho. Shepheard	1
Wm Freareson	1
Mr Foxcrofte	1
Thomas ?Barker	?2
Humfry Jones	1
Tho. Bentham	1
John Stewardson	1
... ...	2
	129

Persons not Chargeable

Thomas Fletcher	1
Tho. Yeomans	1
Ralph Bearde	1
Wm Burrowes	1
Ralph Alsibrooke	1
Wm Symms	1
Tho. Symms	1
Widd. Farman	1
Widd. Stewardson	1
Robt Claver	1
John Bayley sen.	1
Jane Pinder	1
Rich. Stables	1
Tho. Tatum	1
Joseph Day	1
Rich. Cockerham	1
Wm Tatum	1
Widd. Dilks	1
Tho. Matkin	1
Tho. Sowter	1
Thomas James	1
widd. Smith	1
widd. Fisher	1
Rich. Mowbray	1
Wm Meakyn	1
Wm ?Crosly	1
Abraham Bloodworth	1
Henry Hawlsworth	1
Rich. Rowbotham	1
Katherine White widd.	1
Adam Potter	1
Anth. ?Claver	1
Robt Deddicke	1
Wm Sowter	1
Ralph Robinson	1
Elizabeth Bradshawe	1
Thomas Maddocke	1
Widd. Day	1

Tho. Whelpdale	1
Widd. Potter	1
Wm Jackson	1
Robt Sowter	1
Thomas Crofts	1
Godfry Newton	1
Francis Page	1
John Smeathers	1
John Newton	1
Peter Page Jun.	1
John Sowter	1
Fran. Hawley	1

harths decreased

Margarett Bradshaw	3
Mr. Ralph Rossington	1
Mr. Wm Broadhurst	3
Hen. Orme	2
Wm Bullocke	1
Widd. Swift	1
Wm Lees	2
	63

(1v.)

Snelston

Persons Chargeable

Mr Benett	11
?Alice Litton widd.	1
?Lawrence Sutton	1
Ralph Doxie sen.	2
Jo. Tunnycliffe	2
Tho. Dakine	1
Tho. Telloe	1
Luke Seaverne	2
Ralp Doxie Ju.	1
Jane Jackson	1
Jo. Doxie Jun.	1
Mrs Anne Wilson	4
Wm Keeleing	1
Robt Wharton	1
Tho. Brunt	1
Wm Brunt	1
Nicholas Seaverne	2
Wm Walton	1
Tho. Coxon Jun.	1
Thomas Maddocke	1
Symon Stone	1
Rich. Heape	1
Rich. Allen	1
?Moadd Doxie	1
Edw. Coxon	1
Edw. Ashton	1
Wm Bill	1
Elizabeth Fernall	1
John Doxie sen.	1
Jo. woodhouse Jun.	1
John Wharton	5
Tho. Doxie	1
Ralph Tunnycliffe Jun.	2
Wm Allen	1
Jo. woodhouse sen.	1
Tho. Johnson	1
Nath. Dakine	1
Law. Reeve	1
	60

Persons not Chargeable

Rich. woodward	1
Robt Greensmith	1
Wm Cowper	1
Francis Roome	1
Tho. Braddocke	1
Rich. Wharton	1
Ellen Kinson	1
Rich. Hall	1
Thomas Coxon	1
Thomas Boyer	1
James Atkyn	1
Humfry Warren	1

John Roe	1
	13

Yeaveley

Persons Chargeable

Mr Joseph Harpur	2
Walter Stidman	1
Thomas Ould	1
Rich. Jankinson	1
Fran. Calvert	1
Robt Stronge	1
Wm Hallam	1
Wm Tompson	1
Ralph Lankester	1
Thomas Hudson	1
Tho. Stone	1
Wm Gaunt	1
Tho. Keeleing	1
Geo. Frost	1
Wm Marrott	1
Geo. Hodgkinson	1
Tho. Tipper	1
John Fare	1
Tho. Smith	1
Tho. Jackson	1
	21

Not Chargeable

Mr Joseph Harpur	2
Rich. Jankinson	1
Fran. Calvert	1
Robt Stronge	1
Wm Tompson	1
Tho. Hudson	1
Wm Gaunt	1
Geo. Frost	1
John Lancaster	1
Geo. Hodgkinson	1
Tho. Watton	1

Ralph Cotten	1
Tho. Jackson	1
	14

Bartonfeilds

Chargeable

John Merrey Esq.	10
Mr Hugh Rawlinson	3
Henry Atkyn	1
Fran. Burton	1
	15

Not Chargeable

Robt Cheatom
Tho. Lee
Widd. Mather

(2r.)

(Alderw)osley (& Ash)lehay

Chargeable

Jo. Lowe Esq.	6
Mrs Jone Lowe	4
James Winfeild	3
Mrs Spencer	3
Wm Vallance	2
Tho. Thacker	2
Wm Cockerham	2
John Storer	2
Anth. Chadwicke	1
?Wm Storer sen.	1
Wm Storer Jun.	1
John Storer	1
James Adams	1
John Adams	1
Anth. Thacker	1
Willm Wall	1
Roger Hollingworth	1
Anth. Storer	1
James Rowland	1

John Spencer	1
John Lichfield	1
John Smith	1
Robt Bomer	1
Mr Carryer	2
Ralph Hogton	1
Elizabeth Wall	1
Rich. Thacker	1
Robt Sellor	1
Robt Wall	1
Robt Tophe	1
Rich. Chadwicke	1
Henry French	1
Jo. Cheadle	1
John Chadwicke	1
Wm Hellott	1
Edw. Kirkland	1
Geo. Armefeild	1
Thomas Sutton	1
Wm Wood	1
Robt Byard	1
John Fletcher	1
Luke Vallance	2
Ferdinando Lowe gen.	2
John Buxtons	1
Edw. Allen	1
Anth. Higgott	1
Anth. Chalsworth	2
Victor Pottor	1
Sam. Bradshawe	1
Lettice Pickard	1
	70

Not Chargeable

Edw. Wigley	1
Robt Byard Jun.	1
Rich. Pottor	1
Edw. Kirkland	1
Luke Vallance	1
Anth. Chalsworth	1
Anth. Thacker	1
John Storer	1
John Alsopp	1
Thomas Allen	1
Tho. Bonsall	1
Wm Smith	1
Rich. Gregorie	1
Widd. Bath	1
John Winfeild	1
James Adams taylor	1
John Fowkes	1
James Alsopp	1
(blank) wagstaffe	1
Mr Carryer	1
	20

Hilton

Chargeable

Geo. Toby	1
Tho. Higgs sen.	2
Tho. Marshall	1
Tho. Harrison	1
Mary Harrison	1
Arthur Lathbury	2
Wm Shirley	1
Robt Heacocke	2
Wm Kirkham	1
Rich. Kirkham	1
Jo. Shirley sen.	1
Arthur Shirley	1
Fran Mansfeild	1
John Terrey	2
Robt Yonge	1
John Prime (?Prince)	1
Rich. Burton	1
Wm Swan	1
John Toby	1
Mr Jo. Wakelyn	6

Tho. Harrison	2
John Ellyott	1
Rich. Hill	2
Tho. Higgs Jun.	1
Wm Rose	3
John Shirley Jun.	1
Tho. B...	1
Wm Wood	1
	41

Not Chargeable

Thomas Lathbury	1
Michaell Holliway	1
John Yonge	1
Henry Fearne	1
Wm Scale	1
Tho. Mansfeild	1
Alice Adam	1
Arthur Pryme (?Prince)	1
Fran. Metham	1
Thomas Wawen	1
Wm Wilson	1
Henry Warren	1
widd. Loton	1
Widd. Oxford	1
Joseph Frances	1
Robt Smith	1
John Mansfeild	1
	17

(2v.)

(?Muggin)ton (?Mercas)ton

& ... Ireton

Chargeable

Mr Saunders	9
Robt Harrison	1
Hen. Lane	1
Mr Pole	4
Wm Cockaine	3
Tho. Burton	2
Wm Woodcocke	1
John Browne	1
Hen. Atkyns	1
Humfry Beeson	1
Rich. Vickars	2
Jo. Slacke	1
Jo. Browne	1
Widd. Boham	1
Wm Bott	1
Henry Moseley	1
Wm Jobbitt	1
Rich. Durden	1
Wm Jankinson	1
Hugh Hill	1
Symon Yates	1
Fran. Wetton	1
Tho. Mabley	1
Tho. Garrett	1
Jo. Garrett	1
Thomas dakine	1
Tho. Stillington	1
John Peach	1
Geo. Boham	1
Widd. Ashton	1
Robt Beeson	1
Wm Wiberley	1
Thomas Cooke	1
Hen. Pickeringe	1
Wm Fox	1
Godfry Brunt	1
?Evans Barnes	1
Germane Pole Esq.	8
Sam Dakine	1
Katherine Wallis	2
Geo. Cowper	1
Wm Ryde	1
Edw. Moseley	1
Gilbt Wallis	2

Rich. Kirkland	1
Joseph Som(m)ers	2
Roger Kirkland	1
James Greaves	1
John Wallis	1
Wm Fitchett	1
Thomas Ault	1
Robt Slacke	1
John Kirkland	1
	78

Not Chargeable

Fran. Orchard	1
Widd. Astle	1
Rich. Vickars	1
Widd. Mabley	1
Rich. Gretton	1
Widd. Turner	1
Robt Bainebridge	1
Alice Smith	1
Widd. Bentley	1
Widd. Bayley	1
Tho. Kirkland	1
Gilbt Cutbeart	1
Wm Cutbert	1
Wm Bradshawe	1
	14

Ednaston

Chargeable

Mr ?Banckes	2
John Morley	2
Rich. Foane	1
Wm Fidler	1
Robt Stone	1
Arthur Browne	1
Thomas Hurd	1
Thomas Cotton	1
Tho. Peach	2
Rich. Stone	1
	13

Synfen & Arlaston

Chargeable

At the Hall	12
John Clarke	1
Widd. Clay	1
Widd. Hegge	1
Abraham Hegge	1
	16

Not Chargeable

Rich. Rose	1
Jane Holmes	1
	2

(3r.)
(Stanley)

Chargeable

Edward Vickars	1
Rich. Bridges	1
Geo. ?Cordin	1
Edw. ?Winray	1
Mr darbyshire	1
Wm Bancrofte	1
Robert Wright	1
Nicholas Kirkby	1
Edw. Winray sen.	1
John Burges	1
Geo. Buxton	1
Anne Sidney	1
John Hancocke	1
Tho. Richardson	1
	14

Not Chargeable

Edw. ...	1
Nicholas ?Kirkby	1

John ?Burges	1
Geo. ?Cordin	1
Joseph Wright	2
Robt Holmes	1
Leonard ?Hulley	1
Anne ?Pyott	1
Robt Bird	1
	10

Mapperley

(Chargeable)

Mr Houlden	2
Mr Dickenson	2
Wm Wheatley	1
Joseph Wright	1
Ralph Hodges	1
Fran. Hodges	1
Rich. Hodges	1
John Buxtons	1
Thomas Wheatley	1
John Hodges	1
	12

Hollington

(Chargeable)

Rich. Bakewell	2
Robt Smith	1
Tho. Burrowes	1
Tho. Withnall	1
Fran. Morley	3
John Greaves	1
John Millington	2
Arthur Bakewell	2
Rich. Mabley	2
Edw. Deddicke	1
Tho. Hoone	2
Mr John Charlton	1
John Peach Jun.	1
Fran. Parker	1
Mr John Warde	1
Rich. Bond	1
John Peach	1
	24

(Not Chargeable)

John Barker

Wm Baker

John Hinde

Nicholas Winfeild

John Dibell

Langford

(Chargeable)

Sr Edw. Cooke	27
Mr Jackson Rector	7
Mr Huxley	3
Tho. Brundon	2
Nicholas Goodale	2
Fran. Hopkin	2
Law. Rolleston	3
Wm Langford	2
Geo. Crichlowe	1
Wm Wright	1
Peter Bryan	1
Wm Burton	1
John Rolleston	1
Tho. Middleton	2
Tho. Pearson	1
Geo. Bomer	2
John Parker	1
Joseph Langford	2
Robt Hurd	2
Wm Aulte	1
widd. Peate	1
Robt Brookhouse	1
Henry Gregson	1
Wm Gregson	1
John Rideings	1

John Pottor	2
Charles Forman	1
John Higges	2
Rich. Rigley	1
John Rigley	1
Nicholas Morley	1
James Morley	1
Tho. Merryman	2
Wm Burton	1
Wm Bond	1
Tho. Baker	1
James Chatterton	1
	84

(3v.)

(Belper)

(Chargeable)

(five entries illegible)

Henry ...	...
Tho. ...	?2
L... ...	...
?John ...	1
John ?Glewe	1
?Mr (?Wm) ?Ollarde	1
Fran. Smith	1
?Mr (?Mrs) Downes	1
Tho. Williamson	1
Peter Ferne	1
?Widd. Woodward	3
John ?Robinson	?1
John Bridges	?1
?Roger Hodges	1
Wm Walker	1
Wm Webster	1
Widd. Wilde	1
Robt Ryley	1
Thomas Bridges	1
Widd. Taylor	1
Geo. Butler	1
Tho. Browne	1
Anth. Williams	1
Robt Barker	1
Widd. Swifte	1
Rich. Steere	2
John Watson	1
Tho. Browne	1
Wm Taylor	1
Mary Webster	1
Willm Goodwin	1
Wm Worth	1
Robt Williams	1
Fran. Woodward	1
Tho. ?Butler	1
Geo. ?Swifte	1
Nicholas Butler	?1
James Jackson	2
Geo. Smith	1
Tho. Swifte	1
Rich. Milward	1
Rich. Launder	1
John Williams	1
John Spencer	1
Tho. Sellars	1
Geo. ?Gratige	2
Anth. Wright	1
Mr Bruckshawe	1
Widd. Green	2
Godfry Lichfeild	1
Rich. Swifte	1
John ?Launder	1
Willm ...	1
Wm ?Annable	1
Peter Hunter	1
John Booth	1
John Annable	1
John Barber	1
Wm Barber	1
John ?Barbar	1

Tho. Felkine	1
Edw. Harrison	1
widd. Fletcher	1
Rich. Milward	1
Wm Simpson	1
Fran. Jackson	1
Fran. Jackson	2
Wm Hall	1
Humfry Collin	1
Robt Calwood (?Colwood)	1
	85

(Not Chargeable)

(four or five entries illegible)

?Anth. ?Walker	...
Widd. ?Walker	...
Peter ?Walker	...
...?Harrison	...
?James Ould	1
James ?Berkine	1
John Mellor	1
Rich. Walker	...
Robt Bolton	...
Thomas Simpson	...
Rich. ?Brisard	...
John ?Og...es	...
Barthol. ?Taylor	1
... Webster	...
Rich. Jackson	...
Peter Alsopp	...
Phillipp Stringham	...
Fran. Beardsley	...
Barthol. Bradbury	1
Walter Jackson	1
Widd. Clarke	...
...kin Sims	1
	27

4r.

H(olbroo)ke

Chargeable

John Gregory	1
Wm Franceys	1
John Fletcher	1
Rich. Haughton	2
Tho. Cowpe(?r)	1
Symon Simpson	1
John Harvy	1
Henry Browne	1
John Lockoe	1
Wm Roe	1
Henry Bradshaw	2
Wm Pownall	2
Henry Hutchinson	1
John Norman Jun.	1
Jo. Norman sen.	1
James Gregory	1
Robt Fletcher	1
John Watton	2
John Moore	1
	23

Not Chargeable

John Taylor	1
John Bell	1
Nicholas Roe	1
Jane Hooton	1
Wm Shardlowe	1
Wm Taylor	1
Tho. Slater	1
Anne Tomlinson	1
Robt Turner	1
Wm Cowper	1
Grace Tomlinson	1
Anth. Burr...	1
John Morton	1
John Scragge	1

Robt Gamble	1
Jeremiah Chambers	1
	16

Heage

(Chargeable)

Geo. Pole Esq.	8
Mrs Pole	4
Mr Tho. Thacker	2
Wm Cawdale	1
Widd. Hanson	1
Robt Toplis	1
Jo. Jepson	1
Wm Simes	1
Elias Simes	1
Robt Holland	1
Geo. Speed	1
Wm Bulloke	1
Jo. Porter	1
Rich. Buckland	1
John Adam	1
Wm Roome & widd. Roome	2
Walter Buckland	1
Geo. Sterland	1
Symon Ratcliffe	1
Anth. Storer	1
Tho. Fletcher sen.	1
Tho. Fletcher Jun.	1
Jo. Hanson	1
Geo. Fletcher	1
Jo. Storer	1
Jo. Lichfeild	1
Widd. Beardow	1
Jo. ?Thacker	1
Sam. ?Noden	1
Jo. Noden	1
Henry Walter	1
Rich. Beardmore	1
Edw. Raynes	1
Anth. Ryley	1
Isaac Beardmore	1
Jo. Brothers	1
Humfry ?Worrell	1
Wm Smedley	2
Abra. ?Shaw	2
?Rich. Steare	1
?Wm ...	1
Wm Robinson	1
Sam. ...	1
Tho. ...	1
... ...	1
... ?Burgin	1
... ?Orgill	1
	60

(Not Chargeable)

Thomas Sprant	1
Geo. Bland	1
Tho. Stopard	1
Jo. Stopard	1
Rich. Mason	1
Robt Booth Jun.	1
John wheatrofte	1
Wm Poyser	1
	8

(Ash)

(Chargeable)

... Sleigh Knt	12
... Wilkinson	1
... ...	1
?John ...	1
... Allen	1
	16

(4v.)

Trusley

Chargeable

Richard Coke Esq.	13
Mr Tho. Folkingham	3
John Reeve	2
Wm Eaton	1
John Gaunt	1
Wm Millington	1
Rich. Taylor	1
Mary Holbrooke	1
Mr Charles Hope	7
Tho. Campion	1
Rich. Hudson	1
Anne Hutchinson	1
	33

Not Chargeable

Tho. Scullet	1
Edw. Bryan	1
	2

Twyford & Stenson

(Chargeable)

Mrs Harpur	7
Mrs Hewband	7
John ?Ston (?Sten)	3
Wm Warde	1
Symon ?Bristoe	1
Wm Brigs	1
Geo. Holmes	1
Gervace Adams	1
Wm ?Wild(e)r (?N...ld(e)r)	1
Wm Taberor	1
John Hawkesley	1
John Shipman	1
Edw. warde	1
Tho. Jerrome	1
Roger Wright	1
Rich. Hingley	1
Robt Brownell	1
Widd. Hancocke	1
	32

(Not Chargeable)

Willm Chambers	1
Widd. Burley	1
Widd. Starbucke	1
Wm Burley	1
Mary Reynold	1
Wm Beare	1
Jo. Gibson	1
Fran. Davie	1
Jane Sarson	1
Tho. Neale	1
Wm Weeder	1
Jo. Jerrome	1
	12

Stidd

(Chargeable)

Fran. Colwich gen.	4
Thomas Hall	1
Gervace Kinder	1
Walter Ashton	1
	7

(Not Chargeable)

John Tarleton	1
Widd. Tarleton	1
Elizabeth Bull widd.	1
Mary Shorthose	1
	4

Kedleston

(Chargeable)

Sr Jo. Curzon	22
Marke Hope	4

John Sowter	1
Widd. Windley	1
John Dawes	1
Jesp. Tantum	1
Tho. Bentley	1
Wm Sowter	1
John Millington	1
Tho. Byard	1
Tho. Hutchinson	1
Rich. Blood	1
	36

(Not Chargeable)

Widd. Sowter	1
John Windley	1
Fran. Hulland	1
Jane Hulland	1
widd. White	1
	5

<u>Somersall Herbert</u>

(Chargeable)

Mr Fitzherbert	9
Rich. Stubbing	6
Mr B...ke	3
Jo. Bowringe	2
Wm Gallimore	2
Fran. Lawrance	1
Edw. Turner	1
Edw. woolley	1
Henry Moseley	1
Tho. Jankinson	1
Edw. Whitrance	1
Willm ?Ayres	1
Wm Bacon	1
Mary Tunnycliffe	1
	(31)

(Not Chargeable)

Geo. Fletcher	1
Wm Holmes	1
Anne Freare	1
Wm Aston	1
Wm Bladen	1
Edw. Wootten	1
Tho. momforte	1
	7

(<u>5r.</u>)

<u>Dovebridge</u>

Chargeable

The Lady Milward	15
Mr Hen. Cavendish	11
Mr Milward	9
Mr Tho. Milward	6
Mr Geo. Glen	4
Mr Rich. Gilbert	4
Mr ?Mathaes	1
Jo. ?Fawleeringe	3
Wm Milward	1
Wm ?Plummer	1
Rich. Pratty	2
Tho. Smith	2
Wm Higgs	2
Mr Roger Fletcher	4
Tho. Duros	2
Mrs Anne Milward	2
widd. Fletcher	3
Margarett Bill	1
Tho. Wilde	1
Anth. Michell	1
Ralph ?Kinder	1
Francis ?Parker	2
Walter Gilbert	2
Tho. Wall	1
Wm Savage	1
Jo. Savage	1

Wm Alcocke	1
Tho. Chapline	1
Rich. Wall	1
Joh. Wall	1
Wm Boulton	1
Robt Boulton	1
John Wall	1
Isaac Hill	1
Rich. Broadbanke	1
Wm Palmer	2
Robt Lees	1
John Moore	2
Jo. Osborne	1
Edw. Slater	1
John Marshall	1
widd. Rowbotham	1
willm Smith	1
Hen. Alcoke	1
Hum. Wall	2
Jo. Palmer	1
Jo. Wright	1
Cutbert Boulton	1
Mr John Hall	1
Jo. Pratty	1
Jo. Palmer	2
Widd. Adams	2
Widd. Buxton	1
Rich. Stubbings	4
Widd. Pryme	2
Jo. Bould	1
Edw. Madeley	2
Rich. Robinson	3
Rich. Copestake	2
Wm Alsopp	1
Tho. Roberts	1
	131

Not Chargeable

(none)

Foston & Scropton

(Chargeable)

Tho. Rossington	3
John Eld	4
Geo. Hodgkinson	1
Tho. Barloe	1
Wm Pike	2
Hugh Barloe	1
Robt Scattergood	1
Wm Moore	2
Wm ?Bookeley	1
Abra. Hall	1
Widd. Hodgkinson	1
Rich. Browne	1
John Warren	2
Wm Mountgomery	3

('Chargeable' continued on m.5v.)

(Not Chargeable)

Jo. Asperry	1
widd. ?Lorte	1
Widd. Siddale	1
Ralph Barloe	1
Tho. Barloe	1
Tho. Bartram	1
widd. Alsopp	1
Edw. Greene	1
Jo. woodward	1
Jo. Ford	1
Tho. Barnes	1
Ralph Twigge	1
Robt Lee	1
Edward Shawe	1

('Not chargeable' cont on m.5v.)

(5v.)

Chargeable

Sam. Orgill	1
John Gelley	1

Edw. Ligoe	1
Tho. Rowbotham	1
?George Trigge	2
Geo. Powes	3
John Barloe	1
Robt Berkin	2
Katherine Norwood	1
John E... of the yate	1
Tho. Barloe	1
Jo. Baldwine	1
Rich. Hodgkinson	1
Tho. Allen	1
Robt Yonge	1
Jo. Archer	2
Wm Chowlerton	2
Wm Maccrory	1
Robt Hunt	1
Rich. Archer	2
Tho. Bate	1
Jo. Wright	1
Rich. Buxton	1
Wm Furnice	1
Tho. Archer	1
Widd. Wood	1
Mr Charles Agard	12
James Jenings	2
Fr. Harrison	2
Nicholas Pike	2
Edward Wright	1
Tho. Swenson	1
Wm Moseley	1
Wm Jackson	2
Gilbt Moore	1
Raph Carter	1
Rich. Woodward	1
Thomas Salt	1
Jo. Gelley	1
Charles Greene	1
Tho. Wright	1
Wm Hieron	2
Rich. Lorte	2
Widd. Higgs	2
	93

Not Chargeable

Hen. Orgill	1
Jo. Bennett	1
Tristram Smith	1
Widd. Houlden	1
Robt Siddale	1
Robt Greene	1
Dorothy Short	1
Tho. Turner	1
Hen. Middleton	1
Jo. Gelley	1
Rich. Gelley	1
Wm Webb	1
Jo. Turner	1
?Sym. Byker	1
Wm Turner	1
Wm Salt	1
Jone Twist	1
Tho. Morecrofte	1
Anne Morecrofte	1
Ralph Barton	1
Robt Evens	1
Tho. Tunnycliffe	1
Clemt Houseley	1
	37

<u>Sapperton</u>

(Chargeable)

Wm Soute	1
Robt Fearne	1
Rich. Averell	2
Robt Jackson	2
Fr. Jackson	2
Wm Fox	1

Widd. Bennett	2
Fr. Warde	6
Widd. Goodale	1
Widd. Battey	1
Jo. Bamford	1
	20

(6r.)

Sudbury

Chargeable

Geo. Vernon Esq.	15
Mr Sturges Minister	7
Edw. Greatrax	1
Stephen Woodings	1
Widd. Hill	2
Widd. Coates	2
Nicholas B...ter	1
John ?Worslowe	1
James Stubbs	1
John Greatrax sen.	1
Francis Blundell	1
Wm Scott	2
Jo. Wetton	3
John Noone	1
widd. Alsopp	1
Tho. Botham	1
Jo. Botham	1
Edw. Blacke	1
Widd. Hall	1
Jo. ?Plimner	1
Mr Rich. Bate	6
Edward Woodward	1
Wm Hurd	1
Fr. ?Bukley (?Bickley)	1
widd. Palmer	1
Tho. Palmer	1
Hen. Upton sen.	1
Mr Gilbt Wakelyn	6
Mr John Bancks	1
Edw. Madeley	2
Walter Plimmer	1
John ?Sleigh	1
Wm Ferne	1
Wm woolley	1
wm Lockoe	1
Sampson Catton	1
Vernon Pearson	4
Tho. Rawbone	1
Hen. Bladen	1
Wm Boyer	1
Nicholas Harrison	1
John Bladen	1
Thomas Bladen	1
Tho. Madeley	1
Geo. Twigge	1
Edw. Chaloner	1
Tho. Benett	1
James Platts	1
John Alsopp	1
James Allen	1
Henry Goodale	1
Edw. Tompson	1
Wm Madeley	1
Wm Harrison	1
John Greatrax	1
	94

Not Chargeable

Wm Kenderdine
Tho. Elliott
Hum. Gaunt
Rich. Benett
Tho. Tomlinson
John Ault
Rich. Woolley
Wm Noone
Robt Morton
Robt Muskett

Widd. Momford	
Widd. Falconer	
Tho. Plim(m)er	

Headaston

(Chargeable)

Sampson Alkyns	1
Tho. Alkyns	1
Wm Hurd	3
Wm Chatterton sen.	1
Tho. Hughson	1
Wm Chatterton Jun.	1
Tho. Smith	2
Mr Abra. Smith	2
Fran. Wardle	2
Rich. Coape	1
Robt Hood	2
Nicholas Hurt	1
John Gretton	1
Mr Tho. Sheldon	2
Wm Salt	2
Joseph Frost	2
Wm Ashton	1
James Ashton	3
Wm Sharwin	1
Joseph Peach	1
Wm Moore	3
Tho. Ireland	1
Geo. Wood	2
	37

(Not Chargeable)

Robert Bowman	1
Geo. Blore	1
Wm Harris	1
Widd. Matkyn	1
Rich. Pycrofte	1
Fr. Bacon	1
Edm. Bacon	1
Tho. Chatterton	1
Widd. Pegge	1
Geo. White	1
	10

(6v.)

Norberry & Rosson

Chargeable

Bassill Fitzherbert Esq.	18
Mr Nath. Williams	6
Nicholas Boswell	2
James Frost	1
Jo. Oldaker sen.	1
Wm Bentley	1
Wm Milnehouse	2
Peter Bill	3
Rich. Hibline	1
Rich. Coape	2
Law. Richardson al(ia)s Brewer	1
Tho. Bill	1
Jo. Mole	1
Fr. Keene gen.	6
Rich. Bill	1
Tho. Hibline	1
Geo. Wood	1
Tho. Dakine	1
John Oldaker Jun.	1
Rich. Morrice	1
Jo. Hibline	1
Ignatius Greensmith	1
Anth. Greensmith	1
Charles ?Waste (?Wash) for Hen. Jacksons house	1
Edw. Hurd	2
Robt Bill	3
Tho. Coape sen.	1
Gilbt Pedley	1
Rich. Harrison	2
Tho. Coape Jun.	2

Hen. Bayley	1
Tho. Laughtenhouse	1
Nicholas Harrison	1
Tho. Harrison	3
Robt Lowe	1
Wm Palmer	1
Geo. Dakine	1
Tho. Gill	1
Norbury Mill	2
	79

Not Chargeable

Wm Heathcote	1
Anth. Slater	1
Widd. Palmer	1
Fr. Palmer	1
Jo. Dakine	1
Wm Rowbotham	1
Jo. Cotton	1
Tho. Cotton	1
	8

Etwall

(Chargeable)

Sr Sam Sleigh	18
Mr Jo. Jackson Viccar	4
(altered to 3 later?)	
Tho. Barker	1
xfer Saxon	1
Tho. Wilson	1
John Hope	3
Mr Tho. Trubshawe	2
Jo. Baker	1
Mr Wm Browne	1
Wm Eaton	2
Joseph Heacocke	1
Tho. Clarke	1
Robert Hanford	1
Hum. Milnehouse	1
Fr Kilborne	1
Mr Fr. Pilketon	3
John Browne	1
Tho. Gilbert	1
Ralph Moore	1
Geo. Eaton	1
Elizabeth Campion	1
Mr Ralph Benington	4
Michaell Beare	1
Wm Peach	1
John Orme	5
Widd. Lees	1
Jone Keeler	1
Widd. Knight	1
Wm Vickars	1
Sampson Woolverton	1
Lancelott Stanley	2
Hen. Cantrell	1
Mathew Wilson	1
John Feazand	1
John Hingley	1
Anth. Turner	1
	70

(Not Chargeable)

Tho. Kirkham	1
Tho. Tatum	1
Tho. Berkin	1
Luke Hadfeild	1
Tho. Harrison	1
Tho. Tatum Jun.	1
Widd. Scott	1
Wm ?wilkesson	1
Wm Smith	1
Wm Neild	1
Wm Ward	1
Tho. Clarke	1
Jo. Heywood	1
	13

(7r.)

Alkmanton

Chargeable

Mr Barnesley	4
Nicholas Laughtenhouse	1
Widd. Allen	1
John Cowley	1
Thomas Shenton	7
Thomas Benett	1
Tho. Walker	1
Tho. Copestake	1
John Robinson	1
John Burton	1
Widd. Chatterton	1
	20

Not Chargeable

Tho. Allen

Braylesford

(Chargeable)

Mr Draper	6
Tho. Bakewell	1
Edward Pegge	1
Tho. Taberer	1
James Bakewell	1
Mr Polles	4
Wm Browne	2
Mr Osborne	6
Wm Warde	2
Rich. Dedicke	1
Fr. Callingwood	1
Mr Love	4
Thomas Peach	1
Wm Peach	1
Ralph Salt	1
Hen Brookes	3
John Foane	1
Robt Aulte	1
Hen. Smith	3
Tho. Astle	1
Tho. Jeoffery	1
Mrs Aston	2
Fran. Morley	1
Gilbt Moseley	1
Peter Ault	1
John Jackson	1
John Rowleston	2
Wm Hulland	1
Edmund Marsh	1
Hugh Tolle	1
Tho. Massey	1
Arthur Goodwin	1
Wm Chawner	1
John Reeve	1
Wm Morley	2
Robt Astley	1
Mr Davenporte	5
	66

(Not Chargeable)

Wm Hudson
Wm Bainebridge
Tho. Foane
Tho. Jeoffery
Wm Smith
Wm Pegge
Law. Hinde
Hugh Jobbit
Wm Ault

Radborne

(Chargeable)

Germane Pole Esq.	20
Mr Berisford	6
Vallentine Merrey	2
Edw. Walker	3
Tho. Baker	3

Tho. Hunt	3
Wm Roome	2
Rich. Harrison	1
Wm Hodgkinson	3
Widd. Wilson	1
Tho. Goodale	1
Joane Morley	1
Hen. Stone	1
Margarett Lathberrey	1
Tho. Finney	1
John Draper	1
Edward Hall	1
Edw. ?Scallett	1
Rich. Hardy	1
	53

(7v.)

Marston sup(er) Dove

Chargeable

The Viccaridge	2
John Pownall	3
Bagnalls	3
Tho. woolley	3
Francis Hartle	1
Wm Stubbings	1
Jacob Stafford	1
Tho. Terrey	1
Geo. Spurryer	1
	16
The Towneshipp of Hoone	3
	19

Not Chàrgeable

(none)

Oslaston & Thurvaston

(Chargeable)

Edward Jackson	7
Daniell Jackson	6
Tho. Walker	2
Robt Johnson	1
Tho. Burton	1
James Storer	1
Tho. Moumford	1
Rich. Feazand	1
James Heatherley	1
Symon Smith	1
Widd. Hayne	1
Widd. Heacocke	1
John Reeve	1
Tho. Harrison	1
Wm ?Haugh (?Hough)	1
John Rige	1
John Seale	1
Symon Hayne	1
John Baker	1
Edw. Bakewell	1
Gilbt Wallis	1
Vallentine Jackson	1
	34

(Not Chargeable)

widd. Smith
Jo. Hinde
Robt Shepheard
Tho. Hetherley
Anth. Hetherley
Jo. Radford
Rich. Hodgkinson
Widd. Hallam
Abra. Shawe
Jo. Furnice
Robt Jackson
Widd. Harrison
Luke Fryth
Tho. Eaton

<u>Hatton</u>

(Chargeable)

Symon Throne	1
Fran. Wilkinson	1
Wm Bladen	2
Geo. Bradshawe	1
Rich. Buxton	1
Rich. Astle	1
John Moore	1
Widd. Holland	1
Jo. Parker	1
Widd. Heane	1
Tho. Orton	1
Geo. Ford	1
Rich. Johnson	1
	14

(Not Chargeable)

Rich. Fish	?1
Geo. Heathcote	1
Fran. Pryme	1
John Hall	1
Robt Jackson	1
	5

<u>Sutton</u>

(Chargeable)

Wm Hawkes	1
Hen. ?Hawson	1
Jo. Peach	1
Tho. Atkyns	2
Mr Francis ?Rowe	4
John Fearebrother	1
widd. Boldwine	1
Wm Woodward	2
Rich. Statham	1
Geo. Boldwin	1
Tho.Johnson	1
Wm Boughay	1
Wm Dakine	5
Mr Tatum Vicar	4
Tho. Milne	1
	27

(<u>8r.</u>)

<u>Hulland</u>

Chargeable

Alton hall	6
Robt Toplis	2
Hen. Cockerham	1
Widd. Storer	4
Rich. Watson	1
Ellen Webster	1
Hum.Webster	1
Robt Webster	3
John Gamble	2
widd. Lomas	1
Robt Mellor	4
Robt Annable	2
Wm Aulton sen.	1
Wm Aulton Jun.	1
Widd. Storer	1
John Aulton	1
John Gamble sen.	1
Geo. Pickatt	2
Ralph Smalley	1
Rich. Warde	1
Widd. Warde	1
Rich. Smith	1
Robt Mellor sen.	4
Robt Olliver	1
Jo. Cockerham	1
Wm Smith	1
Tho. Beeson	1
Wm Robinson	1
Wm Beeson	1
Hen. ?Webster	1
Robt Murfin	1

Wm Milward	1
Rich. Cheadle	1
Robt Smales	1
Law. Wetton	1
Tho. Newton	1
James Johnson	1
Jo. Gamble	1
Tho. Wagstaffe	1
Margarett Day	1
Mr Wm Byram	3
Tho. Webster	1
Sam. Webster	1
Jo. Milward	1
Robt ?Hanson (?Henson)	1
Ralph Johnson	1
Robt Cockaine	1
Tho. Smales	1
James Aulton	1
Wm Coley	1
Wm Webster	1
Wm Und(er)wood	1
John Drable	1
Wm Dicken	1
widd. Mellor	1
Jo. Elliott	1
widd. Bond	1
Peter wilcockson	3
Geo. Hill	1
Wm Webster	1
Ralph Burton	2
Jo. wilcockson	1
widd. wilcockson	1
widd. webster	1
Jo. wilcockson sen.	1
Widd. Smith	1
Wm Webster	1
Anth. Steeple	1
Jo. Blood	1
Tho. Austine	1
Wm Harison	1
Wm Dedicke	1
Jo. Hitchcocke	1
Robt Webster	1
Joseph Webster	1
	100

Not Chargeable

Geo. Barker
Fr. wardloe
Tho. Pegge
Jo. Wardloe
Jo. Whittles
xfer Millinton
Peter Mannors
Wm Sommers
Robt Crofte
Edw. Wright
John Hanch
Widd. Brocksop
John Knott
Jo. Harison
Rich. Alkyn
Edw. Barloe
Robt Brocksop
widd. Bingley
Tho. Greaves
Jo. Tompson
James Haugh
Wm Smales
Rich. Coley
Jo. Osbiston
James Day
Wm Bott
Fr. Osbiston
Ralph Osbiston
Fr. Day
Tho. Johnson
Tho. Hitchcocke

Wm Wilcockson

Benett North

Fr. North

Fr. Alsopp

Edw. Groves

Henry Cawton

Tho. Fisher

(8v.)

Atlowe

Chargeable

Geo. Alsopp	1
Wm Langdon	1
John Ellott	1
xfer Tomlinson	1
Tho. Ellott	1
Tho. Greatrax	1
Tho. Hood	1
Jo. Tomlinson	1
Tho. Tomlinson	1
Row. Maddocke	1
Hen. Robinson	1
Jo. Hood	1
Geo. Wilcockson	1
Robt Wagstaffe	1
Tho. Latham	1
Widd. Cockaine	1
Ralph Harrison	1
Thomas Wade	1
John Frost	1
Rich. Harison	1
Phillip Browne	1
Geo. Wilson	1
	22

Not Chargeable

Ematt Cowper

Robt Wagstaffe Jun.

Geo. Millington

Robt Dawson

Marson Muntgomery

(Chargeable)

Mr Lowe	6
Mr Peacocke	5
& at Marson Parke	4
Tho. Stubbing	4
Wm Coape	3
Jo. Loton	3
Mr Taylor	2
Wm Ditch	1
John Smith	1
Mr Sheldon	4
Tho. Boyer	3
Edw. Burton	2
Anne Gaunt	1
Jo. Upton	1
Tho. Copestake	1
Tho. ?Harrison	?5
John North	?2
Rich. Bryan	1
Jo. Townesend	2
Hum. Wood	1
Wm Hollis	1
Jo. Chamberlyn	4
Tho. Ditch	1
Wm woolley sen.	1
James Newton	1
Tho. Wood	1
Jo. Woolley	2
Rich. Conway	4
Wm woolley Ju.	2
Tho. Marsh	1
Wm Hall	2
Wm Browne	1
Rich. Shipley	1
	74

(Not Chargeable)

Tho. Hatton sen.	1
Tho. Hatton Jun.	1
Fr. Landers	1
Fr. Hollis	1
Wm Cowper	1
Jo. Carter	1
Anne Kirkland	1
Robt Hall	1
Rich. Hall	1
Ashton Ethrington	1
John wood	1

(9r.)

Shirley

Chargeable

Mr Shepheard	1
Mr Edward Pegge	3
John Moore	4
Sa(m)pson Bentley	3
Tho. Yeomans	1
Wm Smith	1
Wm Bentley	1
Hum. Pegge	1
Jo. Goodale	1
Wm Hallam	2
Edw. Blake	1
Fr. Haine	1
Rich. Chawner	1
Rich. Marrott	1
Wm Pegge	1
Rich. Pegge	1
Eliz. Heath	1
Rich. Hitchcocke	1
James Yeomans	1
Robt Foane	1
Wm Rigley	1
	29

Not Chargeable

Wm Bowler	1
James Godhelpe	1
Wm Bentley	1
Ralph Smith	1
Rich. Bentley	1
Tho. Okey	1
Gibt Kniveton	1
Wm Salt	1
Jo. Ofley	1
	9

Cubley

(Chargeable)

Mr Soulden	2
Mr North	3
Wm Ryley	2
Jo. Copestake	1
Robt Storer	1
Jo. Copestake	3
Tho. Slater	1
John Blood	1
Fran. Benett	1
Wm Beardmore	1
Geo. North	1
Wm Johnson	3
John Heath	1
Wm Tunnycliffe	1
Mrs Edith Ford & Fr. Fairebrother	2
Wm Harison	1
Jo. & ?Anis Baker	2
Tho. Crichlowe	1
Robt Holmes	1
John Smith	1
Robt Bull	1
Fr. Hall	1
Jo. Baker	1
Jo. Hall	1

Anth. Roberts	1
Wm Ryley	1
	36

Boylston

(Chargeable)

Tho. John	1
Wm Challoner	2
John Coape	1
Jo. Bayley	1
Clemt Challenor	1
Tho. Challoner	1
Eliz. Rowbotham	1
Anne Clarke	1
Robt Challoner	2
Thom. Wilson	2
Hen. Wilson	2
Jo. Wilson	1
Hum. Naesh	1
Roger Worthon	1
Jo. Harpur	1
Margrett Stones	1
Fr. Waste	1
Edw. Johnson	2
Robt Blount	1
Isaac Alsopp	2
	26

(Not Chargeable)

Tho. Heanes
Jo. Harpur
Tho. Harpur
Saml Challoner
Jo. Sharwin
Wm Ragge

(9v.)

Osmaston next Ashburne

Chargeable

Tho. Kniveton	3
Hum. Pegge	3
Jo. Hurd	3
Gervace Prince	2
Wm Goodwin	2
Godfry Beard	1
Hum. Hurd	3
Tho. Beard	2
Zachariah Peach	1
Wm Hurd	2
Tho. Bott	1
Jo. Terry	1
Widd. Wrigley	1
Mr Edw. Love	2
Jo. Freareson	1
	28

Not Chargeable

John Johnson	1
Geo. ?Morgan	1
Wm ?Shene	1
Hen. Blore	1
Jo. Hodgkinson	1
xfer Smith	1
Fr. Smith	1
Anth. Johnson	1
Wm Slacke	1
	9

Church Broughton

(Chargeable)

Tho. Waste	2
James Alsopp	1
Sam. Lowe	1
Jo. Fox	1
Widd. Prince	1

Tho. Cheadle	1
Robt Brinsley	2
Hen. Bradshawe	1
Tho. Barton	1
Rich. Fearne	1
Rich. Ragge	1
Geo. Ragge	1
Robt Jackson Jun.	1
Hen. Eld	1
Wm Parker	3
Tho. Kniveton	2
Robt. Jackson sen.	1
Widd. Alsopp	1
Clem. Barker	1
Cha. Buxton	1
Mrs Peares	2
Sam. Heatherley	1
	28

(Not Chargeable)

Margery Cheadle	1
Tho. Laborne	1
widd. Peach	1
Widd. Flinthurst	1
Widd. Yates	1
Widd. Alsebrooke	1
widd. Smith	1
Jo. whelocke	1
Hen. Alsebrooke	1
James Alsebrooke	1
Jo. Stringer	1
will. Headerly	1
(added later; total originally 11)	12

<u>Rodsley</u>

(Chargeable)

Wm Smith	1
Rich. Bentley	1
Mr xfer Pegge	2
Tho. Yeomans	1
Stephen Parker	1
Tho. Parker	1
Tho. Hinde	1
Wm Jackson	2
Jo. Osbaston	1
Tho. Prince	1
Jo. Sharwine	1
Robt Yeomans	1
Jane Cliffe	1
	15

(Not Chargeable)

Mary Parker widd.	1
Mr Pegge	1
Stephen Parker	1
Wm Pottor	1
Wm Crosley	1
	5

(<u>10r.</u>)

<u>Chaddesden</u>

Chargeable

Robt Willymott Esq.	5
Geo. Goodwin	1
Geo. Holmes	1
Fran. Cockaine	2
Tho. Rice	2
widd. Shawe	1
Tho. Newham	1
John Carter	1
Thomas Gretton	2
William Clarke	1
Edward Clarke	1
Mr Gorge Parker	1
John Roe	1
Thomas Stables	1
Thomas Calladine	1

William Chalner	1
Robert Walker	1
Mis Rowlande	1
Robert Mansfeilde	1
William Whittineham	1
William Chalner sen.	1
Ralphe Cheadle	1
John Morley	1
Widdow Cheadle	1
Richard Roe	1
William Dakin	1
William Tafte	1
John Clarke	1
	35

Not Chargeable

Henry Woodhouse
Edward Johnson
Thomas Adams
Richard Bainebridge
Robt Outram
Robt Martin
Widd. Hill
Robt Smedley
Fr. Bainebridge
Pike Peeter
Geo. Morley
Robt Sheffeild
Rich. Hollingworth
Henry Clarke
Sampson Blackshawe
Rich Staniford
John Brookhouse
Wm Smith

<u>Sturson & Compton</u>

(Chargeable)

John Grace	1
?Oto Slator	1
Robt Buntinge	1
Tho. Slater	1
Tho. Smith	2
Henry Old	3
Rich. Olliver	3
Charles Calver	6
Tho. Foane	1
Law. Kirkland	1
Jo. Toplis	1
Tho. Wheeldon	1
Nicholas Yocksall	1
Wm Browne	1
Ralph Thacker	1
Fr. Toplady	1
Jo. Kirkland	1
Edw. Asbery sen.	1
Nich. Eches	1
Tho. Puffee	1
Tho. Hurt	1
Jo. Forman	1
Tho. Harris	1
Geo. Hough	1
Tho. Bradshawe	2
Wm Lewis	1
Geo. Wilcocke	1
Robt Jeoffery	3
Miles Becke	1
	42

(Not Chargeable)

Robt Parker	1
Rich. Rigley	1
Kath. Cole widd.	1
Jo. Milward webster	1
Jo. Johnson	1
Tho. Eches	1
Joane Bott widd.	1
Ralph wood	1
Eliz. Taylor widd.	1

Ralph ?Hemus (?Hennis)	1
Wm Spalton	1
Widd. Gallen	1
John Rich	1
Jo. Alsopp	1
Wm Smith	1
Jo. Dixon	1
Susanna Smith wid.	1
Jo. Morgan	1
	18

(10v.)

Bradley

Chargeable

Fran. Meynell Esq.	18
Mr Mason	2
Henry Jackson	1
Will. Greenwood	1
Wid. Hill	1
John Morley	1
Hen. ?Bucrons	1
Jo. Millor	1
Hum. Harris	1
Jo. Goodwin	1
Wm Willis	1
John Orme	1
Tho. Leight	1
Jo. Bancrofte	1
Wm Ellott	1
Tho. Alsopp	1
Willm Willis Jun.	1
Cha. Copestake	1
Ro. Mason	1
Jo. Wood	1
Hum. Ashton	1
Wm Kirkland	1
Anth. Copestake	1
	41

Not Chargeable

Widd. ?Vudwood	...
Widd. Jackson	...
Widd. Bromwell	1
Widd. Kerkland	1
Paul Lorte	1
Geo. Hambleton	1
Ra. Okeley	1
Ste. Forman	...
Geo. Lorte	1
Widd. ?Hattersich	1
Tho. Beldome	1
Geo. Waste	1
Edw. Orme	1
	13

Yeildersley

(Chargeable)

Mr Pegge	7
Mrs Whitehall	3
Mr Lees	4
John Somers	1
Edw. Stone	1
Wm Waste	1
John Slater	1
Tho. Smith	2
Hum. Browne	1
Edw. Stone	1
Robt Kirkland	1
John Pegge	1
Miles Becke	1
Wm Doe	1
Geo. North	1
Hugh Tipper	1
Wm Hall	1
Rich. Austine	1
Edw. Austine	1
Wm Smith	1
Wm Cloves	1

Wm Bramfeild	2
Tho. Ashton	1
Edw. Greenhaugh	1
Lawrence Meakin	1
Jo. wasshington	1
	39

(Not Chargeable)

Tho. Peach	1
Wm Gadsby	1
John Brunt	1
Nathaniell Sharwood	1
Widd. Blore	1
Widd. Hurd	1
Ellen Browne	1
Tho. Brunt	1
Jo. Keeleing	1
Geo. ?Sumers	1
John Bowne	1
Jo. Eyre	1
Tho. Forman	1
	13

Dalberry Lees

(Chargeable)

Ralph Bull Rector	3
Fran. Fowler widd.	4
Jane Fowler widd.	1
Wm Moumford	3
Rich. Hankinson	2
Wm Eaton	1
Tho. Hankinson	3
Dorothy Botham wid.	1
Tho. Campion	1
Wm Ridshawe	2
Robt Bowler	1
Edw. Blood	1
Dorothy Maulton wid.	1
Edw. Pole	1

Hen. Ault	1
Tho. Foane	1
Gervace Brough	6
Ellen Barks widd.	1
Anne Taylor widd.	1
Ralph Hill	1
	36

(Not Chargeable)

Wm Blood	1
Dorothy Newham	1
Hen. Newham	1
Wm Hanford	1
Widd. Bradbury	1
John Hunt	1
Jo. Newham	2
Robt Blood	1
Wm Haine	1
Geo. Bradbury	1
Dorothy Bradbury	1
	12

(11r.)

Breadsall

Chargeable

Roger Morledge	...
Robt Wright	...
Ren. P(ind)er Jun.	...
Elizabeth Flamsteed	1
Ren. Pinder sen.	2
Tho. Cheshire	1
Jo. Mason	2
Mathew Morledge	1
Tho. ?Scooley	1
Hum. Hill	1
Jo. Ufton	1
Eliz. Burrowes	1
John Burrowes	1
Wm Armefeild	1

Mary ?Mainesley	1
Jane Heywood	1
Wm Towle	1
Hen. Stanley	1
Ralph Porter	1
Wm Hibbert	1
Jo. Pickeringe	1
John Moore	2
Robt White	1
Jo. White	1
Peter Sarson	1
Rich. Mason	1
Wm Jackson	1
Robt Jackson	1
Jo. Pegg	2
Anth. Walker	4
Jo. ?Jordan	1
Tho. Inglesant	1
Jane Hibbert	1
Rich. Portor	1
Tho. Bamford	1
Wm Walker	1
Mr Geo. Hill	4
Law. Clarke	1
Francis Turner	1
Tho. Pegge	1
Edw. Wright	1
Wm Yates	1
Law. Sherwood	1
Rich. Baker	1
?Vic. Bradshawe	3
John Robinson	1
John Portor	1
Hen. Creswell	1
	62

Not Chargeable

John Bayley	1
Robt Kerrey	1
Rich. Kerrey	1
Jo. Hunter	1
Tho. Shirley	1
Elizabeth Hill	1
Tho. Moore	1
Anne Grace	1
Arthur Drinckwater	1
Wm Cator	1
Robt Johnson	1
Robt Adams	1
Anne Meakin	1
Wm Morledge	1
Arthur Hill	1
Rich. Shawe	1
Anne Haines	1
Tho. Jackson	1
Rich. Bayley	1
Rich. Bradbury	1
Wm Norman	1
Thomas Hibbert	1
Rich. Mafell	1
	23

<u>Shottle & Posterne</u>

(Chargeable)

Tho. Cawton	1
John Spendlove	1
Wm Pottor	1
Widd. Pottor	1
Willm Wilson	1
Ralph Wilson	1
Nich. Wilson	2
Ralph Dowley	1
Edw. Hopps	1
Wm ...linson	1
Wm ...dley	1
Jo. Aulton	2
Rich. Poyser	1
Edward Wood	1

Widd. Eyley	1
James Chadwicke	1
Tho. Poyser	1
Edw. Smedley	1
Phillipp Smedley	1
Robt Goodwin	1
Robt Jackson	1
widd. ?Kidey	1
Tho. Watson	1
Rich. Watson	1
Daniell Cawton	1
Widd. Fletcher	1
Tho. Holmes	1
Tho. Cockerham	1
... Wilkinson	1
?Robt Hibbert	?1

('Chargeable' continued on m.11v.)

(Not Chargeable)

Jo. James	1
Widd. Allen	1
Rich. Allen	1
Jo. Siddon	1
Widd. whitrance	1
Widd. ?Hunt (?Hurt)	1
Wm Hunt	1
James Beardsley	1
John Greene	1
Wm Rowlston	1
Robt Walker	1
Widd. Spencer	1
Jo. Buxton	1
Widd. Hibbert	1
Rich. waterfall	1
Eliz. Bunting	1
Geo. Poyser	1
Tho. Wood	1
Jo. Rowland	1
Jo. Redfearne	1
Rich. Bramley	1
Mary Ashmore	1
widd. Dedicke	1
Jo. Greene	1
Edw. Kiddey	1
widd. Bramley	1
Widd. Bramley (sic)	1
Eliz. Bramley	1
Wm Shore	1
Hen. W...son	?1
... ...	1
Anne ...	1
Widd. ?Boulton	1

('Not Chargeable' continued on m.11v.)

<u>11v.</u>

(Chargeable, continued)

(Four or five entries illegible)

... ?Fletcher	1
... Drable	1
John ?Garrat	1
John ?Willesall (?Waterfall)	1
... ...son	1

(Forty entries illegible except for some hearth figures)

Ralph Gratton	?1
Jo. ?Smith	1
Wm ...	1
Tho. Hand	2
Wm Eyre	1
Jo. White	1
Wm Cowper	1
... Smith	1
... B...	2
... ?Winson	1

(Three entries illegible, but each with one hearth; total hearths figure ends in '9')

(Not Chargeable, continued)

Rich. ?Hallam (?Haslam)	1
Geo. ...ton	1
Wm ?Brunley	1
Geo. Hallam	1
	37

HIGH PEAK HUNDRED

1670

Derby Public Library, Derbyshire Collection, DC 9955

(<u>Title page</u>)

The Hundred of High Peake

Hearth money

John Wheeldon &
Hugh Wheeldon

<u>1</u>

The Hundred of high Peake
The number of fire hearths
as followeth

<u>Ashford</u>

William Millnes senior	3
William Millnes Junior	3
John Greaves	1
Thomas White	2
William Low	3
Thomas Ragg	1
Samuel *White* Wright	1
Thomas Toplis	1
John Wright de Elme	1
Thomas Langford Jun.	1
Francis Backer	2
William Thorpe hall end	1
Gervas Torre	1
Robert Hoolme	1
Edward Brewell	2
Richard Wright	1
William Brewill	3
William Thorpe Lane end	1
Elizabeth Toft	1
William Heward of stocks	2
Robert Thorpe	1 Ret
Richard Oxspring	1
Widdow Goodenough	3
John Greetbatch	6
John Wright Taylor	1
William Finney	1
Thomas Wright Graser	3
Willm Finney for ?horynson house	1
George Cowper Church Dale	2
Widdow Goodwin	2
John Harrinson	3 Ret
Thomas Wright Cutler	4
John Cooke	1 *Ret*
Mr Hollinshead	3 Ret

<u>2</u>

John Wright Shoomaker	1
John Oxspring	1
George Harris	1
For the Free schoole	3 Ret
Richard Swindill	1
George Rigard	1
Widdow Heward	2
Richard Millnes	1
Richard Greene	4
William Heward	1
Willm Wright fenill street	2
Edward Jackson	1 C
John Hayward of fould	2
Edward Wright	2
George Jackson	1
George Hage	1
William Boores	1

John Beastall sen.	2	
Richard Johnson	5	
Francis Fallose	1	
John Scikes	1	
	1-15-0	
	3- 4-0	

3

Moniash

Mr Sheldon	3	
Mr Dale	2	
Thomas Harrison	3	
Mr Ridiard	2	
James Cocke	2	
John Johnson	1	
Hugh Elye	1	
John Goodwin	1	
Richard Lee	1	
Edward Harrison	1	
Richard Bowne	1	
Widdow Carder	1	
Ralph Crichlow	1	
William Allbott	1	
Nich. Moore	1	
James Mellor	1	
Roger Ball	1	
Richard Hibberd	1	
John Alcocke	1	
Widdow Goodwin	1	
Edmund Bagshaw	1	
Thomas Bowne	1	
John Bartholomew	2	
William, Earle of Devonshire	4	Ret
Henry Lightfoot	1	
John Gratton	1	
Hugh Bome	1	
Richard Child	1	
Edmund Plats	1	
Joseph Goodwin	2	
Francis White	1	
George Frost	1	
Leonard Frost	2	
Ellias Barker	1	
Arthur Goodwin	1	
Ellias Barker for shore house	1	Ret
Francis Hibberd	1	
Tho. Newton	1	
Hugh Redferne	1	

4

Tho. Inglesunt	1	
Richard Naylor	1	
George Goodwin	2	
	2-16-0	

Longson

Mr Wright	11	
Frances Hodskinson	1	
Widdow Sheapard	1	
Tho. Heathcoat	1	
James Scamerdine	1	
Widdow Swindle	2	
Henry Scamerdine	1	
William Hallowes	1	
Francis Plats	1	
Joanas Creswell	1	
Robert Plant	1	
John Blackwall	1	
Widdow Bettney	1	
John Beard	1	
Mr Richard Spencer	3	
William Fernyhough	1	
Edmund Blackwall	1	
William Dowley	2	*Ret*
Humphrey Welles	2	
Nath. Burton	1	
Francis Needham	2	
Arthur Heathcoat	1	

William Low	1	
John Dakin	1	
William Haslam	1	
Lawrence Tomlinson	1	
Richard Hancocke	1	

5

Widdow Blackwall	1	
William Allen	2	
Widdow Hodskinson	1	
Barnold White	1	*Ret*
William Cloose	1	
John Flint	1	
Richard Wright Jun.	1	
Thomas Bagshaw	1	
Thomas Sellors	1	
Barnold Spencer	1	
Thomas Tomlinson	1	Ret
Robert Tomlinson	1	
Thomas Hodskinson	1	
Widdow Bland	1	
William Hodskinson	1	
John Heyward	1	
William Flint	1	
Henry Plats	1	
Robert Belcke	1	C
Richard Foolow	1	C
Godfrey Foolow	1	C
	3-5-0	

Rowland

Francis Bagshaw	1
James Bland	1
John Hardey	1
Thomas Low	1
Francis Brightmoore	1
John Bland	1
John Ashton	2
Richard Jepson	1
Robert Bland sen.	1

Hoolme

William Eyre Esq.	9
John Clay	1
Abraham Berisford	1
John Berisford	1
John Gardiner	1
Ellias Bradbury	1

5 (bis)

Parte of Great Longson

William Winscombe	1	
William Slacke	1	
Henry Wright	1	
John Cocker	1	
Henry Tomlinson	1	
Widdow Clarke	3	
Widdow Hully	1	
William Naylor	2	
John Tomlinson	1	
Henry Plates	1	Ret
Widdow Clarke	1	
Robert Jenkinson	1	
John Frost	1	
William Hodgskinson	1	
Richard Wright sen.	1	
George Garlicke	1	
Hugh Hyeld	1	
Willm Sellars for a halfe yeare	1^{s}	
	2-5-0	

Wardlow

Ralph James	1	
Francis Licklin	1	
George Hodskinson	1	
John Foulgiam	1	
Elizabeth Wright	1	Ret

Francis Bramwell	1
Rowland Low	1
Thomas Hoolme	1
Godfrey Hoolme	1
Edward Peake	1
John Robinson	1
Widdow Peake	1 Ret
Henry Bramwell	1
Thomas Bennet	1
Abraham White	1
William Buxton	1
Edward Frost	1
Widdow Tomlinson	1
Richard White	1

6

Arthur Skidmoore	1
Christopher Ludlam	1
George Hoolme	2
Widdow Burges	1 Ret
George Frost	1
John Stone	1
Stephen Hunt	1
Peter Holme	1
James Royton	1
Widdow James	1
	1-10-0

Sheldon

William Barker	3
Henry Harrison	1
Anthony Goodwin	1
John Mellor	2
William Frost	1
Ralph White	3
Katherine Boores	1 Ret
John White	2
Roger Dale	2
Arthur Needham	1
Thomas White	1
Edmund Dukens	1
Hugh Hadfeild	1
Edward Beighton	1
John Goodwin	1
Hugh Sheldon	2
John Atkinson	2
Tho. Dukens	2
John Frost smith	1
Edward White	1
Hugh Harrison	1 Ret
John Taylor	1

7

John Cowper	1
George Hayward	1
Phillip Powner	1
Joseph Barker	1
George Frost	1
Francis Beighton	1
	1-18-0

Received by Edw. Needham late
Collector the sum of 8^{li}. 14^{s}. 0^{d}
of this Towneshipe

Viewed by John Wheeldon & Hugh
Wheeldon Collectors
John Chapman Const
George Harris Constable

Baslow

Edmund Marston	2
Robert Rowland	2
John Mattley	2
Anne Bowler	3
James Marple	1
Thomas Heaton	1
George Ragg	1
Robert Marple	1

William Groudy	2	William Smith	2
James Noton	1	William Norman	1
Robert Marston	1	George Asborne	1
Robert Gregory	1	Adam Barker	2
Roger Dam	1	William Taylor	2 *Ret*
Alex. Dam	1	Robert Wilson	1
Robert Hagge	1	John Norman de Juling	1
John Bradbury	2	Francis Badgley	1
Anthony Bradow	1	Mary Norman	1
Hugh Marston	1	Gervas Randle	1
		Hugh Hagge	3

8

Samuel White	1
John Stafford	1
William Wilson	1
Anne Kender	2
John White	1
Robert Hagge	1
Tho. Goardon	2
Edward Hindman	1
Humphrey Chapman	2
Ralph Cooke	1
John Bowlor	1
Mary Nordon	1
John Smith	1
Thomas Johnson	1
Alex. Johnson	1
John Ragge	1
Lidia Eastwood	2 Ret
William Earle of Devonshire	79
Mr Savill	10
Thomas Statham	4
Adam Wright	1
John Norman	2
Do wood	2
John Tonicliffe	1
Thomas Chrawshaw	1
Anthony Holme	1
Widdow Froggat	1

9

William Haucksworth	1
Elizabeth Norman	1
John Wright	1
Abraham Clay	1
John Gill	1
Edmund White	1
James White	1
Francis Wats	1
Elizabeth Marshall	1 *Ret*
John Wilson	2
John Malldin	1
Widdow Wright	1
John Hagge	1
Anne Norman widdow	1
	8-19-0

Edensor

Mr John Tacey	4
Mr George Birds	5
Phillip Lees	3
Widdow Taylor	1
Richard Bowring	1
Henry Dakins	2 Ret
Widdow Woodard	1
Ralph Marple	1
William Bronsley	1

Alex. Barker	1	
Robert Houme	1	
John Smith	1	
Edward Booth	1	
John Booth	1	Ret
Humphrey Drable	2	

10

Abraham Wheeldon	1	
George Vicars	1	
Edward Cowley	1	
Henry Greaves	3	
William Marcar	1	
*John C...ey	C 1	Ret*
William Lauton	1	
Francis Heward	1	
Gervas Heyward	2	
Widow Walker	1	
Francis Booth	1	Ret
Edward Cowley	1	
William Ward	1	
Robert Lees	2	
Henry Salle	1	
Richard Hartley	1	
	2-6-0	

Calvar Curbar & Froggatt

John Froggat	3	
Anthony Gregory	2	
Humphrey Brushfield	1	
John Stones	1	
Francis Jackson	1	
John Ellis	1	
William Bingly	1	
William Glossop	1	*Ret*
Thomas Gregory	1	Ret
Thomas Grundy	2	
Thomas Hoole	1	
William Habergam	1	
Richard Cooke	1	*Ret*
John Gregory	1	

11

George Ellat	1
John Blackstone	1
Simon Wild	1
William Booth	1
Humphrey Gregory	1
Robert Wild	1
Thomas Badgaly	1
William Cooke	2
John Cooke	1
Humprey Badgaly	1
James Badgaly	1
William Adamson	2
Richard Stevenson	1
Thomas Ellis	1
	1-14-0

Bubnell

Richard Froggatt	4
John Kitching	2
John Bromhead	3
Godfry Heyward	1
John Collier	1
Anne Stevenson	1
Elizabeth Lees Wd.	1
Robert Bromhead	11
George White	3
Robert Dobb	1
William Jackson	1
George Andrew	1
Jane Jackson	1
James Rushton	1
George Harrison	1
Thomas Harrison	1
Richard Lees	1

Hassop

Rowland Eyre Esq.	20	
Richard Noton	1	
George Harris	1	
Francis Crowder	1	Ret
William Harrison	3	
Francis Kneveton	1	
Nicholas Sheldon	2	
Rowland Townrow	1	
William Wilson	2	
Widdow Plates	1	
George Kneveton	1	
	3-9-0	

Calvar

Thomas Froggatt	1	
Henry Gregory	1	
Thomas Cocker	1	
John Froggat	2	
Francis Sellars	1	
Symon Hallam	1	
Thomas Ragg	1	
Godfry Bower	2	
Anthony Gregory	2	
Tho. Wild	1	
John Sharwin	1	
James Gregory	1	
Elizabeth Allwood	1	
Richard Gregory Jun.	1	
Hugh ?Camme	1	
Richard Gregory sen.	1	
Rowland Booth	1	
Henry Furnis	1	
	1-1-0	

13
Pillsly

William Revitt	2	
Francis Rippon	1	
John Boot	1	
Christopher Hoole	1	
George Merrill	1	
Robert Calton	1	
William Calton	1	
Henry Penneston	2	
Henry Heyward	1	
Henry Greensmith	1	
Edward Greene Smith	2	
George Boote	1	Ret
John Madax	1	
John Woodhouse	1	
Roger Pennystone	1	
William Meeland	1	Ret
	0-19-0	

Received by Ed. Needham late Collect(or) out of this township the sum of 35^{li}. 0. 0

Viewed by John Wheeldon & Hugh Wheeldon Collectors
George Ragg Constable

Chelmarton

Richard Goodwin	3
Ralph White	1
Robert Wright	1
Richard Abney	1
Tho. Hodkisson	1
Edward Buxton	2
Symon Buxton	3
George Buxton	1
Robert Longdane	2
Humphrey Barke	1
William Boot	1
Nich. Heathcoat	2
William Buxton	1
William Robinson	1
Tho. Ealy	1

14

Tho. ?Simsoc	1
George Robinson	1
Peter Oullerenshaw	1 s
Tho. Meareman	1
John Dalle Jun.	4
Roger Slattor	1
John Dale sen.	1
Humprey Buxton	1
Tho. Hill	1
Robert Breusell	1
John Drable	1
William Plates	2
John Buxton	4
John Gyte	1
Edw. Buxton	1
Tho. Plant	1
John Drable	1
Edw. Breusell	1 Ret
Richard Ward	1 Ret
Andrew Needham	1
Edw. Dakin	1 s
Tho. Mosley	1
	2-11-0

Kings Sterndale

William Micocke	1
John Woodfen	1
Will. Redferne	1
Edward Londen	1
Will. Bargh	1
Robert Longden	2
Widdow Wardle	1
Henry Dakin	1
Stephen Buxton	1
Edward Buxton	1
William Heathcoat	2
	0-13-0

Cowdale

John Heathcoat	3
George Goodwin	1
Anthony Barker	1
Heathley	1

15

Stadon

Willm Dakin	1
Mr Moorewood	4
Ralph Needham	3
Edw. Bradshaw	1
Anthony Norton	1
George Longdane	1 Ret
John Duckworth	1
Arthur Dakin	1
Rich. Buxton	1
Anth. Ward	1
Widdow Warfield	1
Ralph Humbton	1
	1-3-0

Flagge

William Bagshaw	?1
William Heathcoat	1
George Needham	1
Richard Needham	1
Robert Mycocke	3
James Taylor	7
William Poope	1
Rich. Eyre	1
William Goodwin	1
Phillip Bateman	1
Robert Orme	1
William Plates	1
Katherine Plates	2
James Naylor	2
William Blackwell	1
Thomas Lumas	1

William Milles	2	
Richard Buxton	3	
William White	2	
John Dore	1	Ret
William Dale	1	
Robert Redferne	1	
Geo. Berry	1	
Richard Ward	1	
Ralph White	1	
John Howard (?Heward)	1	
Widdow Longden	1	
Ralph Eyre	1	
George Goodwin	2	
Henry Sheldon	1	
	2-5-0	

16

Buxton

John Ward	1	
Mr Andrew Moorewood & John Gambbll	2	
William Hadfield for John Wilkshaw	1	
William Hadfield	1	
Mr John Maddox	3	
Mr Mich. Heathcoat	5	
Arthur Hill	4	
Rowland Heathcoate	2	
Rich. Jackson	1	
Edw. Barker	1	
Ralph Lumas	1	
Rich. yeomans	2	
Anth. Clayton	1	
George Heathcoate	1	
Thomas Cope	2	
George Dallis	1	Ret
Francis Heathcoat	12	
William Smith	4	
Widdow Mosley	1	
	2-6-0	

viewed by John Wheeldon &
Hugh Wheeldon Collectors
Robt Wright Constable

Wormhill

Mr Adam Bagshaw	4
Edw. Howson	1
William Hodgkinson	1
George Bagshaw	1
Henry Bagshaw	1
Anthony Wright	1
John Wright	1
Anth. Longden	1
Will. Creswell	1
Robert Torr Sen.	1

17

Robert Torr Jun.	2
Widdow Torr	1
Nich. Bagshaw	1
Robert Bagshaw	1
Thomas Goodwin	1
Nich. Rendfearne	1
George Torr	1
Rich. Smith	1
George Longden	1
Francis Buxton	1
Richard Bower	2
Thomas Fletcher	2
Stephen Jowle	1
Robert Torr of the hill	1
Humphrey Thornhill	1
Henry Fletcher	1
Tho. Wibersley	2
Widdow Bramwall	1
Anthony Taylor	2^{s}
George Palframan	1

Willm Palframan	2
Willm Rolinge	1
Henry Jackson	1
John Pott	1
Robert Heyard	1
Henry Heyward	1
Henry Bagshaw	1s
Anthony Kirke	1
Anth. Wright	1
Mich. Heward	1
Alex. Goodwin	1
Robert Longden	1
Widdow Longden	1
Widdow Heyward	1
	2-13-0

18

Mathew Palframan	2
Thomas White	2
Rowland Heathcoat	1
Nich. Palframan	2
Anth. Goodwin	1
Geo. Palframan	1
John yates	1
Rich. Oliver one rent day	2s
Robert Wilson	1s
William Peate	1s
	0-14-0

Presclife

The exec. of Robt Dakin	4
Isaac Wibersley	2
Anth. Ward	1
Robert Ralph Oldfield	1
Geo. Holme	1
Stephen Sheldon	1
Widdow Dakin	1
Geo. Eaton	1
Godfrey Hill	1

Hugh Wiberley	2
John Sellars	1
Ralph Wild	1
Francis Swane	1
Roger Jackson	2
Thomas Torr	1
William Wilkinson	1
William Eyre	1
John Berrey	1
John Simpson	1
Geo. Eaton	1
Ellis *Eaton* Raworth	2s
Tho. Bowden	1 C
	1-10-0

Tadington

John Dicken	1
Tho. Jackson	2
Mr Mellor	1
Edw. Rowland	1
Tho. Slattor	1
George Outfield	1
Gervas White	1
George Dickin	1
William Foxlow	1
Tho. Merrell	1
George Rowbotham	1
John Scoefield	1
Henry Gould	2
Rich. Blackwall	1
Widdow Bome	1
John Bateman sen.	1
Anne Sellars	1
John Nuton	1
John Sheldon	1
Mathew Roberts	1
Widdow Kirke	1
Willm Sheldon	1
Roger Goodwin	1

George Goodwin	1
Willm ?Blackwall	1
Lawrence Moult	1
Henry Botham	1
Simon Mosley	1
Geo. Bouth	2
Tho. Nuton	1
William Orme	2
Tho. Bretner	1
Edmund Hill	1
Robert Innocent	1
Tho. Jackson Jun.	1
Christopher Blackwall	1

20

Robert Rowland	1 C
John Merrieman	1
Jane Jackson	1
Ralph Nuton	1
Rich. Robinson	*2*(?1)
Phillip Robinson	1
Rich. Skidmoore	2
George Bagshaw	1
Henry Webster	1
Hugh Iley	1
Gervas Buxton	1 C
John Stidmore	1 C
	2-13-0

Fearnelee

Rich. Shalcrose	6
Rich. Benet	2
Rich. Ormfield	1
James Hurfield	1
James Row	1
Edward Turnocke	1
James Ford	2
John Shalcrose	1
Rich. Royle	1
John Brookhouse	2
Elizabeth Littlewood	1
Alex. Shalcrose	1
Edw. Ollernshaw	1 Ret
Ralph Cooke	1
Tho. Lomas	1
Tho. Hibberd	1
Henry Later	1
Reynold Pot	1
Nich. Hibbert	1
Edw. Brocklehurst	2
Robert Oliver	2
Peter Low	1
Tho. Redferne	1 Ret
William Cooke	1
Rich. Low	2

21

Geo. Redferne	1
John Holme	1
John Cooke	1
	1-19-0

Fearfeild

Rowland Swane	1
Rich. Oliver	1
Robert Mycocke	1
Hellen Dakin	1
Tho. Kirke	1
John Swinscoe	1
George Fearne	3
John Bennet	1
Rowland Swane	2
Francis Swane	1
Robert Lumas	2
Gilbert Moorewood	1
John Cotrell	1
Edward Dakin	1
John Housley	1

Anth. Wilson	1
Tho. Rowland	1
John Mycocke	1
Robert Erulgate	1
James Mellor	1
Ralph Fearne	1
John Gee	1
Rowland Fearne	1
Willm Naden	1
John Moorewood	1
Mich. Swinscoe	2
Rowland Moorewood	2

22

Mich. Heathcoate	1
Humphrey Clayton	1
Geo. Goodwin	1
John Wainewright	1
Robert Mycote	2
John Goodwin	1
George Goodwin	1
Robert Smith	2
John Hill	1
Roger Jackson	1
Alex. Goodwin sen.	1
Alex. Goodwin Jun.	1
Francis Goodwin	1
Edmund Buxton	1
Ralph Boaden	1
Hugh Needham	1[s]
Edw. Dakin Jun.	2
Willm Swinscoe	1
Edw. Lummas for Nich. Swane	1 Ret
John Housley	1[s]
John Mellor	1[s]
Anth. Wild	1[s]
Edw. Bradshaw	1
Tho. Hawley	1
John Cottrell	1
William Smith	1
Rich. Bennet	1
	3-3-0

viewed by John Wheeldon & Hugh Wheeldon Collect(ors)
John Roggers Constable

23

Hope

The heirs of Mr Wooderoufe	5
William Morten	1
Henry Ashton	1
Robert Burdikin	1
John Ashton for Bocking house	1
Robert Bocking	1
Adam Kirke	2
Henry Hoult	1
Tho. Burdikin	1
Andrew Eyre	1
Francis Briddocke	1
Roger Grant	1
Edmund How	1
Tho. Paramore	*3*(?1)
John Paramour	3
same new builded	1
John Bocking	1
Adam Grant	1
John Burdikin	1
Thomas Morten	1
John Hall	1
Edw. Hall	1
Tho. Eyre	1
John Spencer	1
Robert Bray	1
Adam Slacke	1
Tho. Harrison	2
John Hadfield	1

Marke Woodroofe	1
John Beeley	2
Tho. Morten	1
Rich. Grant	1
Francis Stafford	1 Ret
Hanna ?Ashton wid.	2
Tho. Hoult	1
Rich. Morten	1
Nath. Woodroofe	3
24	
Tho. Bocking new builded	5^{s}
Geo. Eyre	3
Vicaridge house	2
Dorothy Marshall wid.	2
John Slacke	2
Tho. Stevenson	3
Godfrey Grant	1
John Bennet	1
Tho. Slacke	1
Jane Balgay wid.	1
Mr Thomas Hall	1
Tho. Rogers	1 C
	3-12-0

Bradwall

Martin Briddocke	1
Robert Eyre	1
John Downing	1
John Wild	1
Tho. Slacke	1
William Jackson	1
George Slacke	1
George Briddocke	1
Edw. Slacke	1
Tho. Milward	1
John Hurler	1
Edw. Barbar	1
Robert Hall	1
Bagott Hadfield house	1
Ellis Sinderland	1
Henry How sen.	1
Henry How Jun.	1 Ret
George Trickett	1
Edw. Marshall	1
Ellis Midleton	2
Wid. Ashton	2
Robert Offerton	nothing
25	
Robert Midleton	1
Tho. Jackson	1
Rich. Midleton	1
Ellis Middleton	1 Ret
Mary Midleton wid.	1
Dennis Bradwall	1
Ellis Morten	1
Mary Bramwell wid.	1
Mich. Hill	1
Mary Marshall wid.	1
George Andrew	1
Tho. Barbar	1
Edw. Wright	3
Stephen Marshall house	?1
Hugh Bradwall sen.	1
Robert Bradwall	1
Robert Burrowes	1
Adam Furnesse	1
William Hartle	1
Godfrey Marshall	1
William Hall Jun.	1
Joane Hallom wid.	1
Edw. Outfield	1
Anth. Outfield	1
Godfrey Morten	1
Willm Hall sen.	1
Tho. Hall	1
Richard Ragge	1

John Hallom	1
John Wright	1
Adam Padley house	nothing
Jane Bradwall wid.	1
Tho. Marshall	1
Math. Thornhill	1
Humphrey Midleton	1

26

Ellis Bradwall	1
Tho. Bradwall	4
Hugh Bradwall	2
Anne Bradwall wid.	1
Thomas Eyre	1
Ottiuell Smith	1
Widdow Morten	1
Edw. Dernely	1
Robert Hallom	1
Robert Hall	1
Wid. Hallom	1
Martin Middleton	1
Andrew Hallam	1
Anne Marshall wid.	1
Hugh Bradwall	1
Wid. Chalsworth	1
Geo. Hallam	1
Robert Barbar	1
Humphrey Hallom	1
John Hallom	1
Tho. Bray	1
Robert Hallom	1
Nich. Sickes	1
Adam Thornhill	1
Martin Marshall	2
John Middleton	1
Martin Middleton	1
Lawrence Balgay	1
George Berley	1
Wid. Downing	1

John Middleton	1
	4-15-0

Woodland

Henry Balgay gent.	6
Joseph Ward	5
Mr Joseph Eyre & Mr Jerimiah Ward	5

27

Abraham Ward	1
Mathew Berley	1
John Eyre	1
John Berley	1
Christopher Sistwell	1
Mary Morten wid.	2
Tho. & Edw. Eyre for Carr house	2
Crooke hill house	4 Ret
Francis Morley	6
Humphrey Furnisse	2
Willm Pashlow	2
Wid. yellot	2
John Morten	2
Stephen Haigh	3
Edward Ibbutson	2
Wid. Barker	1
Edward Barber	1
Tho. Eyre of the Ridge	2
Godfrey Beard	1
George Brownell	3
Edward Eyre	2
Robert Hall sen.	1
Robert Hall Jun.	1
Willm Hattersley	1
Rich. Hide	1
Thomas Hall	1
Nich. Ibbutson	1
Robert Haigh	1

Robert Tricket	1
Tho. Ey	
	3-6-0

Thornhill

Thomas Skinner	2
Joseph Haigh	2
Francis Wilson	2
Edmund Wilson	2
Robert Poynton	2

28

Mr Edw. Haigh	4
Lawrence Darwend	1
Ellis How	1
Willm Darwend	1
Humphrey Smilter	2
Thomas Wilson	2
Thomas Downing	2
John Bothoms	1
John Darwend	1 pd2^{s}
	1-5-0

Aston

Tho. Balgay gent.	4
Nich. Staley	4
John Haigh	2
Robert Morten	1
Lawrence Trickett	1
John Ashton	1
Tho. yellott	1
Robert Sanderson	1
Robert Darwend	1
John Thornhill	1
Willm Darwend	1
Robert Darwend	1
Thomas Crooke	1
John Eyre	1
	1-1-0

Brough

Robert Middleton	1
Roger Botham	1
Edmund Darwend	1
Rich. Middleton	2
John Marshall	1
Willm Marshall	1
Nich. Hayly	1
	0-8-0

Shattons

Thomas Eyre gent.	4
Anthony Robinson	1

29

Tho. Robinson	2
John Ides	1
Howard Brocke gent.	6
Ellis Middleton	1
William How	1
Robert Robinson	1
Francis Hardy	1
	0-19-0

Offerton

Widdow Glossopp	6
Gilbert Marshall	3
John Heild	1
Anthony Wood	1
Joseph Wilson	1
Abraham Robinson	2
	0-14-0

Castleton

Sam. Cryer minister	5
Henry Kneveton gent.	6
Christopher Staley gent.	3
Jo. Hall of goose hill	3
Richard Torr	3

Robert Hayley	1
Willm Dawson	1
Rowland Needham	1
Roger Hall	1 Ret
Wid. Hall	1
John Hall	1
Robert Needham	1
John Hall of the well	1
Anne How wid.	1
Wid. Hall	1
James Needham	1
Tho. Hall	1
Robert Hall	1
Tho. Creswell	4

<u>30</u>

Tho. Creswell for Bernard Wells house	1
John How	1
Nich. Ashton	1
Ellis How	1
Henry Eyre	1
the same for Phillip Ashtons house	1
Thomas Glover	1
Thomas Marshall sen.	1
Margaret Marshall wid.	2
Tho. Hall Shoomaker	2
Wid. Hall	1
Robert Clayton	1
Thomas Dowson	1
Christopher Jackson	1
Thomas Ashton	1
John Ashton	1
Ellis Slacke	1
Marke Furniss Jun.	1
John Hall de Pindall	1
Tho. Hall son of James Hall	1
Rich. Chalsworth	3
Robert Dakin sen.	1
Robert Dakin Jun.	1
Robert Nall	1
Isacc Bullocke	2
Daniel Stephens	3
Henry Slacke	2
Tho. Marshall Jun.	1
Edward Ashton	1
Christopher ?Jowle (?fowle)	1
Edward Cowper	1
Lawrence Warehurst	1
Rich. Ashton	4
Tho. Royse	1
Robert Lummas	1
Robert Glossopp	1
Wid. Hall	1
Jo. Barbar & Robt Thornhill	3

<u>31</u>

Robert Needham	1
Edmund How	1
Humphrey Nall	1
Robert How	1
Tho. How	1
Nicholas How	1
Ellis Pedley	1
John Tyme	1 Ret
Ellis Barbar	1
Tho. Bennet	2
Wid. Hallom	2
Wid. Needham	1
Robert Ashton	1
Francis Barbar	2
John Staley	nothing
Thomas Jowle	1
Widdow Dyson	1
Tho. Eyre	1
	5-8-0

Louse hill

Richard Hambleton	1
Thomas Barber	2
George Kinder	1
Peter Sidebothom	1
Wid. Harrison	1
Wid. Needham	1
Nich. Cowper	1
John Frost	1
Edw. Hattersley	1
John Tymme	1
Ellis Barber	1
Nich. Bridbury	1
Nich. Kirke	1
Roger Barber	2
Nich. Tymme	1
	0-17-0

Edall

Thomas Hall	3
Edw. Hall	3

32

Nicholas Creswell	2
John Fox	1
Mathew Shore	1
Wid. Barber	1
Thomas Low	1
Robert Burdikin	1
Ralph Barber	1
Willm Kinder	1
John Mellor	1
Thomas Hadfield	1
Robert Carington	1
John Kinder	1
Ellis yellot	1
Rouland Hall	1
Robert Hall	1
Tho. Hall	1
Robert Armefield	1
Rowland Barber	1
Robert Kirke	2
Robert Eyre gent.	2
Thomas How	2
Robert Ridgeway	2
John Barber	1
Robert Eyre	2
George How	2
Gilbert Haucksworth	1
Willm How	1
John Rowbothom	1
Roger Hall	1
Wid. Hall	1
Edmund Hall	1
Wid. Lauton	1
Richard Burdekin	1
Robert Pursglove	1
Edmund Laughton	1
Edw. Wood	1
Tho. Sanderson	1
Robt How	1
John Hadfield	1

33

Tho. Hall of greenelands	1
Robert Hambleton	1
Mr Pickforke	3 Ret
George Barber	1 Ret
	2-18-0

Viewed by John Wheeldon & Hugh Wheeldon Collect(or)s
George Brownell Constable

Glossop

Geo. Hollingworth	1
Mr Booth	7
Mr Wagstaffe	6

James Bagshaw	3
Mr Sandiforth	4
Robert Shoply	1
Willm Sickes	1
Thomas Booth	3
William Dousnopp	2
Robt Robinson	2
John Mellor	1
Robert Bramhall	2
Charles Wagstaffe	2
Samuel Wagstaffe	1
Henry Johnson	1
Tho. Doxon	3
Willm Syckes sen.	1
Willm Syckes iun	2
James Hall	2
Willm Hadfield	2
Edw. Hadfield	2
Thomas Hollingworth	1
Edward More house	2

34

John Didbury	1
Mr Garlicke	4
James Robinson	1
Tho. Newton Jun.	1
William Newton	1
Samuel Hall	2
Tho. Garlicke Jun.	1
Hugh Godward	1
The vicaridge	1
Tho. Wood	1
Wid. Booth	1
Tho. Newton	3
Wid. Garlicke	1
John Garlicke	1
John Disbury	1
Samuel Mellor	1
John Harropp	1
Tho. Wagstaffe	2
Tho. Harrison	1
Wid. Bramhall	1
Thomas Bennet	1
Willm Shuttleworth	1
Wid. Oxly	2
William Wagstaffe	1
Glossopp Mill	1
Wid. Hadfeild	1
	4-6-0

Padfield

John Hadfield	1
Anth. Syckes	1
Robert Hall	1
John Bre	1
George Barbar	1
William Chappell	1
Nich. Bramhall	1
John Bramhall	1
George Bennet	1
Willm Dornaly	1
Tho. Harsion	1

35

Nich. Godward	1
William Rollinson	1
John Dornally	3
George Doxon	1
Wid. Dornally	1
Charles Hadfield	1
John Hadfield	1
Tho. Garlicke	2
Willm Hadfield	1
Joseph Bramhall	1
Nich. Hadfield	1
Edw. Hadfield	1
John Hadfield for bro)	1
Israell Godward	1

John Alsopp	2
	1-10-0

Hadfield

Tho. Hadfield	4
Richard Newton	1
Mr Hadfield	2
Nich. Bre	1
Tho. Haigh	1
Tho. Warhurst	1
John Hadfield	1
Wid. Dornely & Edw. Eyre	1
Robert Bore	1
Tho. Newton	1
John Marshall	1
Thomas Blood	1
Tho. Hadfield Jun.	1
Isaac Knot	1
Joseph Dornely	1
	0-19-0

Pinting

Mr Garlicke	4
Joseph Wagstaffe	1

36

Edmund Sandiforth	1
Newtons de Sha	1
Willm Newton	1
Tho. Bre	1
Rich. Newton	1
Charles Garlicke sen.	1
Charles Garlicke Jun.	1
Thomas Armefield	1
Tho. Booth	2
Willm Newton Jun.	1
Edmund Newton	1
Wid. Cleton	1
John Eyre	1
Tho. Warhurst	1
Tho. Newton	1
Nich. Bre	1
	1-2-0

Whitfeild

Nich. Chalsworth	3
Robert Dousnopp	1
John Harropp	1
Willm Alsopp	1
John Haigh	1
Wid. Bre	1
Willm Bre	2
Robert Robinson	1
John Robinson sen.	1
Geo. Wood	2
Robert Haigh	1
Tho. Garlicke	1
Willm Robinson sen.	1
John Bennet	2
John Waterhouse	1
John Platt	1
Edward Garlicke	1
Henry Hadfield	3

37

Willm Robinson Jun.	1
the same for Tatton	1
John Whitle	1
Wid. Fieldsend	1
Willm Barbar	2
John Bore	1
John Timporly	1
John Robinson Jun.	2
Thomas Bore	1
?Jo. Feildsend de harst	1
	1-17-0

Chisworth

Willm Wagstaffe	3
John Hollinworth	2
George Booth	2
Robert Taylor Jun.	2
George Walklate	1
John Hide	2
John Booth	2
Robert Taylor sen.	1
Tho. Booth	2
Willm Brooke	1
John Robinson	2
Wid. Ridge	1
John Rowbotham	1
Robert Booth Jun.	1
Willm Rowbotham	1
John Beely	1
Jo. Fallow	1
Jo. Incle	1
Wid. Mosley	1
Robert Torr	1
Willm follow	1
Ralpe Mosley for a cottage house	1
	1-11-0

38

Chalsworth

Willm Harrison	1
Geo. Chalsworth	4
Tho. Booth	1
Lawrence Bore	1
William Robinson	1
William Kelshaw	1
Wid. Sheply	1
Tho. Harrison	1
Tho. Booth	4
John Booth Jun.	2
John Booth sen.	1
Willm Godward	2

John Hadfield	2
Tho. Beely	2
Willm Booth	1
Willm Walklate	2
Willm Burdekin	1
Wid. Botham	1
Robert Pidsbury	1
Robert folow	1
Geo. Bore	1
Willm Hadfield	1
Willm Botham	1
Willm Cliffe	1
Thomas Booth for warhurst	1
	1-16-0

Ludworth

Edward Thoryly	2
Willm Booth	2
Wid. Hogg et fil.	2
Robert Hollinworth	1
John Highum	1
Robert Wood	1
Peter Ratcliffe	2
Thomas Godward	1

39

Ellen Hide	1
Ralph Higginbothom	1
Wid. Mosley	1
Bryon Wood	1
Willm Wood	1
George Godward	1
Ralph Hide	1
Robert Hide	1
George Taylor	1
Wid. Walklate	1
Geo. Walklate	1
Ottiwell Beely	1
Willm Wood	1

Honori Godward	1
William Smith et fil.	2
John Bothom for Clough end	2
Robert Bird	1
Willm Walklate	2
Thomas Walklate	3
Thomas Mosley	1
Ottiwell Wood	4
Thomas Bore	1
Robert Taylor	1
John Godward	1
John Henchia	1
Elizabeth Booth	4
John Bothom	1
Willm Goodward	1
George Wood	1
Rich. Higginbothom	1
Ottiwell Wood	1
Wid. Robothom	1
Gilbert Godward	1
John Henchia	1
Robert Bott	1
Robert Booth	1

40

Willm Rolly	1
Thomas Hide	1
Ellis Bowman	1
William Taylor	1
Bartholomew Wood	2
Ottiwell Wood	1
	3-6-0

Symoly

Richard Pearson	8
Mr Morton	3
John Morton	1
Thomas Whytle	1
Nich. Kirke	1

Thomas Hadfield	1
John Jackson	1
Tho. Armefield	1
Ralph Watterhouse	1
James Arretage	1
the same for wid. Dison	1
John Moorehouse	1
John Garlicke	1
Henry Bothom	1
George Hogg	1
William Hadfield	1
Willm Hollinworth	(blank)
	1-5-0

Chunall

John Haigh	1
Peter Adsit	1
William Sheply	1
Thomas Sheply	2
Tho. Harrison	2
Samuel Harrison	1
Robert Robinson	1
	0-9-0

41

Mellor

Mr Cryer for Mellor hall	5
Willm Ratcliffe de Tonecliffe	2
Wid. Ratcliffe	2
Willm Hibert	1
John Ratcliffe et fil.	2
Willm Walkelate	1
Robert Heward	1
George Ratcliffe	1
Tho. Godward sen.	1
Peter Godward	1
Tho. Godward Jun.	3
Willm Hambleton	2
Wid. Hadfield	2

Willm Wood	2
John Henchia	1
Gilbert Ratcliffe	3
Tho. Ratcliffe	1
Robert Cotterill	3
Mr Stafford	5
Mrs Stafford	4
Exec. of German Buxton	3
William Cleton	1
Robert Bagshaw	1
John Hide	2
William Hibbert	1
Willm Higginbothom	1
Hugh Wild	1
Willm Higginbothom	1
Henry Beely	1
James Chytum for heathyhurst	3
James Ridgway	1
Willm Tomlinson	1
James Buxton	1
Roger Wild	2
Thomas Mellor	2
Tristrum Ridgway	1

42

William Jackson	2
William Godward	1
John Godward	1
Henry Stafford	1
Edward Stones	1
Anthony Stafford	3
William Godward Jun.	1
Mellor old hall	5
William Godward sen.	1
Peter Sidebothom	1
Willm Richardson	1
Edw. Bramhall	1
Widdow Godward	1
Lawernce Chatterton	1
Geo. Wood	1
John Rowbothom	1
Willm Hibert	1
John Bowman	1
Willm Stafford	1
James Chytum for Holinsworth house	1
Thomas Shuttleworth sen.	1
Tho. Shutleworth	1
Lawrence Rowbotham	1
	4-17-0

Received by Ed. Needham late
Collect(or) out of this towneship
$21^{li}. 5^{s}. 0^{d}$
viewed by John Wheeldon & Hugh
Wheeldon Collectors
Robert Harvey Constable

43

Tidswall

Mr Meverill	5
Mr Tho. Allen	4
Mr Edw. Ash	6
Richard Cooke	5
John Starr	1
William Outfield	1
Willm Chetam	1
Francis Hosson	2
Thomas Stevenson	2
Tho. Fisher	3
George Palframan	3
George Salt	1
Thomas Hill	3
Nich. Mellor	2
Zac. Greaves	3
William Robothom	2
Lawrence Torre	4
Gervas Gent	4

Wid. Bagshaw	2
Ros. Mellor	2
Edw. Creswell	3
Tho. Hardey	4
Willm Ash	2
Nich. Mellor	6
Gervas Hill	2
Joane Woodroufe	3
Thomas Woodroufe	4
Willm Wardle	1
Willm Burdakin	2
Richard yeald	2
Grace Beversly	1
Abraham Robothom	2
Willm Downes	2
Ellis Outfield	2
Gervas Eyre	2
John Wright	4

Richard Leech	1
Ellis Mellor	3
Robert Allen	4
Edw. Hobson	1
Edw. Harrison	1
Tho. Robinson	1
Robert Wardle	1
Willm Mycocke	1
Edw. Bagshaw	2
Humphrey Hobson	1
Richard Townsend	1
Robert Palframan	2
Richard Swane	1
Rich. Hardey	3
Tho. Palframan	1
Robert Johnson	1
Thomas Mycocke	1
Robert Cleaton	1

44

Andrew Bateman	2
Rich. Townsend Jun.	2
Ralph Staley	1
Rich. Middlton	2
Edw. Hadfield	1
John Goodwin	1
Wid. Hill	1
Ralph Cleaton	1
Robert Walker	3
Roger Bray	1
Edw. ?Hall	1
William Nall	4
Robert Sutton	2
John Beard	3
George Walton	1
William Milner	1
George Bower	2
Elizabeth Allen	3
Roger Goodwin	2 Ret

45

Adam Dosson	1
William Merriman	2
Robert Hosson	2
Richard Millnes	2
Anthony Longden	2
James Robinson	1
Geo. Townsend	1
Geo. Bower	1
Nich. Smith	1
Joshua Stoppard	2
John Bramwell	1
Robert Bagshaw	2
Willm How	1
Adam Hill	1
Tho. Holme	1
Francis Vernon	1
Wid. Sheldon	2
Rich. Hill	1
Robert yeald	1

Rich. Barrton	1
Ellis Hill	1
Jesper Breltnall	1
John Blackwall	1
Robert Bagshaw	3
Henry Furnish	1
Rich. Bennet	1
Willm Jesper	1
Willm Nall	1
John Nall	1
Adam Bagshaw	1
James Solsby	1
Peter Bagshaw	1
Ralph James	1
Wid. Sharshall	3
John Pedley	1
Abraham Bagshaw	1

46

James Milne	1
Francis Bennet	2
Adam Poynton	2
Adam Furnisse	3
Ellis Poynton	1
Willm Poynton	1
Edw. Poynton	2
Robert ?Duraham	2
Rowland Smith	2
Christopher James	3
Edw. Chapman	1
Herculus Poynton	1
Tho. Wood	1
Rich. Roger	1
Thomas Brooke	1
Henry Furnish	1
Wid. Furnish	1
Tho. Houldgate	1
John Hill	1
James Blackewall	1

John Bagshaw	7
John Wilson	3
Edward Anderton	1
Tho. Marshall	1
Willm Shaw	1
Geo. Needham	2
John Bagshaw	1
Rich. Bagshaw	1
John Wilson	1
Tho. Staley	1
John Bowman	1
Marke Chapman	1
George Chapman	1
Robert Wilson	2
Hugh Bower	1
John Slator	1

47

Mathew Thornhill	1
Francis Bagshaw	1
Adam Kirke	1
Edmund Outfield	1
Robert Coop	1
Adam Grant	1
Elizabeth Hallom	1
Ellis Furnish	2
Martin Hallum	1
George Furnish	1
George Sheldon	1
Willm Buxton	1
John Buxton	1
Wid. White	1
Tho. Boaden	1
George Boaden	1
Tho. White	1
William Kirke	1
Geo. Hodgkinson	1
Tho. Torr	1
James Boaden	3

Ralph Cantrell	2
Edw. Bennet	1
Wid. Middleton	1
Robert Needham	1
Willm Peake	1
Tho. Allen	1
Willm Middleton	1
Willm Bennet	1
John Fisher	1
Mathew Barber	1
Tho. Boaden	5
Henry Cantrel	3
Tho. Middleton	2
Tho. Allen	1
Tho. Needham	1
Stephen Mellor	1
Edw. German	1
Edw. Tymperley	1
Geo. Hill	1
Tho. Outfield	1
Willm Nall	1
Andrew Longden	1
Lawrence Fox	1
Geo. Raworth	1
John Merrill	1
Tho. Wright	4
Richard Clarke	1
George Blackewall sen.	1
Willm Hygett	1
Willm Outfield	1
George Blackewall sen. (sic)	1
Humphrey Hill	1

48

Ellis Mellor	1
Willm Finney	2
Syth Hodgkinson	1
Bernald White	3
Wid. Mellor	2
Anthony Pidcocke	1
Ellis Raworth	1
Ellizabeth Pott	1
Francis ?Haw	1
Stephen Browne	1
John Shaw	1
George Raworth	1
Anthony Bromhead	1
Edw. Slacke	1
Edw. Wright	3
Humphrey Blackwall	1
John Bockin	1
Tho. Bockin Jun.	1
Tho. Simpson	1
Edward Jackson	1
Tho. Bocking sen.	1

49

Robert Hardey	1
Philip Radford	1
Samuel Eaton	2
Thomas Morten	1
Arthur Jackson	2
John Creswell	3
Robert Clarke	1
John Hubbert	1
Tho. Wibersley	1
Robert Morten	2
Robert Timperley	1
Rich. Ashton	1
Nich. Palframan	1
Tho. Muchell	2
Rich. Smith	1
Willm Bramwall	1
Robert Bagshaw	1
Robert Low	1
Rich. Blackwall	1
Ralph Fearne	1
Robert Barton	1 C

Benet Barten	1 C
Hellen Outfeild	1 C
Rich. Worthy	1 C
Hump. Torr	1 C
Emmet Nall	1 C
	19-7-0

Viewed by Jo. Wheeldon & Hugh Wheeldon Collectors & Robert Hardey Constable

50

Boaden Midlecalles

Mr Hyde	5
Bartle	1
John Braddocke	1
John Hyde	3
Mr Higgingbothom	5
Willm Downes	1
Robert Armfeild	1
Tho. Fearnely	2
Ralph Fearnely	1
Tho. Leigh Esq. for Parke Hall	3
Wid. Cleaton	1 Ret
Nich. Disbury	1
Wid. yeavely	3
Samuel Watterhouse	2
Thomas Platt	1
Robert Bennet	1
Robert Slacke	2
Tho. Mellor	1
John Mellor	1
George Cotterill	1
John Hadfield	2
Robert Hinchcliffe	1
John Heyward	1[s]
James Tompson	1
Thomas Eyre	2
Thomas Marriot	3
Ottewell Kirke	3
Edmund Downes	3
William Allen	1
Wid. Mosse	1
Randle Bennet	1
Thomas Watterhouse	4
Samuel Hide	1

51

William Hide	1
Willm Beard	1
Robert Turner	1
Thomas Gee	4
Robert Rollinson	3 Ret
	3-12-0

Phossit hambet

Mr Rollinson	4
John Carington	1
Thomas Bradbury	1
Tho. Watterhouse	1
Wid. Whytle	1
Tho. Rollingson	1
Tho. Beard	2
Edmund Barnes	1
Tho. Beard	1
John Hadfield	1
Geo. Hadfield	2
Joseph Tricket	1
John Johnson	1
Lawrence Bennet	1 Ret
Robert Warrington	1
John Heyward	1
Geo. Mellor	1
Thomas Downes	2
Francis Downes	1
George Rollinson	3 Ret
Willm Bennet	2

Lawrence Bennet	1
John Brundret	1
Mr Plat	2
Willm Bridbury	2
	1-16-0

Kinder hamblet

Charles Lingard	1
Edmund Bridbury	2
Ralph Gee	1
Joshua Dewsnop	1

52

Robert Bennet	1
Nich. Wild	1
John Barnes	2
Robert Barnes	2
Lawrence Hall	1
Lawrence Hall Jun.	1
John Watterhouse	2
Ralph Kinder	1
Ralph Watterhouse	1
Wid. Armefield	1
Randle Bennet	1[s]
John Foard	3
John Bennet	1
	1-3-0

53

(blank)

54

Beard

Mr Ashenhurst	7
Law. Pott	2
Francis Stanfield	1
Peter Haugh	1
John ?furnnes (?Turnner)	2
Jo. Silvester	1

Tho. Froggat	1
John Froggot	1
Edward Downes	1
John Andrew	2
Randale Hyde	1 Ret
	1-0-0

Ollerset

Mr Bradbury	7
Thurston Ridgway	2
Widd. Bennet	1
Widd. Rollinson	2
Tho. Downes	1
Edw. Shirt	1
Edw. Wild	1
Tho. Bradbury	1
James Beard	1
John Rowbotham	1
Mr John Bradbury	2
Will. Wild	1
Edw. Downes	1
Tho. Booth	1
Tho. Boare	1
Edw. Boare	1
	1-5-0

Thorset

Mr Robert Bradbury	3
Mr Edm. Bradbury	1
Will. Beard	1
Jo. Keethly	1
Edm. Bradbury	1
Tho. Boadon	2

55

Widd. Ridgway	2
George Beard	1
Will. Goddard	1
Widd. Shuttleworth	1

Jeffrey Bramwall	1
Ottewell Bramwell	1
Edw. Lingard	1
Tho. Beard	1
Marke Tricket	1
Tho. Rowbotham	1
Raphe Heaward	1
Will. Heaward	2
Will. Goddard	1
Will. Rowbotham	2
George Longden	2
Edw. Hyde	1
Henry Keethly	1
Occupiers of Bawck head	2
Will. Barber	3
Law. Robotham	1
John Beard of Hollins	1
Raphe Waterhouse	1
John Bennet	1
	1-19-0

White Hamblet

Mr Cleaton	4
James Boaden	3
Nich. Warrington	2
Nich. Warrington sen.	1
Wid. Carrington	1
Nich. Syckes	1
John Bennet	1
John Wildbrow	1
John Haugh	2
Edw. Boare	1
Wid. ?Boare	3

56

Geo. Shirt	1
Ralph Hibbert	1
Randle Hibbert Jun.	1
Randle Hibbert	2

Robert Board	1
Geo. Higginbothom	1
Robert Armefield	1
Wid. Armefield	1
Ralph Boaden	2
John Higginbothom	1
Wid. Stafford	1
Anthony Boaden	2
Tho. Cleaton	2
Shutleworth house	1
Edward Boare torr top	1
John Beard	1
Willm Beard Gilberry yate	1
John Godward	2
Willm Armefield	1
Willm Beard new milne	1
James Wild	1
	2-6-0

Bugsworth

Mr Carrington	8
Robert Bennet	3
Widow Oliver	2
John Bennet	2
Widow Boaden	2
James Carrington	3
James Brerely	2
George Wright	1
Edw. Plattes	1
George Mellor	1
Francis Mellor	1
Francis Pott	1
Richard Gould	2

57

Willm Bennet	2
Edw. Bennet	2
Mr Jodrells house	1
	1-14-0

Brownside

Charles Kirke	2
Tho. Kirke	2
John Ashton	3
Anth. Ward	1
Charles Ashton sen.	1
Charle Lingard	2
Geo. Kirke for Ed. Hide	1
John Downes	1
John Lingard	2
John Lummas	1
	0-16-0

Chimley

Willm Andrew	3
Willm Carrington	3
Robert Beard	1
Roger Deane	1
Robert Gee	1
John Moult	1
Willm Moult	1
Francis Clarke	1
George Kirke	1
Robert Beard	1
Widow Dakin	1
Edward Boaden	1
Thomas Hadfield	1
John Greene	1
John Godward	1
Willm Bennet	1
John Moult	1
Robert Carrington	1

58

Willm Rollinson	1
George Woolley	1
Willm Bennet	1
John Hadfield	1
Godfrey Lingard	1 Ret
Robert *Ellis* Gib	2
Thomas Kirke	1s
Tho. Boaden	1
	1-11-0

Viewed by John Wheeldon & Hugh Wheeldon Coll(ectors)
Mr Carington Constable

59

(blank)

60

Eyam

Robt Eyre Esq. of Highlow	9
Mary Rowland	1
Dorothy Cowlishaw	1
George Johnson	1
John Hawksworth	1
Tho. Chapman sen.	1
John Drable	1
Ann Merrill	1 C
George Plats	1
John Hall	1
James Moore	3
Edw. Taylor	1
John Danyell	1
Nicholas Danyell	1
Tho. Danyell	2
John Hardy	1
John Ragg	2
Rowland Wilsons house	1
Robt Fiddler	1
Rich Saxelly	1
Margret ?Pillington	1
Martyn Furnise	3
Amye Furnise	1
Elizabeth Wood	1
Francis Thornly	1

Peter Bradshaw Esq.	7
Richard Furnise	2
Francis Garret	1
Widd. skydmore	1
Mary Wilson widd.	1
Willm Crane	1
Rogger Gregory	1
Will. Wilson	4
Robt Fox	1
Francis Blackwall	1
Jo. Swindle	1
Alice Rowland	2
Tho. Wright Gent.	4
Henry Fanshaw	noth.
Will. Baxtris house	noth.
Antho. Raworth	1
John Coe	1
Will. Ainesworth	1
Jo. Wilson	1
Tho. Ragg	1 Ret

61

Robert *Hardey* Thorpe	1
Katherine Wilson	1
Bridget Ash	1
Mr Mompheson	4
Mr stanley	2
Stephen Wild for two halfe yeares	2s
John Abell	1
Francis Whitacre	1
Tho. Taylor	1
Rich. Bockinge	1
Tho. Heath	1
Nicolas Thornely	1
Francis Bockinge	1
Will. Fryth	2
Godfrey Torr	1
Stephen French	1
Christopher Abell	1
Francis Torr	1
John Coates	1
Tho. Torr	1
Phillip Sheldon	4
George Talbot	1
Whyteleys House	1
Robt Slyn	1
Tho. Fryth	1
Jo. Taylor for one halfe yeare	1s
Will. Knowles	1
Row. Merrill	1
Tho. Wild	1
Robt Hill	1
Mathew Morton	1
	5-11-0

Woodland Hamblet

Francis Shorps house	2 Ret
Hugh Rippond	1
Sam. Bennet	1
Row. Swan	1
Tho. Cowper	2
Francis Tomason	1
Widd. Wilshaw	6
Addam Hawksworth	1
George Slyn	1
Widd. Anderton	1
Will. Midleton	5
Will. Scot	1
Tho. Calton	1
Will. Trout	1
Nicolas Heald	2
Jeffrey Taylor	1
Widd. Pearcevall	1
Richard Mosley	1

62

Richard Davison	1

Raphe Frost	1	Jo. Barber	1
Will. Mosley	1	Will. Caps	3
Will. Syddall	1	Tho. Buxton	2
Joane Banes	1	Joshua Websters house	3 Ret
Tho. Smith	1	Francis Garret	1
Tho. Heald	1	John Parkes	1 Decre. Notł
		Widd. Garret	1
Stony Midleton		John Baxter	1
Robt Ashton Esq.	7		
Tho. White	4	63	
Tho. Oxely	4	Widd. Wells	2
George Mason	4	Tho. Froggat	2
Francis Shorpe	2	Henry Seile	1
George Etches	2	Tho. Fletcher	1
Dennis Ragg sen.	2	Jo. Wild	1
Dennis Ragg Jun.	1	George Syddall	1
Will. Frost	1	Will. Heald	1
Tho. Mason	2	Tho. Outram	1
Tho. Rose	1 Ret	Tho. Outram sen.	1
Jo. Hallum	1	Tho. Outram	1
Abram Etches	2	Edmund Slake	1
Tho. Howson	1	Richard Outram	1
Stephen Lees	1	Humphrey ?Olliver Jun.	1
George Swift	1	Peter White	1
Christopher Ragg	2	Henry Maden	1
Robt Madder	1	Francis Brites	1 Ret
Humphrey ?Olliver sen.	1	Widd. Thornehill	1 C
Antho. Hardinge	1		6-4-0
Robt Outram	1		
Robt Roggers	2	**Foolow**	
Robt Thornly	2	John Bennet	1
Tho. Olliver	1 Ret	Margret Bennet	1
Tho. Heald	1	Luke Furnise	1
Humphrey Bates	1 Ret	Luke Morten	1
Robt Brough	1	Tho. Olliver	1
George Hench	1	Jo. Merrill	1
Edw. Fooles	1	Ann Andrew	1
Francis Fooles	1	Ellis Furnise	1
Will. Roberts	1	Will. Furnise	1 Ret

Will. Finson	1
John Hill Gent.	4
Robt Morten	1
Will. Marshall	1
George Younge	1
Stephen Hall	1
Tho. Furnise	1
Tho. Gregory	4
Raphe Barber	1
Will. Morley	2
Jo. Soaresby	1
Raphe Ash	2
Jo. Naylor	2
Tho. Holebrooke	1
James Hall	1
Tho. Barber	1
Peter Hawksworth	3
Francis Townesend	1
Widd. Hall	1
Tho. Wilson	1

64

Isacke Morten	1
Edward Bennet	2
Jossua Hall	2
Robt Morten	1
Mathew Morten	1
John Blackwall	1 C
Jo. Litlewood	1 C
Widd. Joane Hall	1 C
Tho. Barker	*1 C*
	2-10-0

Abney Hamblet

Will. Worrall	1
Francis Marshall	1
Henrye Furnise	2
Will. Furnise	1
George Bagshaw	1
Will. Bradwall	1
Abram Crosland	1
Will. Readfearne	1
Francis Eyre	1
Gervas Hallam	2
Robt Barker	1
Francis Barker	1
John Howe	1
John Bomford	1
Nicolas Morten	1
Robt Dakin	1
Ellis Marshall	1
Robt Readfearne	1
Raphe Townesend	1
Will. Greaves	1
John Bagshaw	1
Tho. Drable	1
Tho. Hall	1
Tho. Bagshaw	1
Rich. Bockinge	1
Will. Hawley	1
Robt Brightmore	1
Jo. Roberts	4
Tho. Warrington	1
Widd. Bingley	1
Will. Knowles	2
Tho. Brushfield	1
Bernard Brushfield	1
James stone	1 C
Tho. Sellars Jun.	1 C
Will. sheldon	1 C
Widd. Dorothy sheldon	1 C
	2-3-0

65

Darley

Mr Columbell	12
Mr John Pott	5
Mr ?Puellen (?fluellen)	4

Stanfield Hall	10	
Richard Milner	4	
George Turnner	3	
Henry Wall	1	
James Roberts	1	
Francis May	2	
Henry Barker	2	
Richard Smith	1	
John Wild	3	
Widd. Hodkin	1	
Will. Parker	?2	
Henry Taylor	1	
Ben. Twigg	3	
Francis Badsley	3	
Jo. Bradley	1	
Jo. Bradley Jun.	1	
Peter Gladwin	3	
Peter Barker	4	
Widd. Oates	1	
George Beastoll	2	
Will. Tomlinson	1	
John Tomlinson	1	
John Parke	3	
Luke Killar	1	
George Bradley	1	
John Steere	1	
Godfrey Taylor for two halfe yeares	2^s	*Ret*
Robt Bradley	2	
Ann Hardey	1	
Nicolas Davis	2	
Henry Roose	1	
Antho. Holme	1	
Henry fearne	2	
Rogger Soaresby	1	
Rich. Hosen sen.	3	
Rogger Oates	1	
Richard Hossen Jun.	1	
Jo. Hosen sen.	1	
James Ball	1	

<u>66</u>

John Steveston	1	
George Wagstaffe	3	*Ret*
Widd. Wheatcroft	1	
Antho. Steere	1	
Widd. Dunn	1	
Jo. Bradley	1	
Will. Ball	1	
Robt Fearne	2	
Rogger Taylor	1	
Peter Parke	2	
John Redford	1	
Will. Prime	1	
Jo. Rowbotham	2	
Rogger Steere	1	
Rogger Viccars	1	
Tho. Harrisson	1	
John Evans	2	
Peter Ball	1	*Ret*
John Willimot	1	
James Dunn	1	
Joseph Wattison	1	
Antho. Wood	2	
Rich. Wilgouse	2	
Humphrey Taylor	1	
George Willimot	1	
Samson Hydon and John Hydon	3	
Widd. Taylor	5	
Robt Pidcoke	2	
Jo. Ellot	1	
John Oxespringe	3	
Peter Haward	1	
Jo. supper	1	
Rogger Turner	1	
Tho. Bentley	2	
John Oxely	4	
John Wilgouse	1	

George Hardey	1	
George Willimot	1	
Rogger Cottrell	1	Ret
Robt Smith	1	C

67

Overhaddon Hamblet

George Broadhurst	2	
Roger Milner	1	
Tho. Boame	3	
George Webster	2	
Tho. Newton	2	
George Greaves	1	
George Langley	1	Ret
John Handley	1	
Humphrey swindle	1	
Huge Jones	1	
Roger Taylor	1	
George Dughty	1	
Francis newton	1	
Rich Readfearne	1	
Will. Hodkinson	1	
Will. Taylor	1	
John Mellor	1	
Will. Tofft	2	
Will. Flancksby	1	
John Brunt	1	
Humphrey Broadhurst	1	Ret
John Bateman	1	
Christ. Staley	1	Ret
Richard Broadhurst	1	decse
Mr Robert Bateman for Will. Walker	1	
John Smith	1	
Mr John Bateman	2	Ret
John Earle of Rutland	48	
Robt Bromhead	5	
Rowsley Milne	1	
Mr Henry Buxton	3	
Edward Stone	1	
Will. ?Newune	1	
Mr Jo. Stevenston	6	
Mr Robt Scholler	3	
Jo. Bowreinge	2	
Row. Maddocke	1	
Francis Ludham	1	
Richard Whithead	1	Ret

68

Simon Scelton	1	Ret
Henry Smith	2	
Tho. Wood	1	
Jo. Gibbone	2	
Widd. Goodwin	2	
John Smith	2	
Row. Mason	2	
John Ashburne	3	
	13-19-0	

viewed by John Wheeldon & Hugh Wheeldon Collect(or)s
Tho. Bockinge Constable

Peake Forrest

Mr Tho. Bainbridge	2	
Ann Morton	1	
Ann Youle	1	
Widd. Hayward	1	
Robt Hallome	1	
Jeffrey Hollinshead	2	
Row. Eyre	1	
Raphe Morton	1	
Will. Winterbotham	1	
George White	1	
Will. Cartledge	1	
Henry Trippet	1	
Will. Ward	1	Ret
Robt Ward	1	

James Ward	1	James Warehurst	1
Ann Bagshaw	1	Robt Needham	2
John Townesend	1	John Vernon	2
Richard Winterbotham	1	Robt Bagshaw	1
Will. Archdale	1	Robt Story	1 Ret
Will. Frost	1	Widd. Watts	1 Ret
John Wilson	1	Nicolas Greene	1 Ret
John Ward	1	Gerrard storrer	1 Ret
Will. Longden	1	John Eyre	1
		James Fynney	1 Ret

69

Tho. fletcher	1
Adam Bucocke	1
Row. Eyre	1
Francis Wood	1
Elizabeth Marchshall	2
John Ridgway	1
Richard Moorehurst	1
Edward Morehurst	1
John Warehurst	1
Tho. Warehurst	1
Tho Pearson	1
Tho. Wood	1
Robt Youle	1
Elizabeth Cleaton	1
Will. Rigley	2
Jane Golline	1 C
Rich Beverley	1
Rich Walker	1
John Wells	1
Tho. Wintterbotham	1
James Birckinshough	1
Godfrey Pearson	1
Tho. Wintterbotham	1
Adam Bagshaw	1
Raphe Wright	1
Will. Peacke	1
Tho. Beard	1
Thurstan Hill	1 Ret

Mathew Tyme	1
John Tyme	1
Humphrey Downes	1 Ret

70

John Lowe	1 Ret
Elnor Wright	1
Francis Wright	1
Ann Fryth widd.	1
Edward Watts	1
Richard Swanne	1
Robt Bagshaw	1
Will. Cocker	1
Martin Hallome	1
Robt Dakin	1
Will. Smith	1
Tho Hill	1
Edw. Lummas	1
Mathew Taylor	1
Ellis Collier	1
Will. Hoyle	1
Raphe Boare	1
Will. Pearson	1
John Smith	1
Jane Heaward	1
Will. Nalle	1
James Peacke	1
Tho. Swanne	1
	4-13-0

Viewed by John Wheeldon & Hugh Wheeldon Collectors

Row. Eyre Constable

<u>Youlgreave</u>

Mr Wilson	3
Mr John Buxton	8
Mr Henry Fox	6
Mr John Whitacre	6
Raphaell Bradbury	4
Josua Swindle	1
John Briddon	4
Ellen Smith	1
George Swindle	1
George Hallowes	2

<u>71</u>

John Coates	1
Hugh Sheldon	3
Francis Tofte	1
Edw. Hadfield	1
Sam. Roberts	2
Dorothy Sheldon	2
John Balcouse	2
Abram sheldon for two halfe yeares	2^{s}
Francis Smith	2
John Goodwin	1
Francis Pickeringe	2
George Coates	1
George Allcocke	1
Will. Ratclife	1
John Wilson	1
Will. Garret	1
Hugh Sheldon sen.	1
John Sheldon sen.	1
Henry Swift	3
Tho. Mosley sen.	1
Edw. Briddon	1

John Mosley	C	1	*Ret*
Henry Roberts		1	
Josephe Hossen		2	
Lawrence Hayes		1	
John Crichlow	C	1	*Ret*
George Brids House		3	
Will. Chadwicke		1	
Humphrey Bridden		1	
Lawrence Whalley		1	
Robt Hall		1	
Rich senior		3	
Will. Coates		1	C
George Newton		1	
Mr George Brids		1	
Francis mans house		1	
Will. Hodkinson		1	
John Rowland		1	
Will. Roberts		1	
George Roberts		2	
Tho. Mosley Jun.		1	

<u>72</u>

Francis Taylor	1
George Tofte	1
Tho. Bowreinge	1
John Sheldon Jun.	1
Will. Wagstaffe	1
Will. Ball	1
Francis Carrington	2
Ann Needham	1
John Stone	1
Will. Listers house	1
James Roberts	4
Will. Smedley	1
George Ashburne	1
John Bradshaw	1
John Wright	1
George Frost	1
Francis staley	1

Widd. Briddon	5
John Wardlow	2
Gilbert Langley	3
	6-4-0

Stanton Hamblet

Mr Will. Bach	11
Mr Richard Calton	5
Joseph Webster	1
George Lucas	2
Rich. Nuttwall	1
Tho. Madder	1
John Allen	1
Rich. Norman	1
John Brakenfield	1
John Slator	1
Humphrey Bradshaw	1
Thurston White	1
George Burds	4
Rich. Chappell	1
Rich Holme	1
John Gladwin	1

73

James Ashburne	1
John Mason	1
Ellen Walker	1
Francis Kempe	1
John Ashbourne sen.	1
John Ashburne	1
Widd. Hawley	1
George Gamble	1
Robt Stearnedale	1
Widd. Stearndale	2 Ret
George Hadfield	1
James Knowles	2
John Knowles	2
John Staley	1
Francis Mosley	1
Will. Bateman	1
George stearndale	1
Will. Langton	1
Will. Mylnes	4
Francis Holme	1 Ret
George Holme	1
Henry Buxton	1
Robt Holme	1
Anthony Holme	1
George Fenton	2
John Wagstaffe	1
Francis Baker	3
Antho. Browne	2
Francis Smedley	1
Will. Twigge	1 C
Will. Brakenfield	1
	3-15-0

74

Winster Hamblet

Tho. Dawes	2
John Slator	2
Dorothy Goodwin	1
Rich. Lummas	1
Gilbert Lingard	1
Robt Sherwin	1
Widd. Syworth	1
Jo. Lummas	1
Rogger Clarke	1
John Hawley	1
John Adams	1
Will.Deane	1 C
Tho. Wheeldon	1
Rich. Cadman	1
Tho. Johnson	1
John Johnson	1
John Roberts	1
Antho. Ann Hampson	1 C
John Sherwin	1

John Adams	1	C
George Parker	1	
Will. Sherwin	1	
Will. Barker	1	
Tho. Sellars	1	
Francis moore sen.	1	
Francis moore Jun.	1	*C Ret*
John Marple	1	
Tho. Dancaster	1	C
Edw. Parker	2	
Francis Parker	1	
John Killar	1	C
Mary Eyans	3	
James norman	2	
John Hudson	3	
Tho. Brunsley	1	
Christopher Wilson	3	
Elizabeth Adams	1	
Margret Blackwall	1	
John Jackson	1	

75

Francis Eyans	1	
Francis Ashmore	2	
Raphe Hawley	1	
Robert Moore	3	
George Hampson	1	
Will. Elliot	2	
Tho. Mellor	1	
Will. Eyans	1	
Rich. Greene	2	
George Allen	1	
Rogger Stone	1	
Alex. Stone	1	
Will. Oates	1	
Elnor Allcocke	1	
Tho Heath	1	
Mary Clarke	1	
John Buxton	1	
George Eyans	2	
Tho Hawley	1	
Ann Toft	1	
Robt Hawley	1	
Rich. Tofte	1	
John Ashmore	1	
Will. Eyans sen.	3	
Antho. Ashmore	2	
Raphe Bowre	2	C
Antho. Reynes	1	
Raphe Roggers	1	
Tho. Staley	1	
Francis Staley	1	
Robt Reynes	1	
Will. Dame	1	
Georg Frost	1	
Mary Hall	1	
George Ruddyerd	1	
Rich ?Enser	3	
Jo. Balycouse	1	
Henry Reynes	1	
Jo. Came	1	
Tho. Hossen	1	

76

Will. Hossen	1	
Rich. Vicars	1	
John Beresford	1	
Rich. Came	1	
Will. Eyans	1	
	5-6-0	

Birchover Hamblet

Mr Adam Eyre	7	
Rich. Berrisford	4	
Rich. Housley	1	
Hen Gregroy	1^{s}	
Will. wowen	1	Ret
Adam smith	1	Ret

Tho. Rouse se	1	
Will. Bullace	1	Ret
Will. Bradley	1	Ret
Rich Bradley	1	
Geo. Shipley	1	
Geo. Dalle	1	
Benj shawe	1	
Tho. Housley	1	Ret
Tho. Rouse Ju	1	
Peter Clay	1	Noth
Georg. Bradley	1	
Tho. shepard	1	noth
John Rouse sen.	1	
John Rouse Jun.	1	
Hum. smith	2	
Wid. wright	1	
Rich. Keeling	1	
Will. Daniell	1	
Rob. Gregroy	1	
Hen. Bradley	1	
John shipley	1	
Will. Walker	1	
Rich. Clay	1	
	1-19-0	

77

Gratton

Adam Woolley	2
Rich. Briddon	1
Humphrey Marshall	2
Rich Longden	2
John Tomlinson	1
Widd. Chipman	1
Will. Milner	2
Henry Gilman	1
Humphrey Bridden	1
James Barke	1
John Twigs	2
	0-16-0

Viewed by John Wheeldon & Hugh Wheeldon Collectors & Tho. Mosley Constable

Bowdon Chappell

Mr Bowdon	8
George shirt	2
Jo. Shirt	1
Tho Low	1
Edw. Greensmith	1
Will. Lingard	1
Will. Barber	?2 (?1)
Mr Ash	5
Jo. Bennet	1
Arnold Kirke	1
Tho Younge	1
Antho. Younge	1
Mr Bagshaw	5
Widd. Greensmith	1
Antho. Jackson	1
Raphe Roson	1
Tho. Hambleton	1
Humphrey Low	1
Jo. Lingard	3
Widd. Lingard	1

78

Tho. Greensmith	1
Rich. Greensmith	1
Rob Gibb	3
Will. Tunsteed	1
John Lomas	2
Nicholas shottall	1
John Taylor	1
Geo. Mellor	1
Mrs Anne Bowdon ridg	1
Greate Bowdon ridg	1
John Cresswell	2
James Carrington	3

Edward Dixson	1
wid. Cresswell	1
Hen. Kerke Junor	1
wid. Kirke ...	2
Tho. Whitehead	1
Tho. Bagshawe	1
Rob. Bagshawe	2
Ralph Lomas	1
Edward Cresswell	2
Tho. Lomas	1
Tho. Kirke	3
Philip Marchniton	1
Geo. Thornehill	4
Hum. Thornehill	1
Geo. Leese & Hum. Thornehill	1
The heires of Tho. Mellor	2
Hen. Mellor	1
Geo. Hall	1
wid. Kirke	1
Tho. Kirke	1
Tho Ridge	1
Edward Barbar	1
James Mellor for halef yeare for one harth increse	1s
Hen Kirke for one Halef for one harth increse	1s
	4-10-0

John Lowe	?5	
Tho. Brammall	1	
Tho. Morten	1	
Tho. Lumas	1	Ret
Rob. Marshall	2	Ret
Hen. deayne	2	
Geo. Morten	1	
Tho. Lumas	2	
Tho. Allen	2	
Geo. Lowe	2	
Hen. Bagshaw	2	
Hump. Marshall	3	
Edward wright	1	
Raynold Turner	1	
Barbarah Moulte	1	
wid. Lowe	1	Reto
Hen. Lumas	2	
Charles Cotterill	2	
Tho. Foxlow	1	
Tho. Lumas	1	
Edward Lomas	3	
Tho. Taylor	3	
Nich. Lomas	1	
Rob Crosley	3	
Tho. Downes	1	
John Ollernshaw	1	
Tho. Bowdon	1	Ret

79

Coumbes Edge

Mr Bagshawe	9
Ralph Bagshawe	1
John Heathcoate	1
Tho. Cowper	3
wid. waynewright	2
Fran. Mellor	3
Antho. Beallott	1
Nich. Bradshaw	2
Nich. Bradshaw sen.	1

80

Tho Bowdon

wid. Cowper	1	Ret
Geo. Lowe	1	Ret
Rob. Haskey	1	Ret
Rich Lowe	1	Ret
	3-14-0	

Bradshaw Edge

Mrs Bowden	5
Nich. Lingard	2

Rob. Tunstid	1	Cr
Antho Hide	2	
Hen. Kirke	2	
Geo. Hodgkinson	1	
Rob. Moult	1	
Rob. Browne	1	
James warrington	1	
Fran. Taylor	2	
Edward Kirke	3	
Jos. Hadfeild	1	
John Kerke	1	
Rob. moult de whitehough	1	
Rob. Bennett	1	
Rich Bennett	1	
Tho. Gee	1	
John Moulte	2	
Tho Marshall	3	
Tho. Bowdon	2	
Francis Mosley	2	
Edward Wright	3	
Jo. Bennet	1	
Will. Carrington	1	
John Ford	2	
Margery Bennet	1	
Edw. Olerrenshaw	3	
Antho. Ollerenshaw	1	

81

Widd. Bennet	1
Robt Ollerenshaw	1
Rich Davenport	2
Mrs Bagshaw	2
Francis Gee	2
Edw. Ash	12
Will. Moult	1
Robt Ollerenshaw	1
John Crosley	1
Edw. Ollerenshaw	1
Francis Botham	1

George Cowper	1	
Henrie Mellor	1	
Joseph Botham	1	
George Marshall	1	
Nicolas Low	1	
Mrs Browne for March Hall	1	Ret
Alexander Jones	1	
Robt shirt	1	
Dorothy Mellor	1	Ret
Edw. Greene	1	Ret
George & Nicol. Bagshaw	3	
Nicolas Smith	13	
Edw. Creswell	4	
George Swindle	4	
George Morten	1	
Jo. Crux	1	
Tho Bagshaw	4	
Robt Bagshaw	1	
John fletcher	1	
Tho Shirt	1	
Nicolas Bagshaw	2	
Jo. Kirke	2	
John Cowper	4	
Mr Wood	2	
Robt Bradley	2	
Elizabeth Cleaton	2	

82

Raphe Ramstar	2
Nicolas Beard	2
Widd. Cooke	3
George Shirt	1
George Wright	2
John Lummas	1
John Redfearne	1
George Ma	7-3-0

Viewed by John Wheeldon & Hugh Wheeldon Collectors & John

Lingard Constable

Hathersage

Mr John Walker	4
John Skinner	2
Francis Bingham	1
Francis Smith	1
Tho. Fox	1
Robt Tomson	1
John Smelter	1
Mathew Furnise	2
Robt Syddale	1
John Steele	2
John Wilcockson	1
George Eyre	3
Rich Skinner	1
John Hugh	1
Antho. Barnes	1
Robt Tomason sen.	1
James Morten	1
Adam Furnise	1
George Ibberson	1
John Heald	1
Tho Frost	1

83

Ann Crosland sen.	1
Ann Crosland Jun.	1
Widd. Barker	1
John Greene	1
Myles Wilkin	1
Robt Yellot	1 Ret
John Syddall	1
Symon Dakin	1
George Cowper	1 Ret
Tho Eyre	1
Humphrey syddall	1
Tho. Furnace	1
Nicolas Yeald	1
John Greene	1
Francis Jackson	1
Tho. Eaton	2*Ret*
Mary Hodkinson	1
Robt Came	1
Tho Litlewood	1
Tho Came Jun.	1
Robt Came	1
John wilcokson	2
Antho. Wilcockson	1
John Fryth	1
John Greaves	?4
Rich Wilcockson	1
John Jesop	1
George Bromhill	1
Tho. Stone	1
John Came	2
Tho Wallhead	1
Tho Clarke	2 Ret
Raphe Bagshaw	1
Tho Marshall	2
Robt Jackson	1

84

Will. Olliver	4
George Eyre	2
Dorothy Syddall	1
Will. Fiddler	1
John Greene	1
Martin Sanderson	1
Mathew Barker	1
Raphe Jowet	1
Tho Worrall	1
Tho Skinner	1
Francis Brownehill	1
Tho. Britlebanke	2
Henry Bromehill	1
John Lee	2
John Hawksworth	1

Georg Berely	1	
Tho. Skimer	1	
John Fox	1	
Law Fidler sen.	1	
Rich Crichlow	1	
Law. Fidler Jun.	1	
John Litlewood	1	
Law. Fox	1	
Robt Greaves	1	
Rich Clarke	1	Ret
Jo. Hawkard Jun.	1	
John ?Goodpeare	2	
Hugh Greaves	1	
Robt Yellot	1	
John Skinner	1	
Francis Tomason	1	
Nicolas Bromhill	1	
Tho. Skinner	1	
George Skimer	1	Ret

85

Francis Tomason	*1*	
George Briddard	1	
Will. Hawkard	1	
John Wilson	1	
Antho. Wilcockson	1	
Robt Litlewood	1	
Will. Eyre	1	
Widd. Turnner	1	
Tho Eyre	4	
Widd. silvester	3	
Henry Hyde	*1*	
George Watersly	1	
Alice Cottrell	1	
Joseph Hall	2	
Rogger Barber	1	
Edmund Barber	1	
Abram Baddely	1	Ret
George Jackson	1	Ret
John Trout	1	Ret
Mr Balgray	4	
John Hawley	1	
John Tinker	1	
John Morton	1	
Tho. Glover	1	
Sara Barber	1	
Georg Hobson	1	Not
Robt Hawley	1	
henry Robinson	1	
Edw. Ibusson	1	
Jo. Cottrell	1	
Emet Ibuston	1	
John Tomason	2	
Georg Yellot	1	
Edw. Morton	2	
George Morton	1	

86

John Boare	1	
George Barber	1	
James Webster	1	
Will. Ibutson	1	
Row. Eyre	1	
Dorothy Kirke	1	C
	8-3-0	

Viewed by John Wheeldon & Hugh Wheeldon Collectors & Thomas Tomason Constable

Backwell

Mr Chr. Lawson	5	
Mr Sevill	8	
Jone Adams	1	
John Twig Jun.	4	
John Heathcoate Jun.	2	
Widd. sheldon	2	
James wood	1	C

George *Hawley* ?Foyles (?Stayles)	1 C	Robt Bateman	3
John Heathcoat sen.	3	Tho. Grammar	4
Francis Mosley	2	Robt Bludworth	3
Will. Riddiard	3	Will. Campion	1
Sam. Barlow	2	Francis Welch	1
Will. Doughty	1	John Clife	1
Hercules Foldjame	2	George Hall	2
Grace Tomlinson	2	John North	3
Edw. Dodson	3	Tho North	2
Tho. Yates	2	John Dickens	3
Will. Sevill	6	Will. Thorpe	1
Ann Swan	1	Tho Woodward	2
Jo. Burton	2	Tho steele	1
Edward Downes	1	Edw. Boolar	5
Henry Tattersall	2	Will. Greaves	2
Robt Bott	3	Francis ?Burton	5
Godfrey Fouljambe	2	Will. Newton	7
		Tho. Geary	2

87		88	
Joseph Britland	2	Mr Nicason	4
Antho. Banks	1	Will. North	3
Will. Broadhurst	1	James Fryth	4
Ellis Barber	3	Francis stearndale	1
John Eyley	4	Mary Heaward	1
Henrie Foldjambe	1	Will. Sevill gent.	2
Ann Goodwin	1	James Listchild	4
(one name struck out)		Tho. syddall	2
Will. Ashton	4	Raphe Howson	3
Will Pidcocke	2	Will. Frost	2
Robert Thorpe	3	Jo. Bukton	2 C
Mary Listchild	1	Will. Motterram	2
Georg Maddocke	2	Francis Whitacre	2
Robt Pidcocke	11	Widd. Johnson	1
Rogger plant	2	Francis Dale	1
Mathew Thorpe	2	John Arrell	2
John Thorpe	3	Widd. Jone Eyley	6
Phillip Robinson	3	Ann Bukton	1
Will. Bludworth	2	Nicolas Thornehill	5

Hugh Newton	1	Mary Toplis	1
Will. Brewell for Robt Clarks house for one half yeare	1^s	George Beastoll	1
Michall Noton	1	(one name obliterated)	
Tho. Upshaw	1 C		11-0-0
Charles Hadfield	1		
Jo Tankin	2		
Bernard White	3		
Edw. foster	1		
Will. Greaves	1		
Francis staley	1		

(Rec)eived by Ed. Needham
late Collect(or for) this
towneshipe the sum of
11 li. 0s. 0d.
(Viewed) by John Wheeldon &
(Hugh Wh)eeldon Collectors
...rd Constab(le)

MORLESTON & LITCHURCH HUNDRED

1670

Derby Public Library, Derbyshire Collection, DC 9956

(Title page)

Hundred of Morleston
& Litchurch

John Bancrofte

Hearth money

(1)

Allestrey

Jn Munday Esq.	?decr. Lm	8
f Mr Gilb. Munday		1
Jn Rossell senior		1
Jn Sadler		1
wm Barke		2
Tho. Brunt		2
Tho. Sadler		1
f Mr Collier		5
Rich. Baker		1
Jn Cator		1
will. Sadler		1
Rob. Burton		1
Jn Harrison		1
Hen. Day		1
Hen. Cowley		2
Wm Raven		1
f Wm Baker		3
Wid. Peate		1
Jn Rossell Jun.		1
Rich. wright		1
Tho. Rossell		3
Will. Soer		2
Hen. Burrowes		1
Hen. Collier		1
Rob. Tomlinson		1
Hen. Soer		1
Wm Frearson		1
Rich. Barton		1
Rich. Bradberry		1
These 4 are Certified for being poor & not payable:		
Wid. Frearson		2
Ed. whelpdale		1
Tho. Higgenbotham		1
Rich. Collier		1
		45

Vewed p(er)nos John Bancroft
& Rich. Riley Collectors
Wm Baker Constable

(2)

Auveston & Booton

f Mr Geo. Allestrey	2
Geo. Woodworth	2
Rob. Cowper	1
Wid. Brearley	1
Hu. ?Site	1
Jos. Hallowes	1
John Rossell	1
f Jos. Newham	3
Rob. Hibbert	1
Wm Hodeskinson	1
Ra. Greatrix	1
Wm Strong	2
Ra. Doeman	1
Ed. Burgaine	1

John Greatrix	1	
Geo. Fibbes	1	
f Mr ?Gerrard Bembrigge	6	
Hen. Allestrey	1	
Wm Robinson	2	
Tho. Warwin	1	
Rob. Bracebey	1	
Geo. Butler	2	
Tho. Robinson	1	
Fra. Wattes	1	
Geo. Sherwin	1	
John Alsop	1	
Ed. Calladine	2	
Wm Rollestone	1	
John Bagnale se.	1	
Jn Bagnale ju	2	
Rich. Killingley	1	
Joh. Lacye	1	
Tho. Adames	1	
	47	

(3)

Rob. Rolston senior	1	
Rob. Rolston junior	2	
Rich. Mear	1	
Tho. Sherwin	1	
Math. whittingham	1	
Tho. Walker	1	
Ed. Shilton	1	
Joh. Muggison	1	
Joh. Martin	1	
Certified for are these 5		
John Jorden	1	C
Ellenor Roberts	1	C
Fra. Lant	1	C
Ger. Right	1	C
Fra. ?Egleston	1	C

Vewed p(er)nos John Bancroft

& Rich. Riley Collectors

Tho. Adames Constable

Aston sup(er) Trent

f Mr Holden Lm	9	
Mr Clarke ?Rect(or)	6	
f Mr Cooper	3	
Tho. Cooper junior	1	
Tho. Clemenson	1	
Rich. Prime	1	
Ger. Killingley	1	
Wid. Buckley	1	
Mrs Davenport	1	
Rob. Watson	1	
Tho. Williamson	1	
Ch. Right	1	
Jn Pryor	2	
Tho. Cooper	1	C
C Rich. Lacy	1	
C ?Jane ?Milward wid.	1	
	47	

(4)

C Ed. Siddon	1	C
C Tho. Follose	1	C
Wm Brownhill	1	
John Clemenson	2	
Wm Laund	3	
Jos. Morley	2	
Char. Rolston	1	
Tho. Newett (?Hewett)	1	
Wid. Gouge	1	
Wm Moor	4	
not finisht 3		
Tho. Bonsall	2	
Geo. Follose	2	
Chr. Fairbrother	1	
Ger. Bancroft	2	
Wm Cowlishaw	1	

C Rob Clifford	1 C
Rich Clemenson	2
Rich. Sheepey	1
C Tho. Cockaine	1 C

vewed p(er)nos John Bancroft
& Rich. Riley Collectors
& Mr ?Cowper High Constabe
These 7 marked with C are
Certified for as poor people

Barrow sup(er) Trent

f Mr Sales	8
f P Mr Beaumant	8
Wid. Pickering	1
James Smedley	1
Tho. Carver	1
Wm Sarson	1
Mich. Smedley	1
Jn Gibson	1
Wid. Ragge	2
Tho. Gilbert	3
Kath. Gilbert	1
wm Steenson	2
Wid. Howett	1
Ger. Bancroft	2
	63

(5)

Wid Lacy	1
Jn Bonsall	2
Jn Alt	1
Wm wilkinson senior	1
Mr Farmer	3
Rob. Henton	2
Roger Harrison	1
Wm wilkinson junior	1
Mich. Smedley junior	2
Tho. Maukin	1

Barth. Lowe	1
Ed. wilkinson	1
Rich. Shaw	1
Wm Starbucke	1
Jona. Jackson	1
Tho. Sharpe	3
Chr. Fearbarnes	1
Jn Steenson	1
Fra. Middleton	1
Jn Clarke	1
Ra. Francis	1
Wid. Bancroft	1

Vewed p(er)nos John Bancroft
& Rich. Riley Collectors
will. wilkinson Constable

Breason

Mr John Samson	7
Wm Walker	2
Rich. Titterton	1
Kath. Eddinge	1
Wm Barton	1
Ch. Jerrome	2
Wm walker	1
	44

(6)

Wm Kinesley	1
Rob. Carter	3
Ed. Bretnall	1
Ed. Gregorie	1
Rob. Dudley	1
Rich. Averye	1
Jn Charleton	4
Wm Adames	2
Ed. Geowett	2
Eliz. Russell	1
Wm Walker	1

Jona. Edinge	1
Wid. Cheavin	1
Wid. Speed	2
Wm Gregorie	1
Wm Cowley	1
John Allin	1

vewed p(er)nos John Bancroft
& Rich. Riley Collectors
wm Kinesley Consta(ble)

<u>Chest(er) Eaton & Quorndon</u>

f Mr Bate	6
Mr Davis	6
f Mr Lister	5
Mr Hope	11
f Tho. Butler	1
Wm Sheepey	1
Jn Sales	1
Wid. Whilton	1
f Pat. Hawley	1
('Mr Parker' added in smaller script after 'Hawley')	
John Pickering	4
Rich. Robinson	1
f Wm Hodeskinson Eaton	3
Tho. Sidesbotham	1
Jn Right	1
Rich. Ratchdale	3
	71

(7)

Jn whitaker	1
Anto. Litchfeild	2
Tho. Heywood	3
Wm Harrison	3
Eliz. williomet	2
Tho. Stanley	2
Hen. Litchfeild	4
Mrs Henshaw	5
Fra. williomet	3
Wid. Morley	1
Wm Tomlinson	1
Wm Edge	1
Fra. Gorse senior	1
Fra. Gorse junior	1
Rob. Curtis	2
f Adria. Munday Esq.	7
Tho. Peirceon se	1
Tho. Peirceone ju	1
Luke vallance	1
Wid. Tabberer	1
Wm Tabberer	2
Geo. Coates	1
Wid. Right	1
Mr walker	5
Wm Fauke	1

vewed p(er)nos J. Bancroft
& Rich. Riley Collectors
wm Tabberer Constable

<u>Clifton & Comton</u>

Geo. Doxey	1
Hum. Orme	1
Hum. Titterton	1
Geo. Frogatt	1
Tho. North	1
Godf. Barton	1
wm Gretrix	2
	6(1)

(8)

Fra. Tarre	1
Rob. Barker	2
Geo. ?Bowne (?Bourne)	1
Jn Bate	1
Wid. North	2

Lingretts farme	2
Wid. Jankinson	2
Rich. Titterton	2
Fra. Tailer	1
Wid. Jankinson	1
Law. Kirkeland	1
Nico. Orme	1
Tho. Old	4
f Mr Hawkesworth	7
Wm walker	2
Nath. Loton	1
Wm Finney	1
Jn Jankinson	3
Fra. Toplis	2
Wid. Toplis	1
Hen. Booth	1
Wid. Booth	1
Fra. Blâke	2
Wm Slator	1
Certified for Rob. Myars	1 C

Vewed p(er)nos J. Bancroft
& R. Riley Collectors
Geo. Doxey Constable

Codnor Castle & Parkes

Tho. Burton esq. ½ ye(ar) 2. the next ha(lf) yea(r) 12. *one halfe of both is*	8
Tho. wild	6
Jn Boltbey	2
Pet. Rollinston	1
	60

vewed p(er)nos J. Bancroft
and R. Riley Collectors
Tho. wild Constable

(9)

Codnor & Loscoe

f Mrs Lowe	3
('Tomlinsons' is entered in a smaller hand after 'Lowe')	
f Jn woolley	1
Ed. Roberts	2
Rich. Manesfeild	1
Tho. wild	1
Jn Sterland	2
Jn Peach	1
f Tho. wilson	6
Tho. Hewett	1
f Mr Clarke	4
Jn Gillott	1
f Rob. ?Scaterfeild	3
Hen. Reynold	1
Jn Rivell	1
f Ch. Dakin	1
Rich. Stafford	1
Tho. walker	2
Jn Brown	1
Hen. Brown	4
Tho. Booley	1
wm Aldred	2
Mich. Day	3
Jn Kirkeland	3
Jn Silcocke	1
f Rob. wild	7
f Ben. Clayton	3
f Rich. Clayton	2
Tho. ?Spebey	1
Jn Clarke	1
Tho. walker	1
Phill. wild	1
Wid. Stubbinge	1
Ra. Radford	4
Jn Searson	2
Tho. wright	1

	7(1)

(10)

f Jn Piggen	1
Wid. Burgaine	1
Ed. Boman	1
f Fra. Tantum	3
Jnath. Tantum	1
Jn Tantu(m)	1
f Wid. Bunting	1
Mr Iron	7
f Chr. Hodges	2
f mr John Dreacoate	3
Arth. Terrell	2

vewed p(er)nos John Bancroft
and Rich. Riley Collectors

Chrich and fritchley

Tho. Smith senior	1
Tho. Smith junior	1
Wm Kirkeham	1
Anto. Johnson	1
Rich. Cellers	1
John Marshall	1
f Anto. wood George wood & Sam wood	6
Ed. Fisher	2
Joh. Flint	1
Fra. Flint	1
Jn Burton	1
Geo. Barnes	1
Jacob Bomer	1
wm Burgaine	1
wm Cumberbatch	1
Thir. Fritchley	1
wm ?Lamme	1
Rich. Radford	1
Sa. vardin	2
Rich. Johnson	1
	50

(11)

Anto. Higgott	1
Tho. Madder	1
Gil. Berisford	1
Wm Smith	1
Wm wood	1
Jn Spencer	1
Geo. Hayworth sen	1
Rog. woodhouse	1
Tho. Marshall	1
Hen. Sowter	1
Tho. Lowe	3
Jn Beard	4
Anto. Reynes	1
Jn Wetton	2
Mrs Roobey	4
Jn Oates	1
Sam. Brown	1
Wid. Elliott	2
Jn Cowlishaw	1
Wm Flint	1
Jn Reynes	1
Hen. Meacocke	1
Jn wild	1
Jn wood	2
Jos. Berisford	1
wm Cocker	1
Anto. Harrison	1
Ed. woolland	1
Tho. Barker	1
Rob. Langeley	1
Wid. Storer	1
Jn Hill	1
Jn Hassallam sen.	2
Wid. Lowe	1
Tho. Ammott	1

Hen. Band	1
	48

(12)

Fra. Freepound	1
Wm Allin	1
Rob. wilcockson	1
Joh. Bigton	1
Jn Sowter	1
Jn vallance	1
Rich. Cheatha(m)	1
Tho. Barnes	1
f Mr Wright fritchley	6
Abr. Holmes	1
Alice Mason	1
Geo. Am(m)ot	1
Hen. wilcockson	1
Rob. Sowter	1
Tho. Smith ju.	2
Jn Burgaine	1
Jn Howorth	1
Wm Swift	1
Hen. Bonsall	1
Th. Elliott	1
Jn Smith	1
Fer. wild	2
James Sharpe	2
Ed. Lowe	1
Wm Buxton	4
Mr Golding	2
Godf. Amott	3
Hen. Bonsall	1
Jos. Horobin	1
	43

vewed p(er)nos J. Bancroft
and Rich. Riley Collectors
John Spencer Constable

Dale Abbey

(13)

f P Mr Powtherill	9
f Mr Wandale of ?Sowters grange	9
Wid. wood	2
Jn Bigges	3
Jn Arnold	2
Tho. Roome	1
Jn Right Baker	2
Jn Right	2
Tho. ?wheatelin	1
Jn Foldiam	2
Ed. Stevenes	2
Jn Hancocke	3
Math. Hancocke	3
Geo. Rigley	1
Mich. white	1
Hen. Frith	1
Geo. Clarke	1
Rich. Prattey	1
Geo. Glover	1
Wid. Hodges	1
Jn Hunt	1
Wid. Baker	1
Rich. Boothouse	1
Ed. Vallence	1
Wid. Garton	1
Ra. Tailer	1
Wm Cooke	1
Anto. wagstaffe	1
Ed. Boswell	1
Rob. Boswell	1
Ed. ?Rolston	1
Jn Boden	1
Rich. Grundey	1
wm Smith	2
Jn Brigges	1
	64

(<u>14</u>)

Vewed p(er)nos Joh. Bancroft
and Rich. Riley Collectors
Ed. Stevenes Constable

<u>Darley</u>

Mr Wm Munday	7
Wm Sharwin	1

<u>Denbey</u>

f Mr williomett	13
f Mr Hen. Smith	4
f Mr Math. Smith ½ year 7	
f Mr Hen. Lowe of Parkehall	4
Tho. Elliott	1
Mr wm Gladwin	2
Grace Bate	1
Tho. Outram	1
John Bealey	1
James Gregory	1
Wm Ryley	2
Ste. Bullocke	1
Jn Greene	1
Rob. Butteredge	1
Math. walker	1
Jone Elye	1
Tho. Horesley	1
wm Stafford	1
Rob. Harvye	1
Jn Ratcliffe	1
Pat. Fletcher	1
Jn Else	1
Geo. Gillott	1
Jn Parkiston	1
Hen. Orme	2
	53

(<u>15</u>)

Wm Hawley	1
James Harrison	1
Wid. Riley	1
Wid. wilson	1
Wm Wilson	3
Wid. wesson	1
Ed. Middleton	2
Wid. Rolston	1
Fra. Horesley	1
Jn Holden	1
Jn Riley	2

vewed p(er)nos John Bancroft
and Rich. Riley Collectors
John Bealey Constable

<u>Derbey</u>

<u>Allsaints parish</u>

Mr Ph. Gerye	7
Tho. Steenson	2
Wm Bunting	2
Jn Sharpe	3
Ra. Soer	4
Mr Tho. Greaves	5
Wid. Tagge	2
Wm Newcome	4
Mrs Whitti(n)gham	6
Fra. Hopkines	2
Jn Marson	2
Ed. Daffe	3
Hen. Moor	14
Mr Green	4
Tho. Basse	4
Wm Smith	3
Wm Eaton	3
Mr Motteram	5
Tho. Chaplaine	3
John Lane	2
	95

(16)	
Tho. Yates	1
Wm Fletcher	5
John Howe	2
John Hill	3
John Francis ju.	4
Mr Jn Francis	4
Jn Calton	2
Doct. Dakin	10
Mrs Allestrey	6
Mr Allestrey for a void house	5
Mr Piggen	2
Mr Tho. Alsop	2
Mr Staniford	3
Mr Levis	3
Mrs Swetnam	2
Rich. Bakewell	6
Mr Chambers	8
Mr Bruckhouse	10
Wm Starbucke	4
Wid. Collier	1
Mr Ed. walker	8
Tho. Hayes	2
Wm Heywood	2
Wm Clay	1
Wm Rolston	2
Jn Heyward	3
Mr Jn walker	4
Mr Lort	4
Mr Jackson	2
Ed. Storer	8
Tho. williomet	3
for a void house	5
Wm Cattle	7
Ser John Smith	7
Mr Robert Bennet	4
Mr Geo. Smith	5
	150

(17)	
Mr Thomas Gery ?*Steward*	3
Mr Harryman	14
Mr Jn walker	4
Mr Tho. Watson	8
Mr Hen. worden	8
Mr Wm Allestrey	13
Mrs Rivett	2
Rich. Greaves	1
Wm Dilkes	2
Marke Adderley	2
Jn Leoper	3
Wm Grantum for 2 ½ year 2	
Mr Sherman	2
Wm Hunter	3
Arth. Jolley 3	
Wm Jellecocke	1
Pet. Jessop	1
Tho. Calfehill	1
John Carter	3
Wm Brownhill	2
Hen. Thorpe	2
Wm Greensmith	1
Jn Wilson	3
1 Jn Jorden for ½ year	
Wid. Becke	2
Wm Draper	2
Ph. Bisse	1
Wm Adderley	4
Hen. Webster	4
Hu. Burne	6
Tho. Fletcher	6
Phill. Parre	4
Rich. Holden	1
Geo. Sowter	2
Tho. walker	4
Mr Joh. Tailer	8
Mr Hanford	4

Mrs Mary Parker	3
Eliz. Houghton	1
Jer. Huntington	1
Mr Fra. Greaves	7
John Stone	3
Mrs Allin	5
	14(7)

(18)

Tho. Stronge	1
Wm yeomans	13
Tho. Jackson	4
Geo. Bacon	8
Ben. Smedley	4
Wm Bruckhouse	4
Jos. Fox	7
Dan. Beatchcroft	3
Mr worden	8
Nath. Dootey	1
Dan. Bruckhouse	3
Mr Tho. Burne	13
Mr Hodeskinson	11
Mr Howell	4
Mr Ballidon	8
Mr Tho. Gudwin	5
Mr Heathcoate	4
Rich. Hopkinson	2
Mrs Corden	4
Mr Tho. Corden	5
John woollet	3
Mr Tho. youle	8
Mr Abell Litchford	1
Jn Bate	2
Tho. Botham	2
Ed. Daintieth	2
Luke neild	4
Jn Twigge	2
Elias Cheadle	4
Sam. Fletcher	1
Jos. walker	1
James Stables	3
John Bancroft	3
Mr Large	6
for a void house	5
Mr williamson	2
Ed. Littlehouse	1
Fra. Smedley	2
Geo. Oldershaw	1
Ed. Robinson	5
	170

(19)

Wid. Stables	1
Rich. Storer	8
Jn Bryar	4
Jos. Moor	3
Jn Moor	4
Tho. Stanfeild	4
Jn Rossell	7
Wm Ragge	2
Wid. ?Mather	2
Gab. Banton	2
Tho. Sleigh	1
Rob. Carter	5
Nath. Cockaine	1
Ed. Goodale	10
Mrs Heywood	13
Rob. Litchford	4
Rob. Fearbrother	1
Rich. Elliot	4
Rich. Knowes	1
Ser. Sleigh	3
Marke Burton	2
Mr Marshall	5
Jn Gerrott	1
Mr Blackwell	5
Mr Adderley	13
Hen. Holmes	6

Sr John Shoer	18
Mrs Surcheverill	5
Mr Sad	5
Mr ward	5
Rob. Burn	2
Mr John Dunedge	11
Jn Smedley	5
wm Frearson	3
Jn Ragge	2
Mr Turner	15
wid. Bennet	1
Ger. Kirbey	2
Wid. Cooke	2
Rich. Mellor	1
Math. Saywell	4
	192

(20)

Jeth. Thornton	7
Mrs ward	4
Jn Dawes	5
Geo. Fletcher	6
Hen. Blinkhorne	3
Mrs Moreton	4
Mr Linnacre	2
Ed. Parker	1
Mr Turner	7
Mr Bateman	10
Ed. Marshall	3
1½ Jn Sheafeild	1
Sam. Cockram	2
Hen. Milnes	1
Randle Jessop	1
Jn Barnes	4
Mr Ham(m)ersley	7
Nath. Thorpe	1
Rob. Sex	2
Mr Hopkin	6
Sam.ward	8

Vinc. Robinson	2
Ste. Staniford	4
John Orme	4
Wid. Hutchinson	3
Cor. Hawsey	5
Jn ward	2
Rich. Burton	2
Bar. Jackson	1
Rich. Hopkinson	3
Jn Marson	2
Mr Osborne	8
Mr Dakin	9
wm Moor	1
John Lane	4
Geo. Blagreave	4
late Mr Flamsteads	4
	143

(21)

Rob. Gamble	3
Tho. Morrice	3
Wid. Clarke	2
Jane Needham	1
Wid. Needham	2
Rich. Challiner	4
Jn Parker	2
Ed. Nash	1
Ed. Beardesley	1
Jn Francis	11
Wm Statham	1
Ed. Kirbey	2

st Werburgs Parish

Jn Dalton Esq.	9
Mrs Tabberer	4
Jn Allin	4
Jn Burrowes	8
Hum. Burrowes	5
Wm Fletcher	4

Sam. Horobin	2
Isaac Jackson	2
Tho. Bruckhouse	2
Rich. ward	2
Mr Allestrey	4
Jn Granger	1
Mr yates	6
Mr wandale	6
Wid. Bruckhouse	4
Rob. wagstaffe	4
Wm Horobin	1
Wm Dawson	3
Adam ?Durnilla	4
Fra. Bruckhouse	1
Solomon Roberts	10
Mr Gisborne	7
Mr Steenson	6
John Sadler	2
	13(4)

Mrs Leeveing	8
David Spenter	1
Wid. Foddering	2
Rob. Cope	1
Roger wheeldon	2
Daniell Gryce	1
Wid. Pepper	2
Jn Harrison	1
Hen. yates	1
Tho. Inkersall	1
Jn Milward	3
Wid. Soer	2
John Stafford	4
Peter yates	4
Jn williomet	3
Ed. Cundey	4
Tho. Stamford	3
Daniell Cooke	1
Ra. Richardson	6
	120

(22)

Gab. Butler	4
Mr wilson	2
Tho. Linney	2
Wm Tabberer	6
Jn Litchford	4
Mrs Morrice	6
Mr James ward	7
Wid. Horobin	2
Mrs Houghton	8
Jn Brockhouse	6
James Sexton	4
Ed. Brookes	2
Hen. Greatrix	2
Sam. Spateman	6
Mr Flamstead	4
Lidea Fowler	1
Jn Squier	2
Wm Clay	2

(23)

Wid. Jackson	2
Tho. Brewin	2
Jn Chesheire	4
Peter Dyas	3
Jn Barlowe	1
Tho. Benskin Gent.	4
Wm Wagstaffe	3
Rich. Leevechild	3
Wid. Radford	2
Wm Roome	1
Fra. Agard	2
Jn Sex	1
Josi. wheeldon	1
Tho. Brookes	3
Nico. Gaunt	3
James Jordan	3
John Norman se.	1

Fra. Hutchinson	2
David Jackson	5
Rob. Hood	6
Wid. Lambert	1
Rob. ward	2
Tho. Sleigh	2
James Bacon	3
Wid. Soer	2
And. Jones	2
Mr Tho. Sleigh	8
Rich. Allin	3
Jn wagstaffe	3
Tho. Jerrome	3
Mr Parker	6
wm Tabberer	4
Jn Right	2
Wm walker	1
Tho. Hardey	1
Ed. Barnes	1
	96

(24)

Rob. Chesheire	5
Wm Horobin	1
Wm yates	1
Chr. Garton	1
Fra. Sleigh	1

st peter

Sr Simon Degge	10
Mr Jn Spateman	7
Mrs Mellor	6
Jn Stephenes	1
Wid. Bloodworth	2
Jos. Heanes	2
Law. Turner	1
Jn Moseley	2
Wm Husband	1
Hen. Mellor Esq.	18
Wid. Mee	4
Jn Meynell	4
Rob. Smith	2
Mrs warren	3
Tho. Smith	2
Anne whitingham	1
Wm Tabberer junior	1
Rich. wright	3
Rich. Hopkin	3
Rob. Nash	3
Wid. Heywood	2
Wid. Meynell	1
Wid. Noton	4
pd 3 Rich. Peale	2
Wm Groves	1
Wid. Pim	3
James Oakes junior	2
Gilb. Oakes	1
Rich. Browne	3
Mrs Alestrey	1
Jn Greatrix	5
wm Dawson	3
wid. Twigges	3
	116

(25)

Mr Cope	4
Wid. Storer	2
Tho. Charge	2
Ed. underwood	2
Tho. Baxter	1
Rich. Houghton	1
Jos. watson	1
Wid. Fisher	1
Jn Right	1
Moses Bullocke	1
Tho. Parker	4
Mr Rog. Newton	11
Wid. welesbey	4

Mr Carter	4
Jn Morley	1
Jn Parker	4
James Knight	1
Jn Simson	1
Wid. Clarke	3
Rob. Gregge	1
Tho. Twigge	1
Wm Smallwood	1
Wid. Carver	2
Wid. Twigge	2
Jn Beighton ju.	4
Luke Oldham	2
Will. Dilkes	2
Mr Adria. Munday	1
Elias Grice	2
Geo. Browne	1
Arth. Jolley	2
Tho. ward	3
Rich. Dawson	4
Wid. Jerrome	3
Joh. Headley	5
Mr Butler	2
	87

(26)

Rob. Jerrome	4
Wid. Dawson	2
Mr Willobey	7
Rich. Eaton	4
Tho. Beebey	2
Mr wright	9
Mr Barton	8
Tho. winter	2
Wid. Browne	4
Mrs Brookes	6
Wid. Carver ju.	2
Hen. whittingha(m)	3
Mr vessey	5
Mr Isa. Plats	6
pd ½ y(ear) Rich. Leach	4
Tho. Gretton	2
wid. Buxton	2
Jos. Gryse	3
James Oakes se	4
Wid. Stables	1
Mr Williamson	6
Wid. Hall	5
Jn Tailer	4
Wm Ragge	1

<u>st michaels Parish</u>

Rob. Rushforth	3
Rich. Bludworth	7
Sam. Massey	8
Geo. Buxton	4
Tho. Oldham	2
Mr Roger Farmer	2
Jn Heywood	2
Ema. Bucknall	4
Mr Leper	9
Rich. Boothouse	3
Mr Machin	3
Mrs Newton	3
Ed. Tawman	4
Tho. Lockoe	1
Jn Burne	4
	155

(27)

Rob. welles	1
Tho. Harrison se.	2
Tho. widdoson	4
Mr Dunedge	4
Mrs Harriman	4
Mr Parker	11
Hen. Vicars	3
Wid. Fletcher	3

Wid. Green	3
Wm Bankes	1
Fra. Norman	1
Tho. Hood	2
Tho. woodcocke	3
Ed. Marshall	3
Tho. Needham	2
Jona. Massey	2
John Nailer	1
Wm Muchill	2
Jn Cundey	3
Fra. needham	2
Tho. Bird	1
Mr walker	5
Ada. Broughton	1
Tho. ward	3
Tho. Cooke	2
Wid. Statham	1
Tho. Jackson	2

st Alkmuds

Mr Sa. Gudwin	8
Jn Litchfeild	2
Mr Frost	2
Sam. Chase	2
Jn Ratcliffe	1
Rich. Tobey	2
Jos. Page	3
wm Page	3
Hum. Botham	3
Wm Barlowe	1
Hen. Pauferryman	1
Mrs Burne	6
Wm Roberts	5
Jn Lancaster	4
Tho. Hutton	3
	118

(28)

Rich. Hawley	1
Tho. Sales	6
Tho. Smith	2
Ra. Thorpe	2
Mr Horsington	9
Rog. Farrin	2
wm Spencer	2
Mr Bolewell	8
Rob. Fletcher	3
Rob. Altrickes	1
Jn Coye	2
Jn welch	2
Mrs Brandrith	5
Mr Brightman	10
Wid. Sadler	1
Rich. Chesheire	8
Mr vessey	5
Rich. Newton	1
Rich. Cheadle	2
Ed. Tabberer	2
Tho. webster	1
Gilb. Smith	1
Sam. Monesfeild	2
Jn Reeve	6
Mrs Gudwin	1
Mr Chambers	1
Mr Jn Mundayes Mill	1
Mr Ben. Parker	5
Jn Jessop	2
Wm Nash	2
Ed. ?wast	3
Con. Hough	2
wm Gillott	3
Anne Bludworth	3
Tho. Newton	2
Tho. Smith	1
Mr Hodeskinson	5
Mr Radford	3
Mr Cooke	3

	121

(29)

Geo. ward	3
wm Atkin	2
Tho. Smedley	1
Mary Derbey	2
Tho. wast	2
Mr Horsington	5
Jane Burne	1
Fra. ?Booke	1
Ed. Page	1
Hen. Knowles	2
Jos. Nelstrope	1

All these are Certified for within the Burrow of Derbey:

Wid. Heacocke	1
Wid. Crabtree	2
Rob. Hunt	1
Dani. Bate	1
Wm Snape	1
Rob. Gretton	1
Tho. Frith	1
Nico. Gretton	1
Phill. Stokes	1
Tho. Gibbenes	1
Jn Reynolds	1
Tho. Charge senior	1
Wid. ward	1
Anne Foane	1
Tho. ward senior	2
Rich. Loue (?Love)	1
Jane newcome	1
Rich. Tabberer	1
Jn Jackson	1
Geo. Brown	1
Tho. Gaskin	1
Clare Bruckhouse	1
Tho. Clarke	1
Jn Mayfeild	1
Wid. Grice senior	1
Rich. Ludlome	1
Eli. Pedley	1
Wid. Fletcher	1
Mar. waine	1
Rob. Smith	1
	(53)

(30)

Wid. Twigges senior	2
Tabitha waine	1
wid. Bayley	1
Isabell Tabberer	1
Wid. simson senior	1
Fra. simson	1
Rich. Moseley	1
Wid. Pureslove	1
Wid. whitingham se	1
Wid. Alsopp	1
Wid Okedale	1
wm yates	1
Wid. Dixon	1
Ann Simson alias Ainesworth	1
Jn Patricke	1
Rich. Sleigh	1
Kath. Edinge ali(as) Simson	1
Eli. Tabberer	1
Joh. Gunthorpe	1
Jane Hallome	1
Wid. Browne	1
Tho. Fowler	1
Dor. Simson alias Poker	1
Wid. wilson	1
Wid. Hackwood	1
Tho. Alt	1
Ellen Fletcher	1

wm Tarrott	1
Julian Finch	1
wm Brownhill	2
wm Barker al(ias) Smith	2
Luke Frearson	1
Fra. Rushin	1
Anne Halsey	1
Grace Stothard	1
Tho. Smith	1
Mary Beardmore	1
Jone Alcocke	1
Sam. Smedley	1
John Houghton	2
	44

(31)

Nico. Ride	1
Mathew Hougton	1
wm Cowlishaw	1
Tho. Kirke	1
Jn Moreton	1
Hamlet Linnet	2
Geo. Allin	1
John Harrison	2
Hu. Thorpe	2
Susanna walker	2
Rob. Butler	2
Tho. Rossell	1
Wm Lancaster	1
wm James	1
Jos. Rossell	2
Geo. Bracebey	2
Joh. Tongue	1
Griffin Birch se	1
Rob. Sharwin	1
Rich. Newton	1
Jn Bentley	2
Tho. Burton	2
Wm Garner	3
Ed. Comins or J. Hea...s	2
Thur. Harrowes	1
wm Cannor	1
Hum. Eaton	2
Tho. Trowell	2
	59

vewed p(er)nos John Bancroft & Rich. Riley with the assistance of severall officers to that place belonging

Dreacoate

Mr Judkin	5
Rog. Satham	1
wm woollard	1
Wilne Hall	5
Mary Jacques	2
wm Peate	3

(32)

Tho. Tongue	1
Tho. James	2
Ger. whitehead	2
Tho. Rossell	1
Tho. Cooke	2
John Rossell	1
Griffin Birch	1
Certyfied for wm Browne	1 C

vewed p(er)nos John Bancroft & Rich. Riley Collectors
wm Wothard Constable

Egginton

Sr Hen. Everye	20
Mr yates	2
Mr Buxton	6
Mr walton	4

Wid. Salte	2
Hen. Duffeild	1
Rob. Mason	1
Tho. Eaton	2
Wm Cantrell	2
Ger. Berrey	2
Tho. Newton	1
Wid. Kilborne	2
Geo. Francis	1
Simon Cantrell	1
Rob. Gilliver	3
Tho. Edwards	1
Anne Brigges	1
Tho. Eaton	1
Tho. Knight	1
Ra. Eaton	2
John Davenport	1
Tho. Mason	1
Tho. wilson	1
Fra. Harrison	1
	71

(33)

Jn Byard	2
Ra. Righteon	1
John Ashton	1
Wid. Allin	2
Mr Clarkson	1
Simon walbarke	1
wid. Earle	1
will Brigges	1

vewed p(er)nos John Bancroft &
Rich. Ryley Collectors
Ra. Eaton Constable

Elveston

Mr Stanope	18
Mr Francis	2
Wm Holland	1
Tho. Pollard	1
wm Lacye	1
James Osborne	3
John Bacon	2
Hen. Davye	2
wm Langford	1
Wid. Reines	2
Wm Pigeon	1
Wm Smedley	1
Wid. Lancasheire	1
Luke Hutchinson	2
Jn Lancasheire	1
Francis halkines	1
Wm Cope	2
Chr. Bentley	1
Ed. Tongue	1
Timo. Richardson	1
James Smedley	1
John Bate	1
Rich. Spencer	1
Jn Chambers	1
Elias Pigeon	1
Mr ward	5
Richardsons house	1
wm Gamble	1
Jn Coxon	1
	6(8)

(34)

Rich. Brearley	1
Wid. Madder	1
Ed. Towle	1
Ed. Coxon	1
Jn Trowell	1
Tho. Bate	1
Geo. Souter	2
Peter Coxon	1
wm Madder	1

Vewed p(er)nos John Bancroft &
Rich. Ryley Collectors
Mr ward Constable

Findorne

Mr ?Pootey	6
Math. Roome	2
Jn Porter	2
Step. Hopkin	1
Wm wildor	2
Anne Fleming	1
Rob. watson	1
wm Goodwin	1
Jn Roome	3
Tho. Ashmore	1
wm Holden	1
Fra. Calladine	1
Fran. Pegge	1
Jn Cooke junior	3
Ra. ward	1
Jn Hawkesley	1
Jn Ireland	1
Jn Cooke senior	2
Tho. Madder	2
Rob. wilson	3
Math. wilson	1
John wilson	4
Tho. wate	2
Jn Litchfeild	1
	54

(35)

Wid. Hopkin	1
Rich. Gretton	2

vewed p(er)nos John Bancroft &
Rich. Riley Collectors
Tho. Hopkin Constable

Heynor

Mr Gooddier	8
Mr Winter	5
Mrs Shepheard	8
Jn Hawkes	2
Rob. Smith	1
Rich. Barwell	1
John Tomlinson	2
John Aldred	2
Ra. Braddocke	1
James Hanmore	1
Nico. Green	2
wm Aldred	1
wm Potter	1
John Osborne	1
Mr Roper	1
wm Pidgeon	3
wm walker	1
Hen. Palmer	1
Wid. Osborne	1
Wm Pilkinton	1
Geo. Shipeston	1
wm Millington	1
Jn Walker	1
Jn Moor	1
Rob. Cheatam	1
The Minister	3
Jos. Ratcliff	1
wm watkinson	1
John Cowlishaw	3
Roger Cheatam	1
John Dale	2
John wilson	5
Ed. Ellott	3
Ed. Eaton	3
Fra. Tantum	3
	77

(36)

Sam. Smeiton	2
Rob. Saunderson	2
Wid. Hodges	1
Tho. Holland	1
Roger Stafford	1
Ch. Oldknowes	1
wm Hunter	2
Rich. Coates	1
Solo. Aldred	1
Nico. Oldknowes	1
Wid. Tailer	1
Ed. Clay	1
Fra. walker	2
These are Certified for:	
Tho. Bestwicke	1
Rog. Stafford	1
Wid. Coxon	1
Dainell Betteridge	1

Vewed p(er)nos John Bancroft &
Rich. Riley Collectors
John Tomlinson Constable

Hopwell

Mr Keyes	5
wid. Peate	2

Horesley

Tho. wilson	2
John Hough	1
John Roberts	1
John wheeldon	1
John Rogers	2
Rob. Alsebrooke	1
wm Agard	1
wid. wheeldon	1
Ed. Seale	1
wm Hulland	1
Jn Bingham	1
Tho. Kirkland	2
	43

(37)

Tho. Kirbey	1
Jn Grace	1
wm Harrison	1
Tho. Radforth	1
Rob. Lacye	2
Chr. Middleton	1
Tho. Starbucke	1
Tho. Armet	1
Wm Hodges	3
Geo. Hatton	1
Rob. Seale	1
Jone Armet	1
Mr Bealey	2
Hen. Hatton	1
Tho. Hunter	1
Rob. Burton	2
Tho. Radford	3
Tho. Tailer	1
wm Somers	1
Rich. wathey	1
Patr. Dickens	4
wm Holmes	1
Rich. Garton	2
Mr Grace	4
Rob. Fletcher	2
And. Jakes	1
wm wood	1
Jn Searson	3
Tho. Rolleston	1
Rob. Radford	1
John Launder	2
Patr. Johnson	1
Tho. Harrison	1
Hen. Harrison	1

Joh. Harrison	1
wm Toplis	1
Jn Toplis	1
Arth. Johnson	1
Geo. Moor	3
John Radforth	2
	61

(38)

Jn Houghton	2
Rich. Ball	1
Tho. Biddle	1
Wid. Radford	1
Char Herper	3
will. wheeldon	1
Thurston Radford	3
wid. Fauke	1
Rich. woodhouse	1
Ellenor Stanley	1
Mr Rob. Parker	2
Wm Saxon	1
Jn wilson	3
Hen. Kerrey	1
Rich. Otwell	1
Hen. Houghton	1
wid. Seale	2
Fra. Sison	1

vewed p(er)nos John Bancroft and
Rich. Riley Collectors
Tho. Kirkeland Constable

Ilkestone

Mrs Gregge	8
Mr Joh. Flamstead	6
Tho. Carrior	3
Tho. wheatley	2
John woollet	2
Geo. Burgaine	1
James wattes	1
Fra. Chadburne	2
Tho. Silles	1
Tho. Gladwin Esq.	2
Tho. Boothouse	1
Hen. Tailer	1
Rich. Harthstone	1
Geo. Goodread	1
Joh. Scooley	1
	60

(39)

Gowen Birch	1
Rob. Burgaine	1
Jn Bretnall	1
Jn Trowman	2
Fra. Roberts	1
Mich. Skeventon	1
Tho. Lowe	3
Fra. Burgaine	2
Jn Gregorie	1
Rich. Hunt	1
Fra. Hunt	1
Timo. Rawson	3
Wm Allestrey	1
Geo. Cocker	3
Fra. Bullocke	2
Jn Shepheard	1
Walter Johnson	1
Jn Blunston	2
Chr. Buxton	1
Geo. Robuicke	1
Hen. Toobey	1
Grego. wheatley	1
Jn Leadbetter	1
Jn Buxton	1
Fra. ?Genne	1
Jn Cowper	2
wm Marshall	1

Mr Dunedge	2
Wid. Smalley	2
Geo. ?waldin	1
wid. Cowlishaw	1
Sam. Roe	2
wid. Leadbeter	1
Jn Marshall	1
wm Leadleater	1
Rich. waine	1
Sam. Gregorie	1
Rich. Day	1
Jn Day	3
Jn Gregorye	1
Jn Cooke	3
	59

(40)

Tho. Birch	2
Fra. Cooke	1
Jn Chapman	1
Jn Straw	1
Ed. Straw	1
Tho. Roe	1
Rich. Ophilus	1
Fra. Kirbey	1
Wid. Tarrat	3
Rich. Tutin	1
Jn Beardesley	2

Vewed p(er)nos John Bancroft and
Rich. Riley Collectors
John woollet Constable

Kirke Hallome

Wm Blunstone se	2
Wm Blunstone ju	3
Ed. Beardesley	3
Jn Faulkner	1
wm Lockoe	1
Geo. Foldiam	3
wid. wood	1
Tho. Titterton	1
Jn Newton	1
Mich. Boswell	1

vewed p(er)nos John Bancroft and
Rich. Riley Collectors

Kirke Langley

The Hall	8
Mr Tho. Meynell	5
Tho. Redgate	3
Mr Fryer	2
Nico. Kenton	2
Ch. Dethicke	1
Fra. Jerrome	3
Jer. Hickling	2
	58

(41)

Tho. Parker se.	1
Anne Pinkin	1
Tho. Grace	2
Wid. Grace	1
Tho. Parker ju.	1
Rose Parker	1
John Smith	1
Jn Malton	1
Rich. Hickling	1
Rob. Hall	1
Wm Bowler	1
Wm Calver	2
Hen. Tailer	1
Jn Fisher	1
Tho. Som(m)ers	1
Petr Hough	1
Jn Redgate	2
Wm Clarke	1

Rich. Tailer	1
Wm Oldham	1
Rob. Dakin	1
wid. Jolley	2
wm Gravener	1
Barth. Fretwell	1
Tho. Dolphin	2
wid. Bomfort	1
these are Certified for	
Ed. Twigge	1
Geo. Dawbey	1
Ed. Foane	1
Tho. Beard	1
Doro. Carter	1

Vewed p(er)nos John Bancroft and
Rich. Riley Collectors
Jn Smith Constable

Litchurch

wid. Smith	1
wm Shepheard	1
wid. Fearne	1
	(39)

(42)

Littleover

Rich. Harper Esq.	10
Tho. Taffey	1
Tho. Peach	1
Geo. Carelis	1
Wid. Holden	1
Wm Hall	1
Rob. Sheapherd	1
Wm Conaway	1
Ste. Shepheard	3
Geo. Porter	3
Hu. Hall	2
Wid. Bennett	1
Wm Porter	1
Tho. Hill	1
Mr Huntingford	3
Hum. Viccars	4
Rich. Tatum	3
Jn Narbury	1
Tho. Burrowes	1
Rob. Botham	1
Geo. Barker	1
Geo. Champion	1
Ed. Holden	1
Jn watson	1
Wm Hodeskinson	1
Wid. Feasant	1
Wm Trimer	1
Law. whitingham	1
Jn Lane	1
	50

Vewed p(er)nos John Bancroft
Collectors & Rich. Riley
Wid. Holden Constable

Long Eaton

(43)

Ed. Burton	1
Wm Howett	4
Rich. Rossell	2
Jn Barker	1
Jn Dodson	3
Jn James	2
Wid. williams	1
Wm Crofts	1
Jn Neild	1
Tho. Ball	1
James Crofts	4
Jn Trowell	1
Rob. walker	3
Hen. James	3

Rob. Goodale	2
Wm Heywood	1
Ed. Burton	1
Ed. Trowell	2
Ed. Barrott	2
Tho. Hollingworth	3
Geo. Bonsall	3
Mich. Smalley	2
Joh. Barrott	4
Rich. Golding	1
Ed. Lacye	1
Wm Trowell	4
Jn Bingham	1
Tho. Mee	1
Hum. Twelles	2
Wm Garton	2
Tho. Abbott	1
Wid. Higgenbotham	1
Wm Clarke	1
Jn Jaques	5
Chr. Talbott	1
Wm Davis	2
Fra. Burton	1
Rob. wilson	2
	74

(44)

Wid. Carter	2
Ed. Blood	1
Jn Trowell	1
Rich. Tabolt	1
Jn wilson	2

vewed p(er)nos John Bancroft and
Rich. Riley Collectors
Mich. Smalley Constable

Mackworth

Mr Ogden	5

Wm weston	2
Geo. Lasseles	1
Wm wesson	3
Tho. Scot	1
Jn Shepheard	1
Randle Ambrose	1
Rich. Palferryma(n)	1
Fra. Dawes	1
Ed. Spencer	1
Rich. Robinson	1
God. Bruckhouse	1
wm Ashmore	1
Jane Draper	1
Gregorie Seale	3
Mr Munday for Pim(m)es	1
Jn Turner	3
Hen. Spencer	1
Jn Bennet	2
Fra. Dawson	1
Anto. Allin	1
wm Loe	1
Tho. Moseley	1
wm Stone	1
Rol. momford	1
	44

(45)

wid. Kirkeland	1
wm Toplis	1
wm Lort	1

vewed p(er)nos John Bancroft and
Rich. Riley Collectors
Will. Ashmore Constable

Marke Eaton

John Munday Esq.	11
wm Peter	1
John Cox	2

Rich. Pauferrima(n)	1
Jn Agard	2
wid. Redgate	2
Tho. Bratbey	1
Alex. Bennett	1
Ed. Hewett	1
Jn Beàley	1
Grego. Seale	2
Jn Bembrigge	2
Jn Tatum	1
wm Spicer	2
Rob. Rolston	1
All these are Certified for	
Wm Knowes	1
wid. Rudgate	1
wm Pickering	1
Ed. Bruckhouse	1
Rob. moor	1
John Meachin	1
Rich. Beare	1
Tho. Bakewell	1
Jn Browne ju	1
Jn Browne se	1
Phill. Munday	1
	45

vewed p(er)nos John Bancroft &
Rich. Riley Collectors
John Bembrigge Constable

Rich. Burton	2
Rich. Earle	3
Hu. Ingram Esq.	2
John Spencer	1
Tho. wade	2
Jn Simnet	3
Jn Moor	2
Jn Gadesbey	1
Anne Stiffe	1
Chr. Crosbey (?Crosley)	1
Paul Hardey	2
Tho. Roome	1
Rob. Ollerenshaw	1
Fra. Bratt	1
Ran. Tatum	1
Will. Bruckhouse	1
Tho. Middleton	1
Nico. Hardey	1
Tho. Adames	1
wm Heywood	1
Mr Cotchett	7
Rob. walker	1
Her. Hardey	1
walt. Gell	1
Eliz. Bancroft	1
Tho. Shirley	1
Tho. Bramley	1
	79

(46)

Mickleover

Mr Jn Hill	9
Rich. Squier	5
Mr Rob. newton	5
Mr Farneworth	4
Geo. wade	3
John Earle	4
Jn Gregorie	2
Jn Butler	4

(47)

Rob. Shirley	1
Jn Campion	1
Jn Hardey	2
Ed. Coxon	1
Jn Spencer	1
wid. Pratt	1
wid. Roome	1
Tho. Pegge	1
wm Bokes	1

Rich. Fitton	1
Rob. Bancroft	1
Hen. Hanson ju.	1
Hen. Hanson se.	1
Tho. Jackson	1
Ed. Bate	1
Tho. Pidewell	1
wm Turner	1
Nico. Crosley	1
Tho. ward	1
wm Hunt	1

Vewed p(er)nos John Bancroft &
Rich. Riley Collectors
John Earle Constable

Morley

wm Surcheverill Esq.	16
Mr John Harper	5
Rich. James	1
John Smedley	1
John Burrowes	3
Ed. Martin	1
Giles Shaw	1
wid. James	1
John Martin	1
Joh. Chrichloe	1
wid. webster	1
Tho. Hibbertt	1
John Stonesbey	1
Tho. Riley	1
	56

(48)

Rich. Brigges	1
Jn walker	1
Rob. Saxon	1
Wid. Shottoe	1
Tho. Siddale	1

Nico. Brentnall	1
Rich. Sharpe	2
Rich. Richardson	1
John Hill	1
John Bird	1
Rich. Goodwin	1
wm Towndraw	1
Geo. Brentnall	1
John Maples	1

vewed p(er)nos John Bancroft and
Rich. Riley Collectors

Ockbrooke

Rob. Piggen	2
Rich. Piggen	3
Rob. Cheavine	1
wid. Bennett	1
Andrew Peate	1
Rob. Holland	2
Chr. Spateman	1
Hen. Smith	2
Tho. Holland	1
John Soar	3
Tho. Cooke	2
Rich. James	1
Tho. Saunderson	2
Tho. Potter	1
Tho. Coope	1
Nico. Stephens	1
wm windley	2
Jn Trulove	1
	43

(49)

Ed. Knight	1.
Jn Right	1
Jn Peate	1
Hen.James	2

Phill. Gudman	1
Jn Stephenes	1
Tho. Birch	2
Ed. Brigges	2
Ed. Hubnall	1
wm Collunbell	1
James Osborne	2
Tho. Frearson	2
Rich. Smedley	1
Wid. ?Bathaley	1
Tho. Piggen	1
Tho. Burch	2
Rob. Smedley	1
Hu. Large	2
Wid. Patricke	1
Rich. Spencer	1
Wid. Blount	1
Chr. Storer	3
wid. James	1
Rob. Green	1
Hen. Hanson	1

vewed p(er)nos John Bancroft and
Rich. Riley Collectors
Tho. Piggen Constable

<u>Pentridge</u>

Mr Horne	4
Mr Licett	5
Jn Tailer	2
Jn Sutton	2
Jn Robinson	1
	48

(<u>50</u>)

Math. Tailer	1
Geo. Fletcher	1
Nico. Tailer	1
Wid. Robinson	1
Rob. Rivington se	1
Rob. Rivington ju	2
Jn Cheathain	1
Jn Roland	1
Rich. whiteaker	1
Jn weightman	2
Lewis Rowland	1
Wid. Water	2
Roger water	1
Ed. Bramley	1
Marg. Cheatha(m)	1
Wm Richardson	1
Wm Annable	1
Jn Topham	2
Tho. Herrald	1
Geo. Beighton	1
Hen. Clay	1
Ger. Clay	1
Hu. Broockshaw	1
Jn wood	1
Chadwickes House	1
Geo. Fletcher	1
Wid. Bramley	1
Rob. Rivington	1
Peter Massey	1
Wid. Dobbe	1
Rob. wheatley	1
Phill. Morrice	2
Rich. Torratt	1
Char. Farmesworth	1
Tho. wild	1
Tho. Tailer	1
Hen. Tailer	1
	42

(<u>51</u>)

Tho. walker	1
Jn Farmesworth	1
Jn Middleton	1

Rich. wid. Stafford	3
Tho. Boltley	1
Ed. Tailer	1

vewed p(er)nos John Bancroft and
Rich. Riley Collectors

Ripley

f Mr Geo. Eyre	7
Rich. Riley	2
Wm Stearland	6
Peter Grundey	2
Jn wathey	2
f Rob. newton	4
f Jn Sutton	2
Wm Kirkeland	2
f Jn Cooper	2
wid. Sheafeild	2
Jn Tomlinson	2
Rob. Stearland	2
Wid. Bateman	2
Wid. Royley	3
Wm Saer junior	1
Char. Hunter	1
Jn Loynam	1
Roger Tailer	3
Jn Smith	1
Mary Saer	1
Ed. Storer	2
Leo. Coates	1
Fra. Bruckhouse and wm Storer	6
f Jn Oates	2
Jn wood	2
Jn Madder	1
wid. Chadwicke	1
Rob. Horesley	1
wm Kenderine	1
Jn Searson	1
	74

(52)

Wm Boltbey	1
Jn Gregorye	1
Math. Sowter	2

Vewed p(er)nos Jn Bancroft &
Rich. Riley Collectors
Jn Cowper Constable

Risley

Anch. Grey Esq.	33
Mr Charleton	4
Mrs Farrington	2
Mich. Holland	2
Hum. Blunstone	3
Wid. Smedley	2
Wm Rawson	3
Jn Burbedge	3
Olliver Carter	1
Jn Peate	2
Jn Smith	1
Wid. Saunderson	1
Jn Smedley	3
Jonas winfeild	1

vewed p(er)nos Jn Bancroft and
Rich. Riley Collectors
Mr Charleton Constable

Sandiacre

Mr Charleton	9
Wid. Tailer	3
Wm Blunstone	4
Wm Bonsall	1
Wid. Chambers	1
Jn Barrott	4
Jn Bostocke	1

Jn Mixon	1
Wm Towle	2
Barth. williamson	2
	93

(53)

Rich. Hallome	1
Jn Roobey	1
Wm Land	1
Jn Dodson	3
Tho. Dam(m)es	1
Jn Samson	1
Jn Falkner	1
Ger. Riste	1
Jn Meakin	1
Jn Cowlishaw	1

vewed p(er)nos Jn Bancroft &
Rich. Riley Collectors
Jn Dodson Constable

Sawley

Sr wm Leech	10
Hum. Bladon	3
Ed. Smith	1
Rich. Towle	3
Tho. Barrowe	2
Fra. Lockoe	1
Rich. Smith	1
Tho. Major	1
wm Abbott	1
Ed. Lacye	3
Tho. Blood junior	1
Rob. Pim	1
Jn Tailer	1
Jn Francis	1
Jn Pim	3
Mr Pim	3
Tho. Elton	1
Ed. Thorpe	1
John Pim	3
Tho. Barrowe	1
vallen. Barnett	3
Hen. Bosworth	1
	58

(54)

Tho. Underwood	1
Wid. Blood	1
Ed. Thorpe or Rob. Randle	3
Certified for Hen. Keeley	2

vewed p(er)nos Jn Bancroft
& Rich. Riley Collectors
Francis Smith Constable

Shipley

Sr wm Leech	11
Mr Lowe	5
Roger Neild	1
Wid. Roe	1
Jn worden	1
Hen. Godkin	1
Geo. Brednall	1
Rob. Brednall	2
Jn Gregorie	1
Dani. Hardey	2
Math. Coulishaw	1
Nico. Spurdey	1
Wm wadelow	1
Geo. Eaton	1
Rich. Corden	1
Jn Cyverne	1
Rich. Motebey	1
Jn woollett	1
Tho. whitworth	1
Tho. Potter	1
wm Smith	1

Phill. Cyverne	1
Wid. Godkin	1
Wid. Baall	2
	48

(55)

Wm Trowman	1
Geo. neild	1
These are Certified for	
Tho. Dewett (?Pewett)	1
Wm Potter	1
Tho. Brentna	1

vewed p(er)nos John Bancroft and
Rich. Riley Collectors
Hen. Godkin Constable

Smalley

John Limney	2
Math. Hill	2
John Smeton	2
Jn Seale	1
Eli. Bennison	1
Tho. Calladine	2
Jn Booth	1
Rich. Holland	1
Vincent Saxon	1
Hen. Smith	2
Jn Buxton	2
Geo. ward	1
Hen. Godkin	1
Tho. Holland	1
Ed. Newton	1
Jn Bramsheire	1
Mr John Bagshaw	2
Rob. Gollin	1
Fra. Calladine	1
Tho. Ma(n)chester	2
Geo. Boote	2

Hen. Bestwicke	1
Tho. Bloodward	1
wid. Crichloe	1
Pat. Richardson	3
	41

(56)

Hen. waters	1
Wm Henrye	1
Jn Scooley	1
James Harvey	1
Wid. Martin	1
Rob. Ellot	1
Wid. Cowlishaw	1
Tho. Calladine ju.	1
Tho. Crichloe	3
Jer. Naggle	2
Ed. Woolley	1
Wid. Porter	1
Tho. Shottoe	1
Tho. Lanchstone	1
Marke Trewma(n)	1
Ed. Saunders	1
Peregr. woodhouse	1

vewed p(er)nos John Bancroft and
Rich. Ryley Collectors
Jn Scooley Constable

Stanton juxta Dale

Mrs Pilkinton	8
Mr Holt	5
Mrs Middlemore	4
Mich. Cowley	3
Mr Benskin	2
Mich. Baguley	2
Geo. Pepper	2
Geo. Riley	2
Jn Singleton se	2

Jn Shingleton ju	1
Jn Osborne	2
Wm Burrowes	1
Rob. Burrowes	1
Hen. Averye	2
Jn Eaton Ju	1
wid. Leper	1
	59

(57)

Wm Peate	1
Jn Clarke se	1
Jn Clarke Ju	1
Wm worthington	1
Geo. Brigges	1
Jn Leper	1
These are Certified for	
Tho. Avery	2
Ra. Gilbert	1
Jn Eaton se	1

vewed p(er)nos John Bancroft
Rich: Riley Collectores
Jn Clarke junior Constable

West Hallome

Mrs Powtherill	20
Mr Horne	7
The Parsanage	4
Jn Tomson	3
Rich. Scattergood	3
Tho. Hanley se	2
Tho. Hanley ju	1
Wid. Darbeysheire	1
Wm Darbeysheire	1
Ch. Kelbey	1
Arth. Barton	1
Luke wright	1
Jn Day	3
Tho. Richardson	2
Wid. Morley	1
Tho. Roe	2
Chr. worden	2
Fra. Hollingworth	1
Wid. Tomson	3
Rich. Hunt	2
Jos. Hodges	1
Rob. Cutler	1
Jn Smalley	2
Tho. Boarbanck	1
Certified Mary Day	1 C
	77

(58)

vewed p(er)nos Jn Bancroft
Rich. Riley Collectors
Fra. Hollingworth Constable

Weston sup(er) Trent

Mr Hallowes	10
Doctor Boilston	8
Geo. Patchett	2
Jn Henshaw	1
Rob. Bryan	3
Rich. Bryan	2
Tho. Swindale	2
Tho. Storer	1
wid. Gilbert	1
Wid. Domoloe	1
Rich. Palferryman	4
Jn Cotton	1
Jn Shelton	1
Jn williamson	2
Wm Domoloe	1
Mary Sleigh	1
Jn Henshaw	1
Tho. Storer	*1*
wm Smith	2

Wid. Bostocke	2
Isaac Whittington	1
Wm Doxey	1
wid. Rose	1
Rob. Lockoe	1
Jn ward	1
Tho. Swindale	1
wm Cooper	1
Hum. Milward	1
Jn wilcocke	1

vewed p(er)nos Jn Bancroft
Rich. Riley Collectors
Tho. Storer Constable

weston underwood

Mr Fr. Burton	4
wid. Ride	2
Jn Marsh	1
Geo. Johnson	3
wm Jeffery	3
	68

(59)

Rob. Horobin	3
Jn Momford	2
Rand. Hanson	2
Nico. woodcocke	1
Hen. Hunt	2
John wallis	1
James Hall	2
Fra. Fisher	1
Wid. Meacocke	1
Jn Howbroocke	1
Wm Hunt	2
Jn Hunt	1
Martin Tunniclife	1

vewed p(er)nos John Bancroft
Rich. Ryley Collectors
Jn Momford Constable

willington

Mrs Meynell	3
wr walton	2
Tho. Hough	3
Gil. Bull	4
Mr Jaques	2
wm Cooke	2
wm wilson	1
Wid. Morley	1
Wid. Lees	1
Anto. walton	1
Tho. Jackson	1
Wid. Hobson	1
Jn Heacocke	3
Phill. Cooke	1
Mr ward	1
Mrs Sales	3
Jn Simnet	1
God. Barton Ju	2
Jn Hanburye	1
Mr Davis	1
Nath. Bowler	2
Rich. Richardson	2
	59

(60)

God. Ford	1

vewed p(er)nos Jn Bancroft
Rich. Riley Collectors
Tho. Hough Constable

Wilne & Sharlowe

Mr Jn Sales	8
Jn Holden	4
Jn Townesend	3

Jn Soer	6
Jn Burgaine	1
Wid. wood	1
Rob. Rolston	2
Jos. Robertes	3
Jn Cowlishaw	4
Wid. Right	1
Jn Russeles	1
Wid. Pim	2
Wid. Burgaine	1
Rob. Bingham	1
Geo. Higgenbotha(m)	2
wm Sandes	1
Tho. Clifford	1
Simon Cripple	1
Jn Grococke	1

vewed p(er)nos Jn Bancroft
Rich Riley Collectors
Geo. Higgenbotha(m) Const(able)

<u>wilstroppe</u>

Mr Roobey	5
Ed. Towle	1
Tho. Tebolt	1
Geo. Lane	1
wid. Locke	2
wid. Turner	1
	56

vewed p(er)nos Jn Bancroft &
Rich. Riley Collectors
Mr Roobey Constable

4468

(Grand total originally given as 4465 at foot of page 60; corrected figure appears on page 61.)

REPTON & GRESLEY HUNDRED

1662

Public Record Office, E 179/245/7

(115r.)

Derb. 8° Octob(er) 1664

I have com(m)anded the petty Constables hereund(er)written that they should attend mee accordinge to my Lord Southamptons & my Lord Ashleys warr(an)t to Sr Willm Boothby with such lists moneyes & certificates as was thereby required from them, but they neglected & obeyed not my warr(an)t being Constables att Mich(aelmas) 1662 in the hundred of Repton & Greisley

Robert Wright Constable of Rosliston & Coton and is in arreare for hearth money at Mich(aelmas) 1662 - 0^{l} 7^{s} 0^{d}

Richard Hunte Constable of Repton hath paid all and is nothinge in arreare

Thomas Abbott Constable of Winsell hath paid all and is nothinge in arreare

Thomas Hampe Constable of Walton hath paid all and is nothinge in arreare

And for the other fyve and twenty Constables in my hundred the certifye mee as in the schedules hereunto anexed

John Cocks High Constable

(117r.)

Greisley

A p(ar)ticular List of the hearthes payable of Gresley cu(m) membris 1662 & have p(ai)d for that tyme and ... that are exempt by the act

Tho Gresley Barronett	23
John Allyn Esqr	8
will. Adams	4
John Adams	3
John Sweane	4
Theophilas Hindmarch	3
John Leedam	1
Tho. Shottwell	1
Tho Peace	1
Richard Gretton	1
Richard Creswell	1

Castle Gresley

Augustin Jackson	3
Robert Clarke	2
Tho. Clarke	1
Tho. Leedam	1
Elizabeth Thurman	1
Robert willson	1
Charles Smyth	1

John ?Lago	1

dunisthorpe

John wakelyn	3
Will. Adams	3
James Taylor	2
Walter Hartell	1
widd Grundy	1
John Shechley	1
Luke woodcocke	1
widd Bakon	1

Okethorpe

George dethicke	2
Joseph wood	2
James Taylor	2
Will. Taylor	2(?1)
Walter Hartell	2
Tho. ?dalney	1
Geo. ?dalney	1
Robert dethicke	1
Walter Tayler	1
Widd. Turner	1
Geo. Turner	1
John Radford	1
Joseph Heare	1
Isack Taylor	1
Isabell Tomlinson	1

Swatlingcoate

Mr ?Thickbroome	3
Will. Henshaw	2
John Knight	1
Cristopher Bath	1
Alice watson	1
Robert Nickolson	1
John Browne	1
Will. Meeke	1
Robert Newbold	1
Nicholas Browne	1
Geo. Plant	1
John Hartle	1
Geo. Pegg	1

These p(er)sons abovewritten have all paid

John Leedam Const(able)

(117v.)

These p(er)sons are exempt according to the act ...

Will. Collier	1
Richard Narwood	1
Widd Newbold	1
Tho. dodge	1
Tho. Smyth	1
Elizabeth Pegg	1
Will. Pegg	1
John Newbold	1
Will. Mason	1
Henry watson	1
Widd. Steele	1
Henry Newbold	1
John Smyth	1
Geo. Lynis	1
John Lavender	1
Richard Horey	1
Tho. Morton	1
Henry Bradley	1
John Browne	1
Will. Newbold	1
Tho. Hewer	1
Richard Hewer	1

These p(er)sons are not within the Act

John Swaine   Thomas Leedam

Oversors of the poore

Abraham Beck

Will. Dallman	0
John Okey	0
Humfrey Dallman	0
Hugh Chawner	0
Widd. Middleton	0
Robert Glascoat	0
Tho. Orton	0
Henry Cantrell	0

Sume is 6^l 11^s

John Leedam Constebell & Churchwarden

(118r.)

8 October 1664

This retorne & ?no other I had from John Leedham Constable of Gresley John Cocks High Const(able) of Repton & gresley

(118v.)

(blank)

(119r.)

A duplicate of the fyre hearthes payable at Stapenhill Mich(aelmas) 1662 and have all paid

John Lucus	3
John Cocks	3
Henry Bee	5
James Fulwood	5
Geo. Lovewell	2
Will. Warryn	2
Will. Brunt	1
Richard Warryn	1
Robert Blea	1
John Pratt	1
Robert Wright	1
Will. Bennett	1
Mabell Sanders	6
Tho. Buckley	6
Rebecka Hatterton	1
Em. Wetton	2
Francis Ilsley	2
Elizabeth Jackson	1
Will. Watson	2
Edward Ilsley	1
Will. Bradford	1
Hugh Porter	3
Henry Low	2
John Martiall	1
John Ilsley	2
Tho. Wright	2
John Wright	1
Francis Warryn	1
Will. Gregory	2
John Wright sen.	1
Sarah Cooke	1
Will. Wright	1
Humfry wood	1
Will. Roberts	1
Charles Henshaw	2
Nicholas Beete	1
Edward Hunt	9
Will. dakyn	1
Will. Eaton	4
Richard Fisher	1
Will. draper	1
Tho. Hassard	1
Tho. wood	1
Widd. Watson	1
Ellen Cooke	1
Will. wright	1
James Ordish	1
Daniell Reeve	1

Som(m)e is 4^l 13^s

Charles Henshaw Constable

William Warren Constables

(119v.)

These names are not payable by Act

James Ardish	1
Ellen Cooke	1
Alice Watson	1
Em. Wetton	1
Will. Warryn	1
John Ilsley	1
Tho. Wright	1
Will. Bradford	1

John Lucas minister
Richard Warren John Watson
over seers of the poore and
Churchwardens
This returne & noe other I had from .
Charles Henshaw Consta(ble)
John Cocks High Cons(table)

(120r.)

A note of All the Fire Harths in
Formarke in the yeare 1662 Michaelmas

Sir Francis Burditt	24 Harthes
Mr ?Fischer	5
John weane	2
John Carver	2
John ?shardley	1

Thomas Carver Constable
Theise have all paid
This retorne & noe other I had from
the Constable of Formarke the 8th
of October 1664
John Cocks High Const(able)

(120v.)
(blank)

(121r.)

A note of all the Fire Harths in
Catton in the yeare 1662 at Mich-
(aelmas) & have all paid

Walter Horton Esq.	15 Harthes
Richard Sheppard	2
Richard Thickbroome	2
Christopher Milnes	1
widdow ?Aulsop	1
Widdow Arnauld	1

Christopher Milnes Const(able)
There are none in his Constablery
that should have p(ai)d but have
p(aid) & none th(a)t are exempt by
the Act
I rec(eive)d this certificate & noe
other from Christopher Milnes
John Cocks High Const(able)

(121v.)
(blank)

(122v.)

(This precedes 122r. here, because
f.122 has been reversed in the bindin

1662

(Wi)llesley cum membris: a list of
fier Hearth paid at michel(mas) 1662

James Abney Esq.	16
Thomas Hall	2
Jer. Hall	1
Francis Chilwell	1
will. Argill	1
John Smith	1
John ?Glover	1
	23

stretton Lefeild

John Brown Esq. for part of the Hall	7
Henry Adams gent for the other part of the Hall	5

Mathew Trigge Clarke	4
Sarah Allen widd.	5
Nath. Mansfeild	2
Joseph Grynn	2
will. yates	1
widd. Browne	1
Tho. Eald	1
wàlter Mather	1
John Stretton	1
John Dalmon	1
Nath. Mather	1
Joy Stretton	2
John Roberts	1
	35

Ravenstone

Walter wolseley gent	9
The Parsonage, mr Harrison	5
mr Samuell Hacksup	5
John Carter	2
John Hood	1
Rich. Lancelett	1
Hen. Blockley	1
Tho. Pratt	1
John Turner	1
will. Bodily	1
John Clarke	1
George White	1
Hughe Holt	1
Tho. Bonner	1
Nich. Newberry	1
	32

(122r.)

Packinton firehearths

Robert Leeson	3
Tho. Roe	3
Isacke Taylor	1
Tho. Swindell	1
John Bakewell	2
widd. Gregorie	1
Izabell Gemson	2
Rich. Smith	1
will. Pickering	1
Tho. Shacoe	2
Jephta Johnston	1
	18

Theis persons following did never pay for fire hearths, being poore in packinton:

Robert Blastocke
Frendship Fletcher
Edward Gregson
John Tirrell
John Tilly
Robt Garland
william kutby
widdow Garland
widdow Hill
widdow Peircy
Susanna ?Cart
Jephta Johnston overseer of the poore of packinton

Theis persons in Ravenston not liable to pay for fire hearths

George Mazon
peeter Mazon
Thomas wayne
James Harvie
widdow shepard
widdow Dudley
william Mals
widdow white
nicholas Newberry overseer of the poore in Ravenston

Theis persons in stretton not lyable to pay for fire hearths:
John Heyfeild
Thomas Bodily
John Stretton overseer of the poore in stretton

Theis persons in willesley not lyable to pay
Michaell Parker
Gabriell Floyd
But widdow Lett in regard hath lately taken land above twenty shillings rent p(er) anu(m) is lyable to pay for the next yeare

Will. Argell Constable of willesley cum membris in the yeares 1662 and 1663
Thomas Hall overseer of the poore of willesley Hamlett
This returne and none other I had from will. Argell Constable octob(er) 8 1664
John Cocks High Constable

(123r.)

Lynton The presentm(en)t of the Constable thereof 1662
hearthes payable by Act ... ... paid

Mr Salt	3
Richard Barth	3
Widd. Callingwood	1
Henry Gryn	1
Widd. Bach	1
Tho. Bradband	2
Widd. Moorehouse	1
Robert Walthall	1
Laranc. Rowell	1
Francis Burton	1
Francis Okey	1
Richard Shorthose	1
John Tompson	1
Phillip Mowsley	1
Geo. Holland	1
Edw. ?Corkett	1
Robert Symons	1
Geo. Starkey	1
John Roberts	1
John Arnold	1
Tho. Burton	1
John Smyth	1
widd. Smyth	1
Michaell Alldritt	1
Robert Knight	1
Richard Seeney	1
widd. Matchett	1
Tho. Symons	1

The marke of Francis Burton Constable

These p(er)sons are not payable by Act

Widd. White	1
Grace Seney	1
Richard Johnson	1
widd. ?Hidoy	1
Joseph Marryot	1
widd. widdowist	1
widd. Salisbury	1

Thomas Bradbent over seear of poore
This returne & no other I Rec(eived) from Francis Burton Const(able) of Linton
John Cocks High Const(able)

(123v.)
(blank)

(124r.)

A p(ar)ticular Accompt of all the fire hearthes within the Constablery of Stanton Ward & Newhall as they were found Chargeable by the Act in the yeare of our lord 1662 And were then paid

	hearthes
Newhall house	14
Robert Burgulon	3
Thomas Smith	3
Robert Smith & Widow Peace	2
Francis Williamson	2
Francis Mason sen.	2
William Whitmore	2
Francis Mason Jun.	2
Widow Heape	2
Robert Heape	2
Widow Wetton	1
John Peace	1
Thirston Tompson	1
William Peace	1
Widow Williamson	1
Richard Bardell	1
Richard Fletcher	1
Thomas Knight	1
Richard Harvey and Grace Morley	1
William Orgill	1
Edward Browne	1
William Parker sen.	1

Stanton Ward

Robert Granger	4
John dakyn	1
Widow Eyre	1
Beatrix Jackson	1
Thomas Wetton	1
William Broadgate	2
Humphrey Jackson	1
Robert Abbott	1
William Swaine	1
	59

John dakyn Constable & Overseer

124v.

A p(ar)ticular of the names of su(ch) persons as were found not chargeable by the Act in Stanton and Newhall in the yeare of our Lord 1662

Thomas Parker	1
Widow Peace	1
Francis Smith	1
Widow Brearely	1
Widow Crosse	1
John Hewer	1
Widow Adey	1
Joseph Shilton	1
Gervice Stafford	1
Charles Hardwick	1
Henry Parker	1
John Heynes	1
	12

John Dakyn Constable and Overseer
Noe Church nor Church Wardens
This returne and noe other I had from John Dakin Constable of stanton
John Cocks High Const(able)

(125r.)

A duplicate of the fire hearthes payable 1662 then paid Michel(mas) 1662 for Chilcoate

Will. Milward Esqr.	16
Mr wakelyn	4
Robert Bayley	5
Tho. Hitchinson	1
Jacob Shilkton	1
Will. Baxter	1

John ?Imons	2
Robert Pratt	2
Tho. Okey	1
will. Harryson	2
will. Bakewell	2
Robert Crosse	2
Tho. Bayley	2
Samuell Terrell	1
Robert Gamble	1
Tho. Browne	1
John Mowesley	1
Cristopher Holden	1
Widd. Baxter	1
Widd. Carver	1
Tho. Taylor	1
Will. Bayley	2
Tho. Bowld	1
Henry Beck	1
david Wilcocks	1
will. Spare	1

William Harrison Constable

(125v.)

Chilcote 1662

These p(er)sons are not w(i)thin Act to pay for

Will. Millward Esqr.	1
John wakelyn	1
Jacob Shilkton	2
Robert Pratt	1
Will. Harryson	1
Robert Crosse	1
Tho. Bayley	1
Robert Bayley	1
Will. Bakewell	1

Robart Bayley Robart Cross Chorch Wardens

This Returne & noe other I have Rec(eived) from Will. Harrison Const(able)

John Cocks High Const(able)

(126r.)

A List of all the Hearths within the Constablry of Croxall & Eddingale for the yeare 1662 And paid then Michel(mas) 1662

Lord Richard Earle of Dorset for Croxall hall	16
mr Hough	4
Tho. Mowsley	2
John Swanne	2
Edw. Mowsley	2
John Browne	2
Margaret ?Pimne (?Prinne)	2
Alice Hatchet	1
James Morgell	2
Tho. wagstaffe	1
Joane Grundy	1

Tho. Collet onely exempted by the Act Mr H ...?vicer Francis Kensall Constable & over seear

(126v.)

This returne & noe other I have from Francis Kensall Const(able)

John Cocks High Const(able)

(127r.)

Newton sooney

A note of the fire hearthes payable 1662 And were then paid michel(mas) 1662

Henry Byard	4
Widd. Fisher	2
Will. Hatchett	1
Tho. dakyn	1
Tho. Bird	1

John Smedley	3
Humpfry Alsop	1
Tho. newton	1
Will. Bateman	1
Tho. Holmes	1
Henry Willson	1
John Spratley	1
Widd. Wayne	4
Tho. Smyth	1
Will. Hakesley	1
Will. dickyn	1
Widd. dickyn	2
will. Garner	1
will. Reynoldson	2
John Shepard sen.	1
John Shepard Jun.	1
Geo. Shenton	1
Richard Reynoldson	1
Geo. Rivett	1
Tho. Hide	1
Mr Wiseman	2
Mis Bryan	2
Robert wright	2
John dickin	1
Tho. dickyn	1
John Symson	1
Francis Atkyn	1
John Wright	1

Some is 2l. 8s.

Thomas Dickin Constable

(127v.)

1662 Newton Soolney

These hearthes are not to bee p(ai)d by Act by them whose names are underwritten

Henry Byard	1
Robert Wright	1
Widd. Newton	1
Will. Reynoldson	1
Widd. wayne	2
John Smedley	1

Over Seers Humphree Alsope Thomas Newton newton solney

This returne and none other I received from Thomas Dikin Constable

John Cocks High Const(able)

(128r.)

Inglebey a list of fier Harths paid at Michel(mas) 1662

Ingleby hearthes payable 1662

Mis Whelpdale	5
Richard Bamford	3
Peeter Joynes	2
Mis Hough	2
Ralph Mowld	1
Jane Heane	1
Sarah Burch	1
John Fisher	1
John Willkinson	2
Richard Joynes	3
Richard Barrowes	2
Gabriell Stanley	3
John Mee	2
Will. Bowlton	3
Nathaniell Martiall	2
Samuell Tasker	1
Tho. dickinson	1
Ellner Joynes	1
John Clews	1
Michaell Allyn	1
Anthony Greene	3

John Fisher Peter Joynes Constable of Ingleby

Some is 2l. 1s.

These names are not to pay by Act

Mis Whelpdale	1

Richard Bamford	2
James Ridgley	1
Ralph Mowld	1
John Willkinson	1
Geo. Smyth	1
Richard Barrows	1
Gabriell Stanley	2
will. Bowlton	1
Nathaniell Martiall	1
Anthony Greene	1
John Clews	1

John Willkinson Tho. Bishop Over-
seors of the poore Church Wardens
There is noe church
This returne & noe other I received
from peter Joynes Constable of
Ingleby
John Cocks High Const(able)

(128v.)
(blank)

(129r.)

1662 Ticknall & Calke

Robert Greenwood	6
John Smedley	5
wm Hutchinson	3
Nicolas Ilsley	3
George Bidulph	3
?Ebnathan Pearston three but one is a kytchin & hath noe hearth	
Robt Gilbert	1
wm ...	1
Edw. Hadfeild one	2
John ?Stetchard fowre but one is falne down	
Thomas ?skermar	1
Joseph Vicars	1
Thomas Greene	1
Thomas Hough	1
Daniell Holland	1
John stanley	1
Thomas Tetley	1
Joseph Bamford	2
widdow ?wilhers	1
widowe ?socken	1
Henry ?Gill	1
James Hough	1
George Gilbert	1
John Symnes	1
Rich. Hill	1
Georgh Hough	1
Oliver Beighton	1
John Sympson	1
Raph Hill	1
John Marriott	?1
Thom. Lynes	1
Tymothy Beighton two but one is falne downe	
Rich. Stretton	1
Rich. ?doore	1
John Bould	1
wm Brian	1
Henry Goodwin	2
Thom. Morley	1
Sam Holland one	1
Rich. smyth	1
Sam. Clare	1
Sam. Potter	1
Hastings Garner	1
Thom. Tafte	1
wm Hanbery	1
John Bakewell	1
Richard Joynes one	1
Thomas ?Richdale	1

(129v.)
(blank)

(130r.)

A note of what Chimneys that are w(i)thin the Act w(i)thin the Constablry of Caulke and paid michel(mas) 1662

Sr John Harpur	23
Francis Wetton	one
John Pime	one
Will. Smith	one
Tho. Owin	one
Tho. Hammond	one
George ?Smith	two
Joh. Bagnell	one
Will. Vernon	one
Widd. ...	
Henry Nuton	one
Joh. Wright Jun.	one
Will. Homerton	one
Ralph Woodhouse	one
Joh. Wright sen.	two
Widd. Hanbery	two
John Coates	two
Simion Heawood	one
Edward Heawood	one
Joseph Heawood	two
Will. Heawood	two

william Smith Constable
This returne I had from william smith & noe other
John Cocks High Const(able)

(130v.)

(blank)

(131r.)

A duplicate of the Constable of Calldwell for fire hearthes payable 1662 all w(hi)ch paid michel(mas) 1662

Mr Barton	9
Mr Holland	2
Widd. Aston	2
Tho. Callingwood	3
Tho. Webster	2
Will. Corbett	2
John Swayne	1
Ed. Shilkton	1
Richard Capenhurst	1
Tho. Baxter	2
Geo. Thrumton	1
Tho. Baker	1
Alice Hunter	1
Henry Gilbert	1
Tho. Corbett	2
John Holland	1
Tho. Harve	1
Tho. Holland	1
John Hargreave	1

Henry Gilbert hath not paid but ought to have paid & hath now paid to mee John Cocks high Constable & I have payd the same to Sr willia(m) Boothby the 8th October 1664
John Cocks High Const(able)

(131v.)

These names are exempted by Act of Parliam(en)t

Mr Holland	1
Mr Barton	1
Tho. Callingwood	1
Tho. Webster	1
Will. Corbett	1
Tho. Corbet	1
Tho. Baxter	1
Henry Gilbert	1
Alice Hunter	1

Thomas Webster T his marke Const(able)

Edward Holland Churchward(en)
This returne & noe other I have
from Thomas Webster Const(able)
John Cocks High Const(able)

(<u>132r.</u>)

A note of the fire hearthes within
the Constablewick of <u>Smithsby</u> in
the yeare 1662 & have paid

Henry Kendall Esq.	12
Mr Smart	2
Richerd Dolman	1
Richerd moore	1
Will. Carver	1
Gabrell Carver	2
nicoless Cockram	1
John Facor	1
Robert Dolman	1
Gilbert Radford	2
John Dodg	1
William Feilds	1
Thomas Petcher	2
Thomas Groves	2
Gilbert Tuiker	1
Cristofor Atkins	1
William Holmes	2
George Berlow	1
widdow Benit	1
Gowen Meaking	1
Joseph Toone	1
Edward Gilbert	1

This returne & noe other I have
Rec(eived) from Gilbert Radford
Const(able)
John Cocks High Const(able)
39 harthes Gilbert Radford

(<u>132v.</u>)

These p(er)sons are exempted by Act
of Parlime(nt) 1662

william Tayler	1
widdow wilkinson	1
widdow Barlow	1
George Tucker	1
widdow Toone	1
John Leedom	1
Robert ?Varnaam	1
william Cibell	1
william Feelds the elder	1
Richerd Johnson	1
widdow Atkins	1
william Smith	1
widdow Pick	1

?Ethiell Smart Minister Thomas
Petcher Gilber Radford overseers

(<u>133r.</u>)

The names of the fire hearthes that
were Chargeable in <u>Melburne and</u>
<u>Newton</u> in the yeare of our Lord
1662 and have paid

Robert Harding Esq.	11
John Radcliff	2
William Muglison	1
Robert Cooper	1
William Osborne	1
Richard Harvey	1
Robert Dexter	1
John Cooper	3
Francis Henshaw	1
Thomas Draper	1
John Ward	2
Robert Martin	1
John Bucknall	1
Jane Rivett	3
Grace May	1
Widow Kirkman	1
Robert Sims	1

John Bacon	1
Gowin Waren	1
Henry Twelves	1
George Weeder	1
John Barrisford	3
John Cantrell	3
Bryan Cantrell	1
Thomas Cantrell	1
Thomas Grey	3
William Kirkman	1
Widow draper	1
John Rayge	1
Thomas Scott	1
Widow Higgin	1
William Birch	1
Robert Greenewood	1
George Addleton	1
William Machyn	1
Thomas Astle	1
William Rose	5
Henry Mather	1
Ferdinando Smith	1
Widow Greenewood	2
Robert Draper	1
Widow ?Wadson	1
John Cantrell	1

(133v.)

Francis Hall	1
Robert Hart	3
John Oreton	1
Edward Kiddeare	1
Francis Ball	1
Richard Cartwright sen.	1
Richard Cartwright Jun.	1
William Cole	2
William Rolston	1
John Hall	1
Francis Monck	1
Joseph Jones	4
Kathreine Knight	2
William Browne	1
John Marshall	1
Widow Heape	2
Widow Bodon	2
Priscilla Brookesby	2
Christopher Pym	2
Beniamin Shevin	1
William Turner	1
Richard Turner	1
Daniell Colson	1
John Kendall	1
Bryan Adcocke	1
Thomas Wood	1
Edward Broomehead sen.	2
Henry Bewley	2
Thomas Pagett	1
Henry Greene	1
Richard Hargrave	1
John Sosleby	1
Edward Hollingworth	1
William Bagnall	1
Thomas Chaddock	2
William Selley	1
John Peate	2
William Peate	1
Thomas Sheepey	1
Joseph Lees	1
Richard Sheepey	1
George Mollybeard	1
Matthew Redwood	1
Thomas Sperrey	1
Henry Lyndopp	1
John Peate	1
William Taylor	1
Thomas Monck	2

(134r.)

Stephen Parker	2
Joseph Garland	1
William Cantrell	1
Henry Hanley	1
John Shevyn	1
John Parker	1
John Ellott	1
Dawson Berrisford	1
Richard Terbott	1
Thomas Carter	1
George Hood	1
James Ward	1
Robert Knight	1
Robert Peate	1
Widow Cooke	1
Bryan Muglison	1
John Charnell	1
John Wilder	1
Widow Cartwright	1
Thomas Roberts	1
Humphrey Woodworth	2
Widow Mellars	1
Thomas Heape	1
William Turner	1
John Walker	1
Richard Millner	1
Mr Fords	14
Mr Vicars	4
Widow Chambers	1
Thomas Woodcock	1
Mr Roberts	5
Hannah Swift	1
Edward Broomehead Jun.	1
John Chambers	1

The totall is 190 hearthes
This returne & noe other I have
from Thomas Roberts Const(able)
John Cocks High Const(able)

Thomas Roberts Constable

(134v.)

A p(ar)ticular of the names of such p(er)sons that were then found not Chargeable according to the Act

Thomas Newbould	1
William Birch	1
William Shipley	1
Thomas Warrein	1
(blank) Pickering	1
Anne Rivett	1
John Scott	1
William Birch sen.	1
John Gybson	1
John Parker	1
Walter Bagnall	1
Samuell Nayler	1
(blank) Gaskyn	1
Thomas donkester	1
John Walker	1
John Wood	1
John Elsey	1
Henry Conoway	1
William Oldcastle	1
Thomas Taylor	1
Jane Winkley	1
William Collington	1
John Cartrick	1
Thomas dale	1
Robert Corner	1
Thomas Alt	1
Hugh Heape	1
Margrett Heise	1
Thomas Taylor	1
Matthew Willyn	1
Abraham Lees	1
John Heape	1
Thomas daniell	1

Widow Conoway	1
Widow Clarke	1
Widow Leaper	1
John Syms	1
Nicholas Walleis	1
Robert Bynney	1
Arthur duffeild	1
Christopher Turner	1
Elinor Smith	1
Edward Walker	1
Thomas doxey	1
George doxey	1
Widow doxey	1
Nicholas Smallwood	1
dorothy doxey	1
William Leigh	1
Widow Mason	1
William Bosworth	1
John Baxter	1

James vicars Minister

John Cantrell and Edward Bodon Churchwardens

Thomas Roberts Constable

(135r.)

1662 Harteshorne

Chargeable hearths that have paid

Mr Tho. Stanhope Clarke	6
Mr John Benskine senior	7
Mr John Benskine Junior	4
Mr Thomas Coulson	8
Mr Richard Hatton & Mr Ullocke for shorthassells	2
Richard Choyce	4
Widd. Chambers	1
Sam. Beighton	1
James Swann	1
Thomas Tetley	1
Willm dithell	2
dorothy Smith	1
Willm Spencer	3
Elizabeth Barwell	1
Richard Gretton	5
Tho. Gibson	1
Fran. Mathewes	1
Nichol. Cotchett	1
John Wetton	2
Mr Sam. Benskine	3
Arthur Taylor	4
Willi. Taylor	2
James Elliott	1
Arthur donithorpe	1
Anne Carter	1
John Ball	1
Mrs Mary Hopkins	1
Thomas Hewson	2
Tho. Hassard	2
John Cantrell	1
John Reynolds	1
Willm Stoakes	1

(135v.)

(blank)

(136r.)

James webster	1
Ellenor wildsmith	2
Ralph Shepheard	5
Richard Spencer	1
John Johnson	1
Geo. Allen	1
Willm Heathcoate	1
John Wilkins	1
Robert Greene	1
	87

Samuell Beighton Cunstable

Will. Allestrey

These are not payable

Charles Foster	2
John daniell	1
darothy Newbold	1
Sara Johnson	1
Robert Knowles	1
william varnhom	1
widdow Hackit	1
william ?Himer	1
John Hewet	1
william Finch	1
widdow Hewet	1
widdow smedley	1
John swann	1

Richar(d) Gretton William
Stokes Churchwardens
This returne & noe other I have
Receaved from Samuell Beighton
Const(able)
John Cocks High Const(able)

(136v.)
(blank)

(137r.)
Mesham hearthes payable 1662
these have paid

Mr Woollerston	5
Mr Hoolton	1
Mr Ullocke	3
Joseph Whitword	1
Widd. Wood	2
Charles Morris	1
Isack Ellott Jun.	1
Humpfry Robotham	1
Tho. Willdman	1
Geo. Smyth	1
Tho. Willdman	1
Tho. Moore	1
Tho. dodge	1
Beniamin Crosham	1
Abraham Hough	1
Widd. Whitmoore	1
Joseph dewsherrey	1
Joseph Norman	1
Samuell Chillwell	1
Henry Mowld	1
James Bach	1
Geo. Smythalls	1
Spencer	1
Henry Walker	1
Will. Tatenell	1
Phillip dodge	1
Will. Wright	1
Nicholas Boyer	1
Joseph Cater	1
Tho. Nurse	1
John Browne	1
Robert Smyth	1
Robert Dexter	1
Will. Narwood	1
Abraham Spencer	1
widd. Pearson	1
Geo. Hill	1
Lonard Whateley	1
Samuel Cater	1
Walter Tayler	1

payable

Tho. Wetton	1
Tho. Smaley	1
Elias Smyth	1
Widd. Smyth	1
Tho. Mosley	1
daniell Elloott	1
John ?Coker	1

Sume is 54s
The Marke of Samuell Chilwell
Constable
This returne & noe other I have

Rec(eived) from Samuell Chilwell
Const(able)
John Cocks High Const(able)

(137v.)
(blank)

(138r.)

A pressentment of the fior harth in Chellaston that pade in 1662 and the names of them that pade

mes Thacker	2
mes whinyates	4
sur John horpur	3
John domelo	1
william arkyne	1
John walker	1
John barratt	1
John oliver	3
henery locko	1
willam rose	1
Richard Turner	1
Henery ?crattes	1
Edard robartes	1
william conper	1
Abraham wollat	1
willam shephard	1
willam knifen	1
John Bancroft	1
John formon	1
Robard ?marely	1
An ?willder	2
John reckles	1
wido reckles	1
Thomas robartes	1
Robard bryon	1
Cristephir Barton	1
simon Barton	1
James pickering	2
Joseph ?Bancroft	1
willam campe	1
Thomas Bonsell	1
Ellin palfremon	1

Simon Barton Cunstable of Chelliston

(138v.)

Hearthes not payable

Will. Twiggs	1
John Groves	1
Tho. Smyth	1
will. Sheldon	1
Widd. deay	1
Widd. hobson	1

John oliver willam Bancroft
Robard Brion   Widd. wilter
Overseeres of the poore
This returne & noe other I have
Rec(eived) from Simon Barton
Co(nstable)
John Cocks High Const(able)

(139r.)

Hearthes payable & have paid The Constable of Swarkeston duplicate Ann(o) d(omi)ni 1662

Sr John Harpur	28
Mr Bowld	6
Beniamin Bowld	4
Lazaras Needham	2
Will. Roberts	2
Tho. Cocker	2
James Fayrfeild	2
John Fisher	2
Beniamin Fisher	2
Will. Bradfeild	1
Robert Sarson	1
Tho. Twichell	1
Edmond Parker	4

John Pym	1
Will. Roberts	1
Henry Wright	1
Jervis draper	6
Tho. draper	2
John Coop	1
will. Carter	1
will. Cantrell	1
Jervis Bancroft	1
Samuell woodcocke	1
John Spencer	1
Widd. Tompso(n)	1
John Sarson	1
*John ?Heane	1*

Some is 31 16s

Edmund Parker Constable

(139v.)

These are not payable by Act

Sr John Harpur	1
Beniamin Bowld	1
Will. Roberts	1
Tho. Cocker	1
James Fayrfeild	1
John Fisher	1
Edmond Parker	1
Jarvis drap(er)	1
John Pym	1
Tho. Glover	1
Widd. Tompson	1
John Sarson	1
John Heyne	1

Mr Samuell Bold Recter

Beniamin Bold Lazarus Needham

overseers of the pore

This returne & noe other I have

Rec(eived) from Edmund Parker

Const(able)

John Cocks High Const(able)

(140r.)

A note of the fire hearthes w(i)thin

the Constablewick of Lullington An(no)

d(omi)ni 1662 The(?se) have paid

Mis Gresley	7
Mr Whiting	3
Will. Page	6
Will. Byard	4
Tho. derby	3
Will. Tavernor	2
Samuell Mosse	1
Tho. Ramsor	1
John Ramsor	2
Beniamin Mowesley	3
Ralph Sheppard	2
Edward Mowsley	2
Cristopher Coton	1
John Millner	1
The house voyd	2
Gyles Benfeild	1
?Hersio. woodcocke	2
Richard Sheppard	2
Edward dallkins	2
Robert Page	1
Tho. Bob	1
Arthur duffeild	1

William Taberner Cunstable

(140v.)

These p(er)sons are exempted by Act

Widd. Bratt	1
Richard Smyth	1
Widd. Kerke	1
Widd. Jorden	1
Raphe Morlow	1
Peter Wetton	1
Richard Cocks	1

Peeter whiting minister

william Taberner Samuell Mosse

Overseers
This returne & noe other I have
Rec(eived) from Will. Taberner
Const(able)
John Cocks High Const(able)

(141r.)

A p(ar)ticular of the fire hearthes payable by Act of Parliam(en)t Ann(o) d(omi)ni 1662 for Appleby all have paid

Mr Kendall	13
John Mowld	2
Richard Walthall	1
Joh. Walthall	2
Richard Wright	2
John Knot	1
Henry Erpe	1
An. Hunt	1
Edward Litherland	1
John Proudman	1
Widd. Spencer	2
Geo. Orton	1
Tho. Heyfeild	1
Will. Prowdman	1
John Wallker	1
John Heyfeild	1
Nicholas Sharpe	1
Tho. Petcher	1
John Pratt	1
Francis Berrey	1
Will. Stokes	1
Will. ?Frisbey	1
Abraham Crosland	1
Mathew Pratt	1
John Widd. Heyfeild	1
Tho. Sweane	1
John Stanton	1
will. Heawood	1
widd. Holding	1
Richard Erp	1
John Parker	1
Richard Mold	1
Abraham Shilton	1
John Middleton	1
John Kinge	1
Will. Willson	1

This returne & noe other I have
Rec(eived) from Thomas Heyfeild
Const(able)
John Cocks High Const(able)

(141v.)

(blank)

(142r.)

A note of the fire hearthes of Osmeston 1662 that are payable by Act of Parliam(en)t all paid

Nicholas Wyllymot Esq.	20
John Potter Clerke	2
John Carter	3
Will. Leaper	3
Will. Sheppard	1
James Stere	2
Will. dawson	1
Tho. Reeve	1
Hamlett Peacocke	1
daniell doxey	1
John Ottiwell	1
John Maddocke	1
James dawson	1
Laranc. Sore	1
Tho. Harryson	1
John Campyon	4
John Steere	1
Will. Ball	1
James dawson	1

Will. Barker	2
James Ayre	1

(142v.)

These p(er)sons are exempted by Act

Will. Baxter	1
Ralphe Coop	1
Widd. Thruchley	1
Tho. Rolston	1
Mary Killdall	1

Mr Potter minister
William Ball James da(w)son Church wardens
Thomas harison Cunstablee
This returne & noe other I have Rec(eived) from Thomas harison Const(able)
John Cocks High Const(able)

(143r.)

A note of the fire hearthes w(i)thin the Constable wick of Brettbey Ann(o) d(omi)ni 1662 That have all paid

Phillip Earle of Chesterfeild	68
Will Wilders	1
Luke Budworth	2
James Budworth	1
Henry Belcher	2
Tho. Willson	1
Will. Roberts	1
Will. Goodwyn	2
Edward Newton	1
James Byard	2
Cristopher dawson	1
John Gery	2
Will. Pratt	1
Will. Millner	2
John Belcher	1
Will. Whatton	3
John Pickeringe	1

The Earle of Chesterfeild hath two chymes pulled downe
John Geary Constable
This returne & noe other I have from John Geary Const(able)
John Cocks High Const(able)

(143v.)

These p(er)sons are not w(i)thin the Act of Parliam(en)t

Gregory Wright	1
Roland Mason	1
Will. Higgobotham	1
Tho. Willis	1

Richerd Pears minister
William Gooding William Roberds overseeers

(144r.)

(16)62 Stanton Juxta Pontem have paid

Mr Hawford	4
Mr Clarke	4
Tho. Clarke	2
O...der Hoult	1
Robert Houlden	1
Edward Brooke	2
John dudly	2
Tho. Bostocke	1
Tho. Smeilly	1
Will. Meakin	3
Joh. Cockin	1
Tho. Bostock sen.	1
Joh. Roberts	1
James Turner	2
will. Charnell	3
John Henly	3
John Spencer	1
John Marshall	1

will. Ratclife	3
An Barron	1
Joh Simson	1
widd. Sheapard	4
Isabel Bakwell	1
Henry write	1

Edward Brooke Constable

This returne & noe other I have

Reç(eived) from Edward Brooke

Const(able)

John Cocks High Const(able)

(144v.)

(blank)

(145r.)

(blank)

(145v.)

not within the Acte

Mathew Brouton

Tho. Neilde

Rob. Wilder

Tho. Tailour

wid. Atkin

Elin Biard

Joh wells

widd. wells

widd. yeomans

Joh ward

Theophill. Hawford minister

william Charnells Edward

Robartes Church Wardens

(146r.)

1662 A presentment of all the hearths payable by the Act within the said Towne of Normanton The have paid

Imp(ri)mas First of all Mr Beamond dixie esqui(re)	Tenn hearths
Mr Philip Prime	Nine
William Stenson	one
William Pegg	one
William Portter	one
Micheall Stenson	one
Edward Taberer	one
John Wilson	one
Mr Hassard	Fouer
Henery Stenson	one
Thomas Jackson	Five
John Wilkinson	one
John Stenson	one
Thomas Holmes	one
Richard ...	one
Henery ?Owarte	one
William Boden	one
Widdow Freeman	one
Widdow Stenson	one
Richard Ball	one
William Moulsworth	one
Mary Emes	one

P(er) me William Stenson Constable

(146v.)

Not payable by the Act

Will. Stenson blacksmith

George Morlidge

Will. Moore

Will. Osborne

widdow Sore

Thomas Jackson John stinson

Overseors of the poore

Wee have noe constant Minister

This return & noe other I have

from William Stenson Const(able)

John Cocks High Const(able)

1662

Public Record Office, E 179/94/378

(22)

Winsell

Mr Dutton	2
Thomas Dutton	1
Henry Fisher	2
Thomas Eaton	1
Robert Fitchett	1
John Fitchett	2
William Clarke	1
Thomas Warde	1
Ralph Sanders	1
John Pegge	1
John Warde	1
Nicholas Crosse	1
Robert Crosse	1
William Bladon	1
Thomas Bladon	1
William Attkins	1
John Veile	1
John Darby	2
Thomas Newton	1
Thomas Walker	1
Joane Henshaw	1
Mr Henry Toune	1
Mr Bunn	1
Thomas Henson	1
	28

Repton

Gilbt Thacker Esq.	13
Mr Ullocke	5
Mr Litherland	4
Richard Pratt	3
Mr Gibt Turner	2
John Gearye	2
Godfry Finton	1
Mr Rathbone	5
Richard Marbury	1
John Warde	3
Roberta Ward vid	2
John Pratt	2
Henry Bishop	1
Henry Wigwall	2
Gilbert Pratt	1
Hugh Turner	5
William Davye	1
George Jenings	1
Feales Pratt vid	1
William Pratt	1
William Bishop	2
Widow Grimble	2
Widow Haynes	...
widow Turner	...
Richard Weate	1
William Bull	1
John Cantrell	1
Widow Ward	1
James Dunstall	3
John Holmes	1
Henry Gilbert	2
George Stubbs	4
Gilbert Cantrell	2
Mrs Hardslye	1
Widow Poyser	1
Henry Hunt	1
Robert Rawlins	1
Robert Bull	1
Godfry Warde	4
John Stone	1
William Jorden	1
Widow Chantrye	1
Thomas Hindly	2

Thomas Shaw	3
Widow Heane	1
Gilbert Carter	1
Richard Meykin	1
Mr Godfry Thacker	3
Widow Carver	2
John Pegge	1
John Morly	2
John Barton	2
Widow Weate	2
Richard Hunt	2
Richard Pratt	1
Gilbt Bull	1
Thomas Bull	1
Henry Weate	1
John Pratt	1
Widow Bladen	1
Katheren Leys	1
John Bancroft	1
Widow Smyth	1
Thomas Salt	1
Robert Heathcote	1
Godfry Rivitt	1
Thomas Bramly	1
Thomas Gilbert	2
William Orchard	2
Thomas Hollington	2
Widow Dalton	1
	133

(<u>23</u>)

(Ms torn: several entries (41 hearths) missing at the top)

John Weate	...
Richard Shephard	1
Widow Weate	1
Sir John Harpur kt att his lodge	5
William Chapman	1
Mr Roades	6
Job Durham	1
Edward Shimerfeild	1
Moses Attekins	1
	192

<u>Roslaxton</u>

Henry Fletcher	1
John Maqueire	1
Mathew Armstrong	1
Christopher Radford	1
Richard Chaplin	1
William Wright	1
Widow Watson	1
Sympson Wigins	1
Thomas Mallabor	4
John Hickman	1
Christopher Palmer	1
Edward Bayly	1
William Wetton	2
Denise Bayley	1
Nicholas Baylye	1
Katheren Grymly	1
Henry Bab	1
Nicholas Dawkins	1
Edward Pawnier	3
Thomas Bate	1
Edward Fleminge	1
Thomas Bondman	3
Lawrence Persall	1
Thomas Rushen	1
William Daulman	2
John Nicklin	2
Richard Rowbotham	1
Thomas Mosely	1
	38

<u>Coton</u>

William Maryott	1
Thomas Smyth	1

John Thickbroome	1
(Ms torn: several entries (42 hearths) missing at top of second column)	
William Ball	2
James Dawson	1
William Barker	2
Gervase Eyre	1
	51

(Note: it is uncertain whether or not the Coton entries are continued on m.24; see Table 2)

1664

Public Record Office, E 179/245/10

(4r.)

Walton upon Trent

Persons Chargeable

John Ferrers Esq.	17
Thomas Bearecroft Rector	4
Sam. Whiteinge	3
Wm Bell	3
John Reynolds	1
Thomas Bould	1
Rich. Dickins	1
Rich. Taylor	2
Rich. Tomlinson	1
Rich. Tebb	1
Tho. Jackson	2
John Hall	1
Thomas Hampe	1
Wm Dickins	2
Robert Jordan	1
John Newhall	3
Humfry Bradfeild	1
Robt Wyatt	1
John Jordan	1
Peter Cotton	1
Ralph Haywood	1
Rich. Hewkin	1
Bridgett Bedford widd	1
Peter Newhall	1
Jane Ironmonger vid	1
Rich. Cowper	1
Ellen Stretton widdow	1
Anne Wetton widdow	1
John Henson	1
	57

Persons not Chargeable

Edward Cowper	1
Sam. Elliott	1
Margrett Boothby vid	1
Tho. Fender	1
Rich. Owine	1
Rich. Ellis	1
Elizabeth Bradfeild	1
Alice Yates	1
Elizabeth Allen	1
Alice Wood	1
Thomas Nevill	1
John Stretton	1
	12

SCARSDALE HUNDRED

1670

Derby Public Library, Derbyshire Collection, DC 9954

(Title page)

Scarsdale Booke

Hugh weeldons booke for
hearth money in the
Hundred of Scarsdale

(1)

Scarsdale Hundred

Chesterfield

Mr Richard Clarke Major	23
Mr James Milnes	5
Mr Richard Marchant	5
Mr John Coupe	7
Mr John Woodward	8
Mr Thomas Britland	8
Mr Anthony Legatt	4
Mr Abell Tilley	4
Mrs Columbell	3
Mrs Jenkinson	1
Mrs Anne Britland	2
Samuel Fowler	3
James Lunn	1
Humphrey Low	2
Mr Robert Stringfellow	9
Mr Hills house	5
Michael Watton	3
Gabriel East	6
Anne Pott wid.	4
Robert Booth	3
Godfrey Ashes	4
John Youle	1
Mr George Ashes	5
Anne Vicars wid.	5
Susanna Frith	3
Thomas Burbecke	2
Mr Francis Moore	6
Mr Thomas Needham	5
Edward Needham	3
Benjamin Heathcoat and Mr Thomas Radford	7
Mr William Newton	7
George Youle	2
Mr Marke Ashley	9
Samuel Higgins	3
William Lee	5
Mary Bowe	3

(2)

Peter Redgat & Willm Thorpe	8
Laurence Oxley	3
Richard Milnes	4
John Allen	8
*Robert Gascoyne	nihill*
Hugh Wheeldon	2
William Webster	2
Nich. Webster	3
Samuel Stones	6
Joseph Stones	2
George Bower	4
Thomas Johnson	3
Mr Hercules Clay	5
John Rose	3
Edward Allen	2
Elizabeth Steere	2
Thomas Rollinson	4
Mr Woodwards house	2

Thomas Wright	5
John Bagshaw	1
Mr Robert Milward	4
Mr Gilbert Heathcoate	6
John Wheeldon	1
Thomas Revell	3
Anne Dowker	3
Edward White	1
Martin Britland	3
Mr Peter Needham	3
Thomas Bennison	1
Mr Peter Parkinson	4
Robert Collier	3
Elizabeth Thorpe	2
Henry Stubbings	1
?Dcor Dicksons house	5
Mr Richard Youle	6
Godfrey Swift Jun.	4
Mr Selbye Mason	3 Ret

(3)

John Ashe Butcher	5
Hugh Farnsworth	1
Edward Moore	3
Peter Riggot	3
Michael Gildon	2
Mr Robert Moore house	4
Mr James Dutton	6
George Stringfellow	1
Mrs Dickins	4
Richard Marshall	4
John Dickens	3
Theoph. Brocksoppe	3
William Moore	3
James Milnes tanner	3
Thomas Greaves	3
Mr Paul Webster	6
Thomas Does	2
John Paramore	1
Peter Stansall	1
John Harwood	1
Godfrey Webster	5
Thomas Holland	5
Mr Edward Wood	10
Robert Bennet	10
William Hayes	5
James Mathewes	5
Mr Newton sen.	5
Samuel Needham	3
Wid. Chowe	3
Mr Clarke	1
Mr Bromley	3
John Hugnall	3
Alice Ashe	4
Mr Merchant *one* two over houses	1
Mr Tho. Eyres Esq.	1
Mrs Brierley	9
Robert Bagshaw	5
John Carter	2
Adam Gill	8

(4)

James Milnes ?Iron.	2
Ralph Nayler	3
William Houghton	3
Francis Haldsworth	5
Tho. Ward	3
Tho. Hanbury	3
Francis Browne	7
Mr John Ashe Apoth.	1
Edward Browne	3
Tho. Dowker	7
Thurston Riveington	4
Robert Dowker	4
Joshua Dale	4
Willm Storrer for Mr Woodhouse (?Wood house)	7 Ret

Samuel Haigh	5
Mr Thomas Booth	6
Gregory Wilkinson	2
Henry Hollingworth	2
Francis Tupman	2
Mr William Forth	6
Mr Hardy	6
Thomas Stevenson	2
Ralph Bowne	2
George White	4
Francis Bagshaw	3
Thomas Denby	2
Daniel Lee	2
Mrs Taylor	31
John Ragsdale	1
Jonathan Slater	4
Wid. Hancocke	3
Richard Flint	2
Richard Allwood	3
Richard Sharman	3
Francis Inman	3
Hannah Milnes wid.	4
Tho. Browne	1

(5)

Anne P...ston	*1*
Richard Purslove	1
Wid. Purslove	2
John Mosseley	2
Gervas Maden	3
Thomas Kirke	1
Dicor Stubbing	2
Anne Manifold	3
William Renshaw	3
George Lee	2
John Oldam & Geo. Booth	3
John Wheatcroft	2
John Greaves	2
William Dawson	2

Samuel Inman	5
Isabell Heywood	3
Anthony Woodward	2
Godfry Swift sen.	1
Godfrey Stansall	3
Anthony Purslove	3
George Riveington	4
Mr Cranes house	4
Godfrey Wostenholme	3
Mr Peter Dowker	6
Mrs Carter	4
Thomas Grangeer	5
John White	2
Mr Thomas Ludlam	3
Wid. Cade	2
Abraham Briddon	2
Mr Millnes Chambers	2
Tho. Inman	4
Gilbert Webster	3
Richard Greaves	2
George Poynton	4
Willm Whelor	2

(6)

Humphrey Goodwin	4
George Slater	2
Joseph Parker	1
Anthony Beastall	3
Welch house	3
William Lee sen.	2
Henry Ashton	1
Henry Haynes	2
Wid. Beerry	2
Stephen Penystone	3
John Hossland	3
Thomas Marsden	4
Godfrey Shaw	4
John Shaw	6
Mr Robert Moore	4

Henry Inman	1
Mrs Garvis	6
John Smith	2
George Tupman	3
William Jackson	2
Christopher Stones	2
Thomas Dutton	3
Henry Damme	2
Edward Jeffery	3
Henry Booth	3
Thomas Spenser	4
Peter Shentall	2
Wid. Watts	3
Richard Wheatcroft and Francis ?Eller for Mr Wheeldons house	*...*
	38-16-0

(two blank pages)

(7)

Scarsdale Hundred

Ashover

Mr Obediah Bourne	7
Mr Richard Dakeyne	3
Gyles Cowley	5
Francis Stephenson	3
George Hodgkinson	2
William Hopkinson	2
Anthony Turner	2
Widdow Wheatcroft	1
Leonard Wheatcroft & Antho. Ragg	2
George Beighton	2
John Wilshawe	3
Christopher Bower	1
Richard Hodgkinson	1
Thomas Haslam	2
John Briddon	1
Edward Ragg	1
John Purslove	1
Mr Sleigh sen.	3
Jo. Redferne	3
William Hodgkinson jun.	3
Francis Sigley	1
Thomas Hitche	1
Henry Waterhouse	2
Robert Fell	1
Edmund Ludlam	1 Reto
James Willmott	1
Phillipe Stubbinge	1
Thomas Millington	2
Mr Joseph Willson	6
William Bower	1
Widdow Bower	1
Christopher Hunt	1
Edward Booth	2
John Buntinge	3
William Allsoppe	1
Phillip Waterhouse	1
Zachariah Newton	1
Henry Bower	2
Francis Bower	1
William Momford	1
Richard Varney	2
Thomas Webster	1
John Barker	2
Henry Townedrowe	?2
?Ralph Momforde	(?1)

(8)

Thomas Wagstaffe	2
Roger Barnes	2
Robert Flint	2
Thomas Stone	2
Anthony Prestwidge	2
Francis Needham	2

John Waterhouse	1
William Townedrowe	2
William Hunt	3
Widdow Barker	1
George Needham	1
Charles Allsoppe	1
John Bankes	1
Widdow Mower	2
Robert Norman	2
Thomas Shemilt	1
John Eastwood	1
Robert Smith	1

Mr Sleigh jun.	6
William Needham	3
Richard Briddon	2
John Bower	4
Widdow Spencer	1
Isaack Hopkinson	1
Mathew Haslam	1
Richard Baken	1
John Buntinge	2
Francis Newham	2
Wid. Lowe	2
Leonard Maxefield	1
Thomas Millward	2
Thomas Hollingworth	2
Robert Allwood	1
Robert Milward	2
Mr Roger Coates	5
John Townedrowe	1
John Farnesworth	3
Henry Prestwidge	1
Thomas Wheelwright	1
Anthony Prestwidge	2
Edward Sykes	1

Mr George Hodgkinson	4
Richard Hodgkinson	3
Robert Parkes	3
George Calton	2
?The Lady Hunlocke	10

(9)

Widdow Jackson	1
Ralph Henstocke	1
Adam Criche	1
Edward Hodgkinson	2
Ralph Mather	1
John Mather sen.	2
Thomas Woodist	2
John Mather jun.	2
Ralph Beard	1
Mary Wasse	2
John Spencer	1
Edward Roades	2
Mathew Boothe	2
Henry Cockayne	1
Edward Henstocke	1
Richard Hole	1
Richard Hand	1
Thomas Hand	1
George Spencer	1
George Cowlishaw	3
Mr Beveridge	2
Robert Gregory	1
Henry Henstocke	1
William Hopkinson	1
George Ragg	1
Thomas Nightingale	1
Thomas Allen	1
Mr Owtrem house	2
Roger Hollingworth	1
Henry Andrewe	1
John Gregory	3
Widdow Buntinge	1
George Barker	1
Gyles Hopkinson	1

George Bower	3
Adam Beardsley	1
Hugh Clay	1
Thomas Cantrell	1
Ambrose Hibbard	1
Henry Evaratt	1
John Cantrell	1
Robert Tomlinson	1
John Riggot	1
George Hodgkinson	2
Edward Allen	1
Godfry Basford	1 *Reto* C
Anthony Wood	1
Thomas Goodale	1
	£ s d
229 harthes	*11 9 0*
	(ms torn)

10

Alfreton

Allexander Stannope Esq.	16
Mr John Jolley	5
Edmund Meymott	3
Robert Jackson	3
William Round	1
John Hathwell	1
Rowland Sudbury	2
Francis Falconbridge	1
Widdow Dobb	2
Christopher Holmes	4
John Fallconbridge	1
Richard Willcockson	1
William Rossell	1
Andrew Hoolen	1
nothing Charles Farnsworth	1 Cer.
John Clarke	1
Richard Burneham	1
William Greene	1
John Jackson	2
Robert Wright	2
William Greatraxe	5
Widdow Coates	1
Cornelius Launder	3
Thomas Fletcher	2
Widdow Byfeild	1
John Gyles	1
John Uston	2
Rowland Allsoppe } John Lowne }	3
William Dunnington	2
Henry Simpson	2
William Carden	2
William Jepson	1
John Dutton	1
Thomas Burneham	1
Charles Deane	1
Mr Oatefield	2
Thomas Mower	1
George Varneham	1
Richard Mycocke	1
nothing George Hollis	1 Cer.
Abigall Turner	3
Robert Taylor	1
Isabell Browne	2

(11)

Robert Storah	1
Godfrey Kirke	2
John Kirke	4
nothing Thomas Mower	1 Cer.
Rowland Saxton	1
John Crosse	2
Roger Saunders	1
Mary Turner	4
William Browne sen.	1
John Foster	1 Cer.
Mary Turner	1 Cer.
William Browne jun.	1

Edmund Meymott	1	
Christopher Mower	1	
James Tarratt	2	
Thomas Coe	1	
Edward Bankes	1	
Widdow Turner	1	
Michaell Eyre	2	
William Wrightman	1	
John Beresford	1	
Thomas Bullocke	1	Cer.
Edward Wood	2	
Edward Williamson	1	
Edward Fousley (?Housley)	2	
Richard Harvey	1	
Widdow Burnehame	1	
Thomas Hunter	2	
John Uston	2	
Mr Horne for Plumetree house	1	
John Breilsford	1	
Jónas Fallcónbridge	1	
Seth Wood	3	
Michaell Mosse	1	Cer.
Thomas Hunter	1	
Henry Hunter	2	
Edward Revell	1	
William White	1	
Christopher Searson	1	
James Bacon	1	
Richard Harvey	1	
Widdow Topham	2	
William Hallam	1	
James Bore	1	
Godfrey Cheetam	1	

(12)

John Brunt	1

George West	2	
Thomas Wharton	1	
John Parker	1	
William Clarke	1	
John Brothwell	2	
Widdow Doe	1	
John Ufton	1	
William Wollat	1	
Robert Hoult	1	
Francis Draycott	1	
Christopher Berisford	1	
William Williamson	1	
Edward Fitchrandolphe	3	
Thomas Hodgkinson	2	
Peter Fetherstone	1	
Richard Ufton	1	
Richard Bland	1	
Thomas Walker	1	
John Walker	1	
Robert Tompson	1	
Francis Machell	1	
Michaell Mosse	1	
Thomas Wharton	2	
Richard Harvey	1	Cer.
John Brunt	1	Cer.
Thomas Walker	1	Cer.
Francis Blood	1	Cer.
Robert Tompson	1	Cer.
Francis Macham	1	Cer.
John Lowne	1	
Edward Burneham	1	
Robert Oearedish	*3* 1	
	£ s d	
179 harthes is	*8-19-0*	
	9-13-0	

Shurland & Higham

Mr James Wright	6

Mr Allsoppe	6
Mr Goodwyne	3
Richard Kirkeham	2
Martiall Fell	2

(<u>13</u>)

John Ludlam	2
James Strutt	2
William Buntinge	1
George Alsebrooke	1
John Hasland	1
Mathew Hopkinson	1
Robert Hollingworth	1
Thomas Bennion	1
Roger Alsebrooke	1
Anne Newton	1
William Newton	1
Henry Robinson	1
William Beardsly	1
Thomas Waterhouse	1
Peter Turner	1
John Revell	1
William Stones	1
Robert Hunt	1
Edward Hunt	2
John Theetes	1
John Wright	1
William Stocks	2
Francis Foljambe	1
Richard Cooper	2
Elisabeth Greaves	1
William Harwood	1
George Prestwidge	1
Francis Granger	1
Edward Barker	1
Widdow Bower	1
Thomas Ellis	1
Edward Curtise	2
John Lowe	7
Edward Parkes	3
Francis Parkes	3
Peter Calowe	1
William Bower	1
Elisabeth Holmes	2
Obediah Boote	3
James Bingham	1
William Shawe	1
John Sherbrooke	2
John Benbridge	1
Robert Lee	1
John Roades	1
Simon Greene	1
Widdow Soresby	1
	£ s d
86 harthes	4 5 0

(?6 shillings obliterated)

(<u>14</u>)

<u>Eckenton</u>.

Doctor Gardner	10	
Georg savage	6	
Georg Hatersley	1	
John Gregory	3	
Tho. storkey	3	
sam. Faram	1	
Will. sale	1	
Barbra Treeton	1	Noth
Joane Kirkby	1	
Will. Machen	4	
Will. sales	3	
Robert shooter	2	
Widdo. Rotheram	3	
Widdo. stones	?1	
Joseph Beeley	1	
Hen. Sales	2	
John Kesteeven	2	noth
Rob. Walton	2	
John Harwood	2	

Rob. Wilkes	1	Will. Butcher	2
Johnathan Treeton	2	John Clarke	2
George smith	1	Tho. Booth	1
Rob. Frith	5	Rob. Cowley	2
Will. Malam	1	John Webster	1
Tho. Billam	4	Rob. Jackson	1
Will. Rodger	2	Rich. White	2
Will. Taylor	1	John Auchiffe	1
John Fowden	1	Widdo Allen	6
John. Redfearne	1	Rich White Jun.	1
Will. Hewkin	1	Will. Brucke	1
Fran. Leathwicke	2	Will Crawley	1
Rich. Litlewood	1	John Earnshawe	2
Rob. Cowley	1	Widdo. Townsend	1
Will. Pittes	1	Rob. Mymott	1

(15)		(16)	
Peter Booth	2	Will. Riveington	1
Robert Carver	1	Tho. Hodgson	1
Ralph Leake	2	George Whittworth	2
Widdo. Ridward	1	John Kirkby	2
John Webster	1	George Turner	4
Ellen Chapman	1	Tho. Heynes	1
Tho. sanderson	2	Widdo stanniforth	4
Rich. Taylor	2	Will. Kirkby	2
Will. Feildhouse	1	Vincent Turner	2
George Tomson	4	Tho. Hooson	2
Charles Clay	2	Fran. Bullas	1
George sitwell Esq.	13	Tho. Cruck	1
John Wigfall	11	Tho. Andrewe	2
Mrs Poole	10	Rob. Turner	2
Mr Frances Poole	7	Tho. White	1
Mr Crumpe	2	George stanniforth	1
Will. Newbould	1 noth	Max. Renshawe	2
John Mymott	1 noth	Garvas Rooke	3
Rob. Townsend	3	Elizabeth stanniforth	2
Mary Haslam	1	Tho. Turner	1
Rich. Cade	1 noth	Tho. Litlewood	1
Mathew Munks	1	Widdo savdge	1

Rob. stanniforth	2
Widdo Leake	5
John Turner	2
Elizabeth staniforth	1
John stanniforth sen.	2
John stanniforth Jun.	2
Hen. Garsett	1
Rob. Jackson	1
Tho. Beetson	2
Tho. Richardson	2
Tho. staniforth	1
Edw. Turner	1
John Andrewe	1
Hen. Andrewe	1
Edw. Andrewe	2

(17)

Rob. Boothe	3
Tho. Britlebanke	1
Tho. Rawson	1
John Wilson sen.	2
John Wilson Jun.	4
Rich. Hawksworth	1
stephen Beardsall	1
Tho. Booth	2
Will. staniforth	1
John Mullins house	2
Mr Hen. Kent	5
John Motteram	2
Hen. Hancock	1
Natha. Clay	2
Widdo. Rotheram	1
Gilbert Rotheram	2
George Boothe	1
Tho. Turner	2
Tho. Camme	2
George savidge	2
(one name obliterated)	
Fran Jones	1
Tho. Robinson	1
Widdo Tomson	1 noth
Tho. Turner	1
John Hancocke	1
Rob. stacy	1
Edward Leadbeater	1
Will. story	1 noth
Rich. Taylor	1
Rich Towndrowe	1
Georg Rippon	1 noth
Hen. Boothe	1
Rich Hobson	1
Will. shooter	1
Tho. Parkes	1
Tho. Chatborm	1 noth
Tho. Marriott	1
Mathew Dawson	1

(18)

Henry Bromhead	*1* noth
Rich. Boothe	2
Mr Steenson	3
John Taylor	1
Ralph Anderton	2
Will. Unwiyn	1
Natha. Creswicke	3
Will. Hobson	2
Mr Billam	3
Tho. newbould	2
Will. Crookes	1
Tho. Bunting	*1* noth
John Cade	2
Joseph Lockwood	*1*noth
John Bunting	1
Widdo Cowley	1
Widdo Greene	1
Tho. Unwyn	1
Rob. Boulsover	3
Tho. Boulsover	1

James Lee	2
George shooter	1
Rob. Higgenbotham	1
Hercules Cowlishawe	1
Tho. Westerne	1
John Newbould	2
Will. Bierley	1
John Litlewood	1
John Bingham	1
Tho. Bower	1
John Gervis	1
Mr Michal Burton	7
Mr Joseph stones	9
John Cade	1
John Turner sen.	1
John Turner Jun.	2
John staniforth	3

(19)

Mr Frances Ludlam	4
Henrey Haslehurst	3
Frances Haslehurst	1
Walter Whiley	1
Isaack Fentam	2
Anthony Kirby	1
	£ s d
harthes 338 is	*17.18.0*
	18-12-0

(one page blank)

20

Bramton in morton

Cornelius Clarke Esq.	12
Mr Geo. Heathcote	8
Hen. Folgambe	4
Geo. Calowe	4
will. Hibert	2
Peter Calton	6
John Barlow	1
Geo. Ashe	2
will. Newbould	1
Geo. Collis	1
John Stearnedale	2
John Bennet	1
Jer. Martine	3
James Buxton	2
will. Robertes	2
Elizab. Clay house	2
John Doe	2
John Hollis	2
will. Heaywood	1
Tho. Ashe	4
Geo. Bowre one decrese	2
John Williamat	1
James watkison one decrese	2
Tho. Greaves	1
Anne Fanshawe	2
wid. milnes	2
Tho. Cunday	1
Geo. Barloe	1
Geo. Hodkins	1
Peter Hibert	2
Geo. Newbould	1
	£ s d
harthes 78 is	3.18.00

(21)

The Towne of Barley

Mr Rob. Mowre	7
Mrs Marey Hall	7
Fran. Mower	7
Mr Godfrey Owterm	5
Fran. Owterm	4
Fran. Fowler	2
Geo. Hancocke	1
Rob. stevesson	2
Tho. Parker	1

Hen. Fowler	3
Hen. woostenholme	3
will. mowre	2
Edward Legas	3
Uxor Catton	2
Hen. and George Goodwine	4
will. Barghe	2
James Newton	1
Peter webster	2
will. spooner	2
Geo. Blackwall	2
Tho. Bennet	1
Tho. Tipping	3
Godfrey Travis	1
Geo. Hardista	1
John Hardista	2
Abraham Earnshaw	1
Char. Kirkland	1
will. Hancocke	1
John Cowper	3
George Cowper	1
Char. Greensmith	1
Fran. Hollily	1
Hen. ?Hancocke	*1*
Rob. Pidcocke	1
Geo. Calton	2
Geo. Hey	3
Geo. ?mellor	*1*
John Frost	2
Rob. stevenson	3
Lane End House	3
will. Curtis	1
will Heath	2

(22)

Tho. Ogdain	3
John stevison	*1 Ret*
Hen. wells	1
Tho. Taylor	1
Fran Garston	*1 Ret*
	£ s d
harths 101 is	5.1.00

Beachife

Edward Pegg Esq.	14
Rob. Foxe	3
Hen. Noe	1
Rich. Hand	1
Marke Foxe	1
Tho. smith	1
Rob. Hudson	2
Abra. Brownehill	1
Alis Goddart	1
John sonbey	1
Jane Hancocke	1
Richeard Ridge	1
Antho. Crooke	1
John Jonathan Cowley	1
Anthoney Foxe	1
	£ s d
Harths 31 is	1.11.00

(23)

Litle Normanton

Mr Allwood	4
John mariot	1
John Allwood	1
Ralph Tagge	1
Tho Brocksop	1
will. Richardson	2
Relph Tagge	2
Tho Reason	1
will. Towndar	1
Tho. Towndar	1
Fran. Allwood	1
John woodhouse	1
Rob. Tagge	1
Eliz. Cooper	1

	£ s d
harths 19	0.19.0

(24)

Calow

Tho. Cotrill } Mrs wagstafe }	5
Tho. stubing	4
James watkinson	3
John Bennet	3
Fran. Oxley	1
wido. Watson	1
Rich. watson	1
Thomas watson	1
Rob. watson	1
will. Flecher	2
Hen. Curtis	1
John Watson	2
Math. Ashe	1
Hen. Gearvis	1
Rich. Halleiy	3
will Brealesford	1
Fran. Oxley	1
Geo. singleton	1
Joseph shackloke	1
John Higgenbotham	1
Fran. Marshe	2
Geo. Higgenbotham	2
	£ s d
harths 39 is	1.19.00

(25)

Brackenfeild Wasington

John spateman Esq.	10
Mrs Revell	11
Rob. Hill	1
will. Beighton	1
Fran Tomlinson	1
Thomas wright	1
Tho. Keirkland	1
will. Masland	1
Ellen Orme	1
Rich. Taylor	4
Edward Hunt	2
John Grifstead	1
Edward wright	1
Mrs Newton	2
will. Fletcher	1
Geo. Radford	1
widd. Gregory	1
James swifte	1
Abrah. Hallos	2
Zac. Roper	1
Tho. Allen	1
will. Hill	1
widd. Haslam	1
Tho. Calowe	1
Geo. madder	1
widd. Hole	1
Rob. wright	2
Geo. wright	1
will. Handley	1
Lenouard Hunt	1
(one name obliterated)	
John Evarard	2
widd. walker	1
Tho. keynes	1
Tho. watkinson	1
Rich. marsh	1
Edward Barker	1
Josh. knowles	1
will. Foxe	...
will. Hill	...
Thomas Bramley	...
Tho. Bennet	...
	...
	£ s (d)
harths 69 is	3.9.(0)

(26)

Clowne

mr mace	4	
Tho. Johnson Retorned	3	Re
Geo. wilkson	1	
Rob. Baker	4	
Rich. Tompkin sen.	5	
Hen. wilkson	1	
John Redfearn	1	
Nich. Richardson	3	
John Butcher	4	
Tho. martin	1	
will. woodhed	3	
Dorothy Tidman wid.	2	
John wilson	2	
Tho. Butcher	2	
Rich. Tompkin Jun.	3	Re
will Johnson	2	
Rich. Croshawe	2	
will. shipman	1	
Rich. Thorneley	4	
will. Hage	5	Re
Geo. Johnson	1	
Godfrey watkinson	4	
John Hides	2	
Edward ?Buther	1	
Edward waynwright	2	
James watkinson	3	
Edmund woodhead	4	
Rich. Madin	1	
Tho. Kitchin	1	
Rich. Hurst Jun.	1	
Fran. sharples	2	
Geo. morton	1	
widdo. Barker	2	
Fran. Butcher	2	
Ralph Lambert	1	
Rich. Gravay (?Granay)	1	
Hen. Granay	1	

	£ s d
harths 72 is	*.....00*
	4 -3-0

(27)

southwinfeild Okerthorpe

Mr Emaneuwell Halton	7
Anthoney soton	2
Geo. Clarkeson	1
Mathew Plates	3
widdo. Thorpe	2
Geo. smithhorst	3
John Wilshaw	2
John Lambert	3
Tho. Plates	3
Anthoney Gefrey	1
Nicho. williamson	2
Hen. hellott	2
Hen. williamson	1
John Bludworth	2
Edward Vardin	1
Geo. Gonson	1
Rob. mather	1
Geo. Taylor	2
widdo Blithe	1
mr ?Cothes	3
Mrs Newton	6
will. Hearyes	2
widdo. ?Batman	1
mr sterley	3
widdo Tomlinson	1
John Harvy	1
will. Hodges	4
will. Mellars	2
Rob. Tomlinson	2
Fran. Machen	1
widdo sudberey	2
Rob. Newton	1
widdo Redford	2

Hen. smith	1
Tho. Browne	1
Mary Radford	1
	£ s d
harths 74 is	3.14.00

(28)

Newbould

Mr Geo. Milnes	6
Rob. Poynton	3
Fran. Moore	3
Rich. Hancocke	2
sebis Marcorum	1
Fran. Allwood	1
Geo. shearman	4
John spure	3
widdo Browne	2
John Webester	1
Hugh Beastall	1
Hugh shearman	1
Michaell Browne	1
will. Chowe	1
Tho. Tomlinson	2
mr Hen. Foulgambe	6
Rich. Webster	2
John shore	1
will. Leey	1
will. Haye	2
Geo. Ashe	3
widdo Ragge	2
will. Calow	2
will. sawer	3
Edward Goodwin	2
Peeter webster	2
Thom. Haye	1
James shawe	2
John Browne	2
Godfrey webster	3
Rich. Nayler	1
mathew webster	2
Rob. Redfearn	1
sam. Fowler	4
Paule Flecher	1
Rob. Johnson	1
will. sanford	1
Tho. Saxbey	1
Fran. Passe	1
John Curtis	1

(29)

will. webster	2
Tho. wood	1
will. shearman	2
Geo. Johnson	2
(one name obliterated)	
Rob. Levicke	2
	£ s d
89 harths is	4.9.00

30

Blackwall

mr John wilkinson	3
John Marriott	2
John Turner	2
Tho. Kite	2
John Boote	1
John Brucke	4
Edward smison	2
Obediah Boote	3
mr John Richardson	7
John wileson	2
John Ufton	1
will. Eyre	2
will. Thorpe	2
Tho. Thorpe	1
Godfrey Richardson	1
will. Thorpe Jun.	1
Tho. Buckland	1

John strut	1
mathew welsh	2
widdo Calowe	2
Rich. Buckland	2
widdo Foxe	1
Richard strutt	1
will. Coe	1
John Morley	1
Randaleph Boultby	1
John Blythe	1
John smith	2
John Haslam	1
widdo Thorpe	1
Edward Boote	2
will. Boote Jun.	1
will. Keirkland	2
mr Allsop or John Brunt	1
Edward Clay	1
	£ s d
harths 61 is	3.1.00

(31)

Killamarsh

John Turner	1
Geo. ward	3
widdo Kesteevien	2
Rob. Champin	2
Fran. Atkin	1
John Ward	2
Nicho. Adkin	2 Re
will. Plates	1
wid. Lee	1
will. Moore	1 Re
John Cooper	2
James ?Golland	3
wid. ?Golland	1
John Dobbe	1
Tho. Coole	1
Rob. Hatersley	1
wid. Harris	2
John Poole	2
Rob. Booker	1
Godfrey Harris	4
Rob. Hurst	1
Tho. Howldworth	2
Rich. Hall	1
Tho. Bilum	3
Rich. Whithead	1
Hen. Browne	1
John White	2
wid. Murfin	8
Rob. Harrison	2
Rob. Hewitt	1
Cris. Hill	1
John Turnor	1
wid. Morton	1 No
Humphrey morton	1
will. Water	...

(32)

Cris. Rutherford	1
John Harris	3
will Hall	1
Rich. Hanley	1
Fran Crookes	1
Tho. Worthington	1
Cris. Atkines	1
John wright	1
Will. Porter	2
Geo. Huggill	1
wido. Burd	1
will. Machen	1
Godfrey Harris	2
	£ s d
harths 74	*3.14.00*
	3-18-0

Morton

Mr Edmund Nixon	5
Tho. wilde	4
Rob. Heald	1
James Haveracke	1
James sidden	1
Edward Taylor	1
Arthur Milnes	1
Rob. Turner	1
Ralph smith	2
Tho. Clarke	1
Rich. Eyre	1
Edward Eyre	1
Will. Eyre	1
will. smith	2
James Parsons	2
John Dobbe	4
will. Tallence	1
Cris. Marrott	1
will. Bankes	1
Rich. Hartley	2

(33)

John Barlowe	2
John Eyre	1
John Melores	1
Geo. Beardall	2
Tho. Ragge	2
Tho. Lynam	1
will. Kyrkes house John dobb	C 2*Re*
wid. Kyrke	2
Tho. Hurt	2
Godfrey wasse	1
John Oldam	1
Ralph Hartley	1
will. Parsons	2
Geo. Ragge	2 no
Tho. Alsebrooke	2

wid. willson	2
Rich. wilson	3
will. winge	2
Rich. Barlowe	1
Doctor Berisford	7
Tho. wood	1
Tho. wilson	1
James Brough	2
James Braylsford	1
Theop Ashbury	2
Rob Clay	1
will. shorte	1
Tho. Hilton	1
James Pendleton	1
Geo. Beardall	1
John willson	1
Dorothy Braylsford	1
Edmund Brocksoppe	2
Rich. watkinson	1
Geo. savadge	3
Rich. Ashmore	3

(34)

Hen. Ashmore	2 Re
Rob. statham	1
Rob mottershawe	1
wid. Browne	1
Edward Ragge	2
John shawe	1
John Cowper	1
Geo. Ragge	2
John Alwood	1
John Braylsford	1
Rob. Parsons	1 No
James Askey	1
wid. Askey	2
	£ s d
harths 106	*5- 6-00*
	5-13-0

South Normanton

And Pinxton

Fran. Revell Esq.	15
mr Fulwood	2
Geo. stubing	3
Geo. Dobb	2
John Marriott	4
will. Fletcher	1
will. Rowbotham	2
Rich. Hodson	2
Rich. Parson	1
wid. wilson	1
John Downinge	1
Fran. Basford	2
Geo. Fostard	1
Tho. Frith	1
James Farrand	2
Rich. Johnson	1
Tho. Marriott	1
Rich Marriott	2
John Marriott	1
Rich. Gent	1
Antho. Oldam	1

(35)

Mathew ?Downinge	2
widdo. Marcroft	1
Tho Benningeton	1
Rob Gibson	1
Cade ?mullider	2
Nicholas willas	1
John spalton	1
widdo Ashmore	1
Tho. spalton	1 Re
Cor. Bowringe	1
wid. Flint	1
Edward Wilde	1
Edward Robinson	2
will. Byfeild	1
Edward Cooke	3
will. simpson	1
Fran. Marsh	1
John Allcocke	2
John sewell	1
Hen. Hatton	3
Rob. Ryley	4
Tho Marshall	5
John Crawshawe	2
Tho. Jackson	2
will. Downinge	2
James Herringe	1
Tho. salmon	2
mr Meeke	2
will. Innosent	2
John Farnworth	3
will. Hather	1
will. Tavener & will. whittaker	2
will. Duffeild	1
Fran. Walton	1
Edward strawe	1
Mich. Lee	1
Edward Rooke Burned	*1 Re*
Barth. Lee	?1

(36)

John Wright Burned downe	(blank)
Tho Machen	1
Richard Tagg	2
Fran. Cooke	1
Tho. Hynde	1
widdo spurre	1
Rich. newton	1
	£ s
harths 114 is	5.*14.0*
	16-0

Could Aston

mr John Reveell	3
mr Andrew morewood	10
mr Thomas Kent	7
Tho. Cartledge	2
Tho. Thorpe	4
John Blyth Jun.	1
John Blyth sen.	2
Tho Newbould	1
James Bradbery	2
Godfrey Burton	2
John woodhouse	1
Antho. Parker	1
Edward Benitt	2
Antho wright & will. mewe	3
John Baines	2
Godfrey Haslam	2
will. Bleyth sen.	1
widdo. Bleyth	1 Cr
Phill. Madin	1
Tho Mitchell	3
will. woodhose	2
Rob. Maden	1
Jonath. Brodbotham	1
Rob. white	2
Tho. Fearnes	1
Rich Marples	1
Geo. Billam	1
Mich. Mosley	1
Geo. Turner	2
(37)	
Rob. Pinder	1 Cr
Mich Burrowes	1
Edward Cooke	1
	£ s d
harths 64	*...*
	3-6-0

Dore and Totcley

Mr Frn. Burton Esq.	4
Cris. yellot	1
Geo. Newbould	2
Rob. Greaves	1
Rich Greaves	1
Cris. Greene	1
Rob. Greene	1
Ralph willkinson	1
Ralph Hepwood (?Hexwood)	1
Fran. woodhouse	1
Lyonell martin	2
Fran. Barker	1
Edward Delton (?Dolton)	2
Math. Boouth	1
James Britland	3
Tho. Fisher	2
Fran. ?Roworth	1
Hen. Greeaves	1
Tho. Dolton	1
will. Greene	2
Rob. Oveliner (?Oveliver)	1
will. woodhouse	2
Antho. woodhouse	1
simon swiffte	1
mr Fran. Barker	5
Antho. Bright	6
Hen. Greaves	3
(38)	
John Morton	3
Charlis Greenewood	2
Fran. Clarke	2
James siddale	1
James Newbould	1
will. stevesson	2
Antho. Cutlove	1
Andrew Milnor	1
John Evanes	1

Rob. Colton	1
Rich Dungmarsh	3
Hugh stephson	1
Tho. Leadbeater	1
Rob Onwin	1
John Dande	2
Rich wagge	3
Hen. Greene	3
Nicho. Hage	1
John Carnill	2
Rob Pindor	1
Geo. Barbor	1
Cris. Berley	1
John Turnor	2
Rich. Redfearn	3
John Greaves more	1
Geo. Britland	2
John Greaves Rosit	1
Rob. woolhouse	1
Anne Fisher	1
Michell Oates	2
Rob. Newbould	1
John Hallot	2
John Honton	1
standales House	1
Geo. Fisher	1
Antho Bright high greene	1
harths 104 is	5.4.0

(39)

Whitwell

Mr Camfeild	8
Mrs Clayton	11
mr smith for the Chamber at the Hall	1
mr smith for Furbicke	4
mr Rodes	7
Geo. smith of ?Burneleas	1
Mr Major	5

John Lee	*Re*
Tho spensor	1
mr Renshawe	4
mr Crosse	3
mr Bradshawe	3
mr Rich. Coates	1
mr Roger Coates	3
John Hadfeild	4
Gam. Fordham	1
John Flower	1
John Bullivant	1
Rich. Harrison	1
John woodhead	2
Antho. Wattes	1
Fran. schoolay	2
Geo. Kentt	1
widdo. Reiney	1
math. Roobotham	1
Mich. Bullock	1
Hugh sissonn	2
will. walker	1
Roger Renshawe	3
Rob. Berne	1
Geo. Revell	1
*Tho. ...	*... Re*
wid. Hurst	3
will. Marchall	1
Fran Milnes	1
John Lambert	2

40

Tho. White	1
Hugh Eyre	1
John mee	1
Margrit sisson	1
John staniland	1
John whithead	1
John Foxe	1
Fran Harrison	1

Rich Harrison	1
Rich. Binney	1
John Haworth	2
Fran schooley house	1
John wildsmith	1
wid. Foxe	1
will. schooly	1
wid. Harrison	1
Geo. Harrison	1
Rich starkey	1
Rich. Crookes	1
John Bulliavant	3
Godfrey Allisson	1
Fran. woodhead	1
Geo. Lane	1
John Read	2
wid. sisson	2
Rob. woodhouse	2
John Foxe	1
John Kenderwell	1
Rich. Reaness	1
mr Rogger Vessey	6
Tho. Marshall	1
Fran. westby	2
	£ s d
harths 128 is	*6. 8.0*
	6-11-0

(41)

Walton

mrs Jenkinson	13
mr Paull Jenkinson	7
Thomas Gouche	2
John Holland	3
Rich. Milnes	1
Godfrey stubing	1
Geo. Brough	3
wid. Oliver	?1
mr Paull Jenkinson Ju.	3
Tho. Nedham	1
Edward Hurst	1
Godfrey Harvey	1
John Heywood	2
Edward Bagshay	1
Rob. Brigges	2
Hen. Harvey	3
Godfrey Beard	1
Martin walton	1
will. Brough	3
Rob. Pyonton	2
Godfrey Brough	1
Paull Hogge	2
Ralph Dakin	1
Tho. Coupe	2
Rich. Hogge	1
mr John Care(?r)	2
sam. Keale	1
sam. Howle	1
stephen Foucher	1
	£
harths 64	3.4.00

(42)

Bramton

Abraham Cressey	3
James Alleatson	1
Cornelius Arnold	4
Cornelius Jackson	7
John Bradshaw	2
Isack Bridon	2
wid. Brucke	1
Antho. Bagaley	2
John Browne	1
Rob. Boute	4
Hen. Allen	2
Rob. swift	1
Gill. watkinson	3
Godfrey Bradshawe	1

Hen. Bright	1
Geo. Bowre	3
Geo. Halland	4
Rob. Barker	3
James Revell	1
Peter Cowley	1
Hen. Browne	1
Tho. Bamford	1
Geo. Bor...	1
Godfrey Bore	2
Godfrey Clarke Esq.	16
mrs Briggit Clarke	7
Ralph Loe	2
Elizabeth Croftes	9
Geo. Calow	1
John Calow	1
Fran. Calow	1
will. shaw	1
Abra. Cunday	1
will. Dobb	1
John shaw	1
James Drable	1
Godfrey Foliambe	3
Deborah Phips	2

<u>43</u>

John Foliambe	2
Ralph Flecher	1
Antho. Haslam	2
Antho Heath	3
will. Hibbert sen.	1
James Taylor	1
Joseph Heath	1
John Hawkeslye	1
John steveson	1
John Hibbert	1
will. Heywood	1
Tho. Riggat	3
wid. Learam	2
Godfrey Leineker	2
wid. Lach	1
James Limm	1
Rob. Roe	1
John Loe	2
mr Mathewman	6
Tho. Midleton	1
Godfrey Midleton	1
Rob. Mosley	2
Rob. Mason	1
Fran. Margenison	1
Rob. Madin house	1
Ralph Mather	1
Rob. Margenison	1
James Midleton	1
Tho. Mellor	1
Tho. Masson	1
wid. Mosley	2
James Hartley	1
John Reading	1
Geo. Revell sen.	1
Geo. Revell Jun.	1
wid. Allwood	2
Ralph Renshawe	2
Cris. Renshawe	1
John Revell	1
Fran. swiffte	7

<u>44</u>

?James shawe	3
Rob. sutton	3
Nicholas swift	2
Godfrey stevison of Hem greene	1
Godfrey stevison Hill Top	3
Hen. scoror one decrese	1
will. Harison	3
Math. symms	3
John stones	4

John stevenson	2
James stevenson	1
Godfrey stephsnson	1
Geo. shawe	2
Godfrey smithe	1
Rob. Turner	2
Hen tomlinson	3
Antho stevenson	1
mr Godfrey watkinson	8
wid wattes of Loades	3
Tho. wattes one decrese	2
Joseph wattes	1
Godfrey watkinson	1
Edman white of more	1
Edman white	1
Tho. white	1
Geo. wilkes	1
Tho. wesstorne	1
Godfrey younge	1
Godfrey wattes Loeades	2
James ward	2
Edward Marshe	1
Rob. Marieneson	1
will. willcockson	1
Rob. Turner	2
	£ s
harths 229 is	*11.9.0*
	11-11-0

(45)

whittington

mr James Hewett	3
Godfrey stubing	5
Geo. sikes	1
Elizabeth Hall	1
Rob. Hewitt	1
James Bellffit	1
John stansall	1
Mary Quicksall	1

Geo. wostenholme	2	
Mary wostenholme	1	
John Hall	1	
Geo. wright	1	
Mary Holmes	1	
stephen Moore	1	
Hen. Lowe	1	de
Rob. Hewitte for Lowe House	1	
John Renshawe	1	
Godfrey Eege	2	
Tho. Ingram	1	
Mr Riveingtons house	5	
John Nayler & Rich Bankes	4	
John Geffrey	2	Cr
John Hynde	3	
Godfrey Beard	1	
Godfrey Hownesfeild	2	
will. Morledge	2	
will. sprentall	3	
Hen. Nealor	1	
solomon Lowe	1	
Ephraim Holmnes	1	
James Eege	1	
John Key	1	
Elizabeth Boeler	1	
Tho. Gillott	2	
Rob. Pearson	2	
Rich Pearson	1	

(46)

Rich. Pearson Jun.	1
Laurence Pearson	1
mr Nchlos sanderson	4
John webster	2
Geo. Plumtree	1
Tho. Gillberthorpe	4
Elizabeth Lowe	2
Hen Lowe for mille	1

James Naylor		2	
Godfrey webster		3	
will. moore		1	
Godfrey Cosen		1	
Rob. Bellffitt		2	
Martin wostenholme		1	
Geo. Roger		1	*Ret*
Hen. Hartley		1	
Antho. Banckes		1	
Tho. dowker mill		1	
Tho. Bottes		1	
Tho. Knowles		1	
Rich. Linley	Cr	1	
Peter webster	Cr	1	
Anne stansall	Cr	1	
Elizabeth Forrist	Cr	1	

Dunston Hamlitt

John Ouldfeild	1	
Fran. swifft	1	
wid. swifft	3	
Edward Pedley	2	
Rob. Eyre	2	
will. woodhouse	2	
Arthor Trickett	1	
John Hunt sen.	*2	Ret*
John Hunt Juno.	1	
Nicholas Milnor	2	
Tho. Hoppe	1	
John Madin	1	
will. Poynton	2	
Laurence Passe	1	
John Roper	1	
John Ouldfeild Jun.	1	

(47)

wid. Hage	2
Tho. Hage	1
Nicholas Thornally	1

Brimington Hamlet

mr Gill Esq.	11
mr will. Milnes	8
John Litlewood	1
mr Bennitt	3
Edward Hadfeild	1
will. Kesteven	1
John Mettam	3
Anne Bingham	1
Tho. Galley	2
Berthe. Joanes	2
Philip Hobson	2
will. Marriott	1
Margret saxton	1
will. Mason	3
Tho. smith	2
Antho. Challnor	1
Geo. Boeler	2
Godfrey Bingham	2
Elizabeth Cartlidge	2
Godfrey widdoson	2
Bartho. Hounsfeild	2
John Bagshawe	2
Bartho. Fretwell	3
Edward Bramall	1
Rob. Hallam	1
dyna smith	1
Fran. Bamall	1
Geo. Bate	2
John Boler	2
Tho. Cocker	1
George Gill	1
Rob. Glossop	1
harths 187 is	9.7.00

(the 7 shillings is altered to 14)

Little normanton with the
?said particular names ...
mr Alwood with 13 particulers

are named here followeth
(added in a different hand)

(48)

Glapwell

Thomas woollouse Esq.	9	
wid. Pawson	1	
Rob. spalton	1	
Fran. Heath	1	
Rob. Haigh	1	
John Hardwicke	1	
Max needham	1	
will. Mason	1	
Rob. Brailsford	1	
Rich. Coope	1	Not
Tho. Colbecke	2	
John searsey	1	
will. Hardwicke	1	
John Hawe	1	
Tho. Tetlowe	1	
will. wheeldon	2	
Tho. whithead	1	
John Hardwicke Jun.	1	
Edmund Brumley	1	
Roger Jepson	1	
Rich. Eyre	1	
Hugh Fisher	1	
will. waples	1	
Hester Clay	1	
Rich. Haslam	1	Not
James Jackson	1	
	£ s d	
harths 34 is	1.14.00	

(the 14 is altered to 16)

Tibshelfe Oxcroft

mr Twentyman	6	
John Holmes	3	
John Clarke	3	
Rich. Parson	2	
John Crofts	2	
will. Morley	3	
John Smith	3	
Lawrence Marson	3	
Hen Townsend	1	
James Hill	1	
Rich Buckland	1	

(49)

will. Buckland	2	
Rich. Turner	1	
Rich Blythe	2	
Rich Buckland	1	
will. welche	1	
Alice Morley	1	
will. Buckland	1	
Rich. Turner Jun.	1	
Cris Moorgates	1	
Tho. Buckland	2	
Tho. Clarke	1	
John ?Mosley Jun.	1	
will. Bingham	1	
Tho. Hynde	1	
Rich. Haslam	1	
Rich. Clarke	2	
Tho stringer	1	
will. Cartwright	1	
will. Adlington	2	
Will. Boote	1	
silvester Hill	1	
John smith	1	No
Tho. smith	1	No
wid. stringfelowe	1	
Rich Morley	1	
will. ?withers	2	
Tho. Woodhead	1	
Henrey Jenkinson	1	
John spitlehouse	1	

Geo. symson	1	
John ?Eudson	1	No
Fran. Alleson Jun.	1	
Fran. Alleson sen.	1	
Will. Alleson	1	
	£	
harths 66 is	*3.6.00*	
	3-7-0	

<u>50</u>

<u>Boulesover</u>

will. deuke of Newcast(le)	36	
The vicaridg	5	
The Parsonage	(blank)	
Geo. Cullambell	5	
will. Brameley	1	
John Hill sen.	2	
wid. Foulkes	4	
Tho Hinde	3	
Humphry spitlehouse	3	
Edward Hinde	1	
Jeffry stubing	1	
Tho. Cusen	1	
will. Fenteman	1	
John Fretwell	2	
wid. warwicke	1	
Rob Machin	4	
John Achors	8	
Tho Butcher	4	
Tho Baker	2	
Tho. stanley	3	
Tho. Taylor	3	
Tho. Northedge	3	
will. Robinson	2	
Edward Backer	3	
Gill. Backer	3	
wid. southworth	3	
John Beely	1	
John Peace	1	
John youle	4	
wid. Backer	2	
wid. youle	2	
Tho. Kitchen	4	
Tho. Mazrine	3	
John Cozen	1	
Tho. smith	3	
Hen. Barlow	4	
Mr John smithson	6	
will. Coozen	1	

(<u>51</u>)

Will. shirtecliffe	1	
Rich Baker	2	
Tho. Willson	1	
Rich. Heaywood	1	
Geo. Hallum	1	
Ridgenall Beely	1	
sam. Levssley	1	
Rob. Ince	2	
Rob. shipston	1	
wid. spitlehouse	1	
James Bull	1	
John stancall	2	
John stasey	2	Re
*Cris. H...	1*	
Rich. Hutchinson	1	
Edward Britten	1	
John Cooke	1	
John Tripit	1	

<u>woodhouse</u>

Joseph willson	5	
Fran. Lache	7	
will. Haye	2	Re
Joseph Jackson	1	
Humphrey smale	2	
Humphrey spitlehouse	1	
Rob. Frithe	1	

Gill Baker	3	
Ralph Flint	1	Re
Tho Green	1	
Tho Godley	1	
Oliver Baker	1	
John shorte	1	
Fran. Allitson	1	Re
John Ludlam	3	
John Duckmanton	?1	

(52)

wholey

John Clarke	1	
mr George Roson	4	
Tho. Poynton	3	
Edmund Beely	1	
Rich Granner	1	
Rich Greene	2	
John sission	3	
John Barker	1	
will. Cozen sen.	1	
John Carter	2	
will. Wardlowe	2	
Hen. Amery	1	
Rob. Thorpe	1	
	£ s d	
harths 204 is	*10. 4.0*	
	10-11-0	

(the 204 seems originally to have been 105 and the 4 shillings 5)

scarclife & Paulterton

mr John Jaquis	2	
Thomas Bromhed	2	
will. Kesteven	1	
John Kesteven	1	
Tho. shipston		
Tho. stepheston	2	
stephen Jeffrey	1	
Rob spray	1	
John Lawrence	1	
Rob Jeffrey	1	
Rob Greaves	1	Cr
Alis spray	1	
John spray	1	
Fran. spalton	1	
John Tomson	1	
John Rauson	1	
widd. ?Cramme	1	
Godfrey stephenson	1	

(53)

widd. Kitchen	1	Cr
will Marr	1	
widdo Haigh	1	
John Bennet	1	
John storth	2	
Rich. woodhead	1	
Edward Taylor	1	
John Heath	1	
Mary Camme	1	
John Greene	3	
Humphrey Clayton	3	
Cris. mellors	1	
Anne sudberey	1	not
will. Kesteven	1	
John Foxe	1	
John Hill	1	
will. Bennet	1	
Rob. Cowley	2	
wid. Hearnshawe	1	
Joseph stanley	1	
Rob Clay	1	
Hen. Roides	2	
Edw. Whittaker	1	
John smoote	1	
will. Bradley	1	Cr

Geo. Heath	1	
Tho Clough	2	
Rob. stevenson	1	Cr
will. Thorneley	2	
Edw. Robson	1	
John Cowpe	1	
wid. Kitchen	1	
Hum. Clayton	3	
Tho. Taylor	1	
John Catlin	1	
will. whitaker	1	
James Blodworth	1	
John Lister	1	

(54)

Timothy Robinson	1	
Will. steenson	1	
Wid. Webster	1	
Tho. Godber	1	
mary Royall	1	
Isaack Ludlam	2	
Rob. Bankes	1	
Tho. Bakon	2	
Fran. nedham	2	
Will. Bradley	2	
John Coggin	2	
	£	
harths 80	4.	0.0

(the 0 shillings has been altered to 5)

Dranfeild

Fran. Burton Esq.	9	
for Mrs Blyth house	8	
Widd. Morewood	7	
Tho. Dand	3	
Geo. stenrode	1	
Agustin Jackson	2	
mrs Mowsley	2	
John stenrode	4	
Mrs Richardson	3	
Mrs ward	2	Cr
Mr Mason for schole	3	
John Bate	3	
vichridg howse	4	
Tho. Fisher	4	
John Rotherham ju.	5	
Tho. stephenson	1	Cr
Tho. Greenewood	3	
John nayler	3	
will Hancocke	1	
mr John Blyth	1	
Tho. Calton	4	

(55)

Geo. Browne	1	
Rob. Browne	1	
Rich. Rewell & his sonne Robert	3	
Anne Downes	1	Cr
Rob. Greenewood	3	
Rob. Masson	3	
widdo. Drable sen.	2	
widdo. Drable Jun.	6	
Anne wright & John wright	2	
Alice wayne & John Bate	5	
James Greaves	1	
Rich. Greaves	1	
Geo. Drable	3	
John Rotherham	3	
Edward Greenwood	5	
Katha. Taylor	6	
John Downes	2	
Gill. walton	2	
John Boorr	1	Cr
Geo. young	3	
Geo. Plattes	1	
steph. wattson	2	

will. Owtrem	4
Harris house	2
Edward smith	1
Rob. Greenewood	
Rob. ward for sowwood house	2
John Carver	1
Rob. ward	1
John Drable	1
Hen. Clay	1 Cr
Tho. Mather	1
soper Lane house	2
Edward smith	5
Fran. Frith	1
Hen. womacke	2
widdo. smith	1 Cr
Thomas Taylor	3
Rich. Taylor	1
will. Harris	1
Jo. smith	1 Cr

(56)

wood house & stubley

mr Tho. Eare	5
Rich Frost	2
Godfrey swift	2
Rotherham Linney	3
Edward Bunting	2
Fran. sikes	2
mr Slater	7
Geo. stevenson	2
Fran. ?Parcker	2
John Mason	3
Geo. Glover	1
Ralph vougham	1
Fran. Cartledge	2
Antho. Mason	1
Antho. Hancocke	3
Edw. Jackson	1
widdo Mellor	2
Tho. Alfreton	1
Hen. Bright	1
Geo. Hancocke	1
Geo. stephenson	3
James Bennet and Geo. ?steynrel	3
Peeter Booth	1
Adam Bromhead	1

Cowley

Tho. Allen	4
Gill. Cooke	2
widdo Naylor	1
Fran. Hancocke	3
Tho. Rogder	1
Arthor Ovsn	1
John Heaworth	1
James Bennet	2
widdo Keirke	1 Re.
John Eyenes	1 Re
Peter Pindor	1
Elen newbould	1
Rob. french	1 Cr
	£ s
harths 222 is	11.2.00

(the 2 shillings has been altered to ?13)

57

Norton

Cor. Clarke Esq.	18
Fran. Barker Esq.	10
mr John storey for Bradway	11
mr John Moorwood	12
mr Trickett	5
nich. stones	9
John storrey for Hasle Borro	11
Rob Ashton	7

Andre Creven	4
mrs Anne Gell	6
mrs Mary wood	5
mr Bleyth	7
Tho. Bullocke	3
John Gillatt	5
John Parker	5
Tho. Bearley	8
John Poynton	3
Tho. Camme	4
Rob. Rowlinson	4
John North	1
Geo. Ourton	5
Antho. Barton	2
John Barten	3
Geo Turner	4
Jos. Barton	4
James Atcken	1
sam. Atcken	4
Edward Hudson	1
Rich. Gillatt	2
Cornelas Clarke	3
John Batte	3
Geo. Martin	3
Tho. Creswicke	4
widdo Bate	1
James Bate	5
Anne Poynton widdo	1
Geo. Renny	2
John Barten	3
John ?Bayse (?Bayge)	3

(58)

John Greene	2
Rob. Greene	1
John Rose	3
Phill. Atkin	2
Edward wood	6
will. Parker	2
Rob. Atkin	1
Tho. waynewright	5
Alice Gillot	1 Reto
Rich. Gillot	3 Reto
Rob. Atkin sen.	1
Alice Poynton	1
Joseph Thornelly	3 Reto
Rouland Parker	1
will. Flecher	1
John north	1
Tho Hall	1
Geo. Orton	1
Will. selvester	1
Tho. Roades	2
John Bowman	1
Rich. Gillot	2
Geo. Nuttall	1 Re
Tho. England	1
Hugh Gothard	3
Tho. wacker	1
Will. Rusell	2
Geo. Anderton	2
Will. Barton	1
Josph Jackson	2
Rob. Tuerner	2
John Bawtrey	1
Will. Throope	1
Cris. Barton	1
Tho. Flecher	1
Nicho. Cartwright	2
John Moore	1 *Reto*
Will. Brownehill	1
Tho. Bigne	2
Will. Patericke	3
Charles Bawer	3

(59)

Widdo spooner	4
Nicho. Cartwright	

Will. Nawles	2	
Will. woolhouse	1	
widdo. Bigni	1	
Joes. Thornelly	1	
Fran. Atkin	2	
Geo. Urton	3	
John Lee	6	
Oliver newbould	1	
Will. Jackson	1	
Rob. Hicke	1	
Widdo. nitingalle	1	
Tho. Jackson	1	
stephen wall	3	
Rob. Brownehill	1	
Edward North	1	
Fran. Reaney	6	
Will. Bate	1	
Rob. willson	1	*Re*
James Bigni	3	
Rich Bowlesover	1	
Widdo Joanes	2	
Will. Bockin	1	
Will. Greene	1	
Tho. Ropper	1	
Row. Gillot	2	
Fran. ?Calton (?Catton)	2	
Edward Wood	1	
mr Roades for the schoole	2	
Will. Greene	1	
Tho. Keworth	3	
Rob. Waynewright	2	
Mat. Clayton	1	
Rob. Clay	1	
Edw. Brownehill	1	
Godfrey Rusell	2	
Antho. Cartwright	2	*Re*
Hen. Andrew	1	
harths 325 is	*16.5.0*	
	16-13-0	

(the 13 has been altered to 14, or vice versa)

60

Stawley

John Lord Frechwell	30
mr Ralph Heathcoate	5
mr John Frogat	7
Fran. Marples	2
Geo. Calow	1
Peeter Murfeild	1
James Frith	1
Tho. Brailesford	3
Godfrey wiker	1
Widdo Cadman	1
Isack Johnson	1
John Mader	2
Rob. smith	2
John Alcrofte sen.	1
John Allcrofte Jun.	1
Peeter Litlewood	1
John Frith	1
John Guddy	1
Peeter Frith	1
Peeter harwood	1
John Goostrey	3
John smith	1
John mader or Peter	1
Will Darby	1
Phill. steele Jun.	2
Phill. steele sen.	2
Peter steele	1
John Wilson	2
Rob Litlewood	1
Peter Cadman	1
Rich. Cadman	1
sampson Cadman	3
Gearvis Browne	2
Peter shipston	1

Gearvis Deare	1
Peter smith	1
Tho. Brailesford	4
Hen. Low	4
Tho Johnson	1

(61)

John Bradwall	1
Peter Parker	2
widdo wodson	1
Will. Hollingworth	2
Chawner house	1
James Royston	1
Rob steele	1
hen. steele	1
Martin Harrison	2
Widdo Farne	1
Rob Hewitt	1
Rich. Juggs	1
mr Rob Browne	2
mr Roger Newham	3
Tho. Roger	1
*sampson Cadman	?3*
John Pickeforke	1
Hen. Norman	1
Tho. Chapman	1
Widdo Hodgkinson	1

John Mason	3
Peter Willson	1
Fran. Heathcote	1
Richard Renshaw	1
Will. Roger	3
Rob. Arthur	2
Rob. Browne	1
Hen. Cade	1
Peter Browne	2
Anthony Renshaw	1
Widdo Frith	1
Tho. wright	2
Will. wright	2
Hen. Galles	1
John Kirke	1
Rob. shipston	1
Tho. starsall	1
John starsall	2
Tho. Turner & John	3
Godfrey Bright	4

(62)

Godfrey Edge	2
Tho. Turner	2
Widdo Bilby	1
John Marshall	3
Widdo Marshall	1
Tho. Johnson	1
Rob. Turner	2
John Hitch	2
Tho. Gee	2
Rich. Jackson	1
Widdo Osborne	1
Rich. Dewhorst	1
Anthony Banin	1
Widdo Booth	2
Hen. Roger	2
Rob. Litlewood	2
Tho. Litlewood	3
John newbould	1
Rich Coates	1
Tho. smith	2
Tho. Pinder	2
John Ellis	1
Will. Roger	2
Wid. Taylor	2
Anthony Huchinson	3
Tho. Preestlow	1
Peter steeven	1
John steeven	2

John Thorpe	1	
Will. Turnor	2	
mr Bowman	1	
John Parker	2	
Fran. Glossop	2	
Hugh Crofte	1	
John smith	2	
Rob Firth	1	
will. Perigo	1	Cr
Geo. Babb	1	Cr
	£ s d	
217 harths is	10.17.0	

(63)

Wingerworth

sr Hen. Humlocke Bor.	14	
Rob. Alsebrooke	2	
Hugh storer	2	
John Fidler	2	
Tho. Ouldfeild	1	
Will. Hurst	1	
Jesper Walker	1	
Hen. Wharton	1	
Tho. Pararmore	1	
Ralph Eastmeat	1	
Will. Mowson	1	
Edw. ?Gibbon (?Gibson)	2	
Nicho. Alsibrooke	1	
Will. Greaves	1	
Gartrude Greaves	2	
Rob Peace	1	
Tho Cowpe	2	
John Ludlam	1	
Hen vickers	2	
Georg Waterhouse	1	
Emanuall Reding	1	
Fran. Webster	1	
Will. scorer	1	
Will. Pursall	1	
Wid. or George Peace	2	
Geo. Rooth	1	*Re*
Rob. Clay	1	
Phillip Child	1	
John Ludlam Jun.	1	
Rowland Greene	1	
Widdo Greene	1	re
Edward Newton	2	
Widdo Cowley	2	Re
Tho Farre	4	
Will. Knowles	2	
John Wattes	2	
sam. Greaves	1	
James Greaves	1	

(64)

Tho. Parker	2	
Fran. Milward	1	
John Damport	1	
Godfrey Gibbon	1	
John Holland	2	
Peter Bennet	1	
Fran Scales	1	
Tho. Thomlinson	1	
Tho Holland	2	
Rob Mellor	1	
Will. Calow	1	ret
Fran swift	1	
Thurstam scales	1	
Tho Gladwin Esq.	6	Re
sam. Rotherham	3	
mr James Webster	5	
Tho. Brealsford	3	
Fran. Clay	3	
Will. steenson	1	
Godfrey Ashley	1	noth
John steenson	1	
James Flecher	1	
Tho. Legg	1	

Tho. Tingle	1
Geo. Ashley	2
stephen Coupe	1
Rich. Wattson	1
	£ s
harths 101 is	5.12.00

4-0-0

(65)

Hasland

Edw. Croshawe	7
Rich. Mossley	3
Fran Hardey Jun.	3
Will. Huchinson	2
Tho. Foulds	1
Will. Marshe	1
Edw. Brocksoppe	2
John Reddige	1
mr Websters House	1
Fran. Hardey sen.	2
Geo. Lowe	2
Fran. Widdowson	1
Ralph Britland	2
Geo. Widdowson	1
Will. Higgenbotham	2
mr shawe sen.	6
mr shawe of spitle	7
mr Wheeldon	5
mr Jenkinson of spitle	7
Tapton Hall	7
Will. Taylor	1
Will. Winchester	1
Fran. Hides	1 noth
Will. Watson	1
Rich. Hides	2
mr Bloodworth	5
Will. Lawrence	1
mr Carre	5
	£ s d
harths 79 is	*3.19.00*

(66)

sutton & Duckmanton

Ncholas Earle of scarsdale	26
mr Tho. Freeman	7
mr Rich. Needham	7
mr Puckering	2
Will. Roberts	5
Hen Chantrey	4
Tho. Allwood	1
John Heath	1
Godfrey Tallent	2
Will. Dowman	1
Tho. Marsh	2
Edw. Arden	1
Nicholas Marsh	1
John Ashbury	1
mr Thomas Taylor	4
Rob. Hardey	4
Roger Richardson	2
nicholas Redfearne	2
Tho. Hill	2 Cr
Will. Walker	1
Rob. Butcher	1
Will. Outerm	1
John Rogers	1
Rich. Bennett	1
Widd. Hobb.	1
Ralph Pickerue	2
Will. Colgreave	1
Widd. Moore	1
Rich. White	2
Rob. Foxe	1
John Bomford	1
Will. Richardson	1
Rob. stauley	3
Ben. Gesling	3
Fran. Butcher	1

Will. Taberner	1
Godfrey Richardson	1
Widd. Rogers	1
Godfrey Flint	1

(67)

Ralph Richardson	1
Richard shawe	1
John sales	3
Fran. Rogeres	2
widd. silvester	1
Will. scales	1
Rob. Lawrence	2
John Tompson	1
Rich. Turner	1
Rob. Naylor	1
John Chapman	1
Hen. Fearne	1
Widd. Brett	2
John Glossoppe	2
Will. Watkinson	2
Edw. Haslam	4
James Mettam	2
Rob. Alwood	2
Peter Bigerstafe	1
Tho. Noble	1
*Godfrey s...nes	...*
	noth
	£ s d
harths 131 is (the 11 has been altered to 13)	6.11.00

Pleasley & Langwith

Mr Leggatt Recto.	4
Rich. Catlin	1
Will. Allen	1
John Matley	1
Widd. Flinton	2
Rob. Thorpe	1
Rob. swincoe	2
James Potter	1
John Longman	2
Widd. Godber	1
Widd. Bankes	1
Curtis Turner	2
Will. Halton	1 noth

(68)

Jeffery ?Vrine	1 Reto
Will. Deane	1
Will. Dodge	1
Widd. syddane	1
Rob. Cooke	1
Roger Farmer	1
Will syddwell	1
Rob. Clay	1
mrs Stuffin	3
John Buttry	2
Roger Wood	1
Mathew Heath	1
Rich Clayton	2
Rich. Barker	3
Tho. Lea	1
Roger Farnsworth ?jun.	1
Mr stuffing	1
John stevenson	2
Fran. Boler	3
Rob. spray	1
Widd. wilson	1
James Renshawe	1
John Cowpe	1
Arthur Barker	1
Peter Wade	1
Widd. Barker	2
Tho. Woolley	1
mr Lupton Curat	3
Fardiand Barlowe	1

Widd. Hatton	1
Tho. Ingoe	1
Will. Vickers	2
Tho. Ardishe	1
James Potter	1
Tho. Frith	1
John syddane	1
Hen. Frith	1

(69)

Tho Mellors	2
John Hughton	1
James Howfindale	1
John Clay	2
Ralph Emuiges	3
Rich Pawson	1
mr Hall	3
mr Pinckney	2
Peter Allen	1
Tho. Binge	1
	£ s
harths 85 is	4.5.0

(the 5 shillings has been altered to 7)

Ounston

mr John Dande	8
mr Fran stevenson	6
mr John Rose	6
mr Ralph Hancocke	5
Ralph Archdale	2
Widdo Chantrey	1
Godfrey Gill	2
Ralph sligh	1
Tho. Jordan Jun.	1
mrs Alics wostenholme	1
Geo. Tabbener	1
Will. Throope	2
Henrey Barker	1
mr Rob. Curtise	2
Godfrey Chantrey	2
Roger Barnes	1
Fran Chantrey	?2
Will. Gill	2
Phillip Barker	1
Robert Browne	1

70

Alice Couper	3
Constance Gill	1
John Rogerse	2
Rob. stevinson	1
Tho Adamson	2
Widd. Lambert	1
James Valles	2
Tho. Jordan sen.	1
Will. Nixson	1
Geo. Trout	1
Tho Outreme	2
John Clarke	3
Rob. Outreme	2
mr Rouland stevinson	3
Hen. Blythe	4
Ralph Bullocke	1
Robert Andrew	1
Peter Turner	2
George Trickitt	1
Widd. Rogers	1
Rob. Penesston	1
Fran. Curtise	2
Peter Greaves	2
John Rennalles	1
	£ s d
harths 89 is	4.9.00

Beighton

Fran. scalles	3
Tho. Allin	1 Cer

mr Tho. Gould	2
mr Lassells	4
Will. scalles	2
Geo. Jessope	1
Geo. Hewitt	3
Tho. Jessope	2

(71)

Nicholas Hallsworth	2
Rich Borras	4
sarah Ellis	1
Will. Lee	1
John Taylor	1
Rob. Taylor	1
Edward Atkin	1
Zachariah Roberts	1
Jane newboune	1
Rossaman Greaves	1
Ralph Greaves	1
nicholas Greaves	2
Will. starbucke	2
Cris. Greaves sen.	2
Will. Richardson	1
Rob. Rodthwell	1
Rob. shirte	2
Fran. Linley	1
Widd. staniford	1
Widd. Hobson	2
Epiphamus Rose	2
Rob. Warde	2
Johnathanan Greaves	2
Natha. Greaves	2
Rob. stanfeild	2
Ralph Wright sen.	1
Ralph Wright Jun.	1
Widd. Law	2
Godfrey Morton	2
Hen. Hobson sen.	1
Cris Greene Jun.	1 Reto
Lucke Ward	1 Cer
Geo. Andrew	1 Ret

(72)

Geo. Haslehorst	2
John Beney	1
Natha. Creswicke	1
Nichlos Mitchell	1
Will. staniforth	1
John Newbould	6
Richard & Robeart Taylor	4
Rob. staniforth	1
seath shipley	2
John Turner	1
John Creswicke	1
seath Boler	1
Tho. moore	1
Edward Bee	4
Mary newbould	2
Will. Otewell	1
Hen. Hobson Jun.	2
John Allen	2
Rob. Hurst	2
Tho. Hurst	1
Rob. smedley	1
Will. Foxe	1
Widd. Foxe	2
Beaghton Millnes	1
Will. Greene waltethorp	1
	£ s d
harths 106 is	*5. 6.0*
	5-12-0

(73)

Balbrough

Frances Roades Borronett	21
Allin Lockhard Esq.	12
mr Brocklehurst	6
mr Ashe	7

mr Marples	6
mr Clayton	8
mr Huitt	8
John slater	3
Rob. Boweman	5
Will. Johnson sen.	2
John stansall	4
Rob. Parr	1
John Milner	2
Rob. Renshall	1
John Thornelly	1
Jarvice shells	1
Rich. Rogers	1
Widd. Holmes	3
Geo. Parr	1
John Fisher	1
Will. Bright	1
Geo. Machen	1
Edward Kent	4
Tho. Jepson	1
Ralph Wood	1
Will. Lethwicke	1
Will. shawe	2
Godfrey Godley	1
Godfrey Machen	2
Valentine Pattison	2
sam. Ingman	1 Reto
Adam Ludlam	1
Fran. Machen	1
Rich. stones	1
Widd. Bately	1

(74)

John Calowe	1
Rob. Rotherham	1
Tho. Chambers	2
mr Nornebell	2
John Chambers	2
Widdo. slater	4
Jarvies stansall	1
solomon slater	1
George Geme	2
Humphrey Key	1
John Pilkinton	2
Widdo. Quottingrave	1
Will. Johnson Jun.	2
James Golland	3
John Clarke	1
Martin siddall	1
Frances Milner	2
George Feepound	1
Richard Belke	1
	£ s
harths 125 (sic) is	7.5.00

(the 5 shillings has been altered to 6)

stretton

samuell wheatcroft	4
John Marriott	1
Ja. Bennet & will. Revell	3
John Johnson	2
Mathew *Webster* Brelsford	1
Widdo Webster	2
Will. shawe	1
John Bowne	1
John Curtise	4
Huyh Wright	1
Edw. Wright	1

(75)

James Turner	1
Fran. Fidler	1
Tho Fidler	2
John Revell	1
Tho. willshawe	1
Peter Ellott	1
Clement smith	2

Laurence Bunding	1
Rich. Glewe	1
Hen. Aldam	1
Cris. Wasse	1
Rich. Milward	1
James Hawksley Jun.	1
James Hawksley sen.	1
Hen. Wasse	1
Geo. Hawksley sen.	1
John Hall	2
Geo. Hawksley Jun.	1
Rob. Cowlishawe	1
Jer. Higgenbotham	1
Tho. Cowlishawe	1
Hen. Cowlishawe	1
Ralph Wasse	1
Rob. Wood	1
Geo. smith	1
Dainell Hall	2
John Beighton	1
Tho. Beighton	1
Edw. Hall	2
Tho. Fouke	1
Rich. Hollilley	2
Mathew Hopkinson	1
Will. Milnes	1
John stoppert	1
Tho. Jackson	1
Geo. Brunt	1

(76)

Rob. Hearnshawe	1
Edward north	1
Will. Hill	1
Rich. Motershawe	3
Peter Redgate	1
Will. Wheatecroft	2
Fran. Folgambe	1
Rich. Hawkesley	1
John Bennet	2
John Barker	1
Jane Lowe	1
Tho. Lee	1
Geo. yeaild	1
John Emorey	1
Ralph Cutt	1
John Watson	1
Edward Bradshawe	1
Will. Blythe	3
Fran. Catton	3
Hen. Purslowe	1
Will. webster	1
Rob. Cowlishawe	1
Hen. Cowlishawe	1
Antho. Ragge	1
Archelus Brelsford	4
John Flecher	1
John Dakin	1
John Mosley	1
John Brailsford	3
steph. Beeley	1
Tho Hopkinson	1
Fran. Foxe	1
Antho Foxe	1
Geo. Bleyth	1
the Ex. of Will. Milward	1
Roger Clarke	1

(77)

Geo. Hopkinson	1
Edward Cantrell	1
Will. Revell	1
	£ s
harths 115 is	5.15.00

(78)

steanesby & Heath

Earle of Devenshire	114

Hen. Pearepynt Esq.	48
mr Tho Breilsford	4
mr Derrey	8
John Oldam	2
Tho. Alstrey	2
Rich. Limbe	1
Hen. Damport	1
Widdo Trout	1
John Clay	1
Rich. Hatton	1
Rob. Peace	1
Will. Claton	1
Widdo. Fox	1
Widdo. Parkin	1
Rich. nuttall	2
Will. Clay	2
John Fisher	1
Hen. Coope	1
Widdo Wilgoose	1
James Hardwicke	1
John Fretwell	3
Will. shipley	1
John stones	2
John Kent	1
John Tagg	1
Widdo Towendrowe	2
mr Wayne	4
Tho. Bredshall	2
Widdo Hardwicke	1
mr Nevill	1
mr Rishton	4
mr P...le	8
Tho. Godbere	4
Roger Hill	7
Will. Watkinson	2
Lenard Tomson	1

(one page blank)

(79)

(headed 80)

Tho. Wright	1
John Wright	1
John Bakon	1
Nath. Bakon	1
Ben. Laming	1
Rich Jepson	3
Widdo Hawe	1
Will. Browne	2
Rich. ?Howdin (?Lowdin)	1
Will. Peson	1
Adam Hallam	1
Will. Hardwicke	1
Rich. Hardwicke	1
Tho. Fearnely	1
John Bakon	1
Hen. Whitworth	1
Will. Clay	2
Arthur smith	2
Rich. Hasllam	1
James Tomson	1
Widdo Fretwell	1
Edw. marshall	2
Tho. Jeffrey	1
Ralph Whittacker	1
John Whitworth	2
John Dixon	1
Will. smith	2

Will. Hardwicke &
John Hardwicke &
Rich sanders &
Will. smith
the Earle of Devensheares
Tenantes & all decreases

274 hearths

£ s
13.14.00

(one page blank)

80

Hounsfeild

mr Tho. Wright	8
Rich. Sikes	3
Godfrey Sikes	2
Fran. Hugill	1
James Brumheade	1
Henry Wostenholme	1
Antho. Barker	1
Ralph Newton	2
Widdow Shawe	1 Nothing
Rich. Broadhead	1 Not.
Hugh Sleigh	2
Henry Peirson	1
Jno. Greene	1
Matt. Roberts	4
Rich. Hartly	2
Widdow *Jackson* Gaskoyn	1
Widd. Ragg	2
Jno. Roberts	3
James Brumheade	1
Ed. Sudbury	5
Will. Outrem	2
Geo. Moore	4
Will. Mosley	1
Tho. Marshe	1
Robt Swifte	1
Antho. Bothom	1
Geo. Swifte	2
Widd. Wright	2
Jno. Oliver	1
Widd. Wostenholme	1
Jno. Wilson	1
Widd. Brelsford	2
Widd. Whostenholme	4
Henry Peirson	2
Robt Barker	2
Godfrey Webster	1 *2 one de
Tho. Brelsford	1
Fran. Lee	1
Arthur Ingmanthorpe	1
Tho. Burton Esq.	12
Robt More	3
Tho. Wilson	2
Ed. shawe	2
Rich. Mower	2

(one page blank)

(81)

Geo. Haywood	1
Robt Keay	2
Arthur Watts	1
Reginald Thorpe	8
mrs Whosteholme	8
Jno. Greene	1
Widd. Ingmanthorpe	1
mr Mich. Burton	4
Robt Mower	5
Tho. Hattersly	1
Henry Barker	1
Widd. Key	1
Michaell Keay	1
Will. Keay	1
Jno. Holmes	2
Rich. Kitchen	4
Tho. Rushen	1
Geo. Tayler	1
Godfrey Dam	1
Widd. ?Parker	1
Jno. Stephenson	1
Godfrey Dam ju.	1
	142 hearths
	£ s d
	7.2.0

(the 2 shillings has been

altered to 3)

(one page blank)

(82)

Barlowe Hamlett

Will. Adawson	3
Robt Mower	5
Elizabeth Plomtree	1
Widd. Peirson	1
Widdow Brumhead	3
Robert Jowett	2
Robt Trickett	1
Tho. Wilson	1
Walter Simpson	2
Tho. Nayler	2
Tho. Bee	2
Geo. Newton	2
Godfrey Ragge	1
Jno. Lowe	1
	27 hearths
	£
	1.7.0
	£ s d
Totall	240.16.00

(the 16 has apparently been written over a 7)

83

Elmton & Creswell

Oliver Woodhead sen.	2
Jno. Woodhead	2
Oliver Woodhead ju.	1
Ed. Woodheade	1
Fran. Butcher	1
Robt Haugue	2
Tho. Newbould	1
Ed. Robinson	1
Jno. Carline	1
Nicho. Archer	1
Rich. Butcher	1
Jno. Wilson	1
Tho. Baker	2
Will. Tue	1
Ed. Bell	1
Oliver Baker	3
Geo. Shorte	1
Widd. Sherson	1
John Mason	1
James Smith	1
Jno. Carter	1
Widd. Kempe	1
Tho. Smith sen.	1
Widdow Bullivant	1
Fran. Smith	1
Antho. Smith	1
Mary Roades	1
Tho. Sidday	1
Robt Foulds	1
Henry Baker	2
Hugh Sissons	1
Fran. Bell	1
	39 hearths
	£ s
	1.19.0

WIRKSWORTH HUNDRED

1670

Derby Public Library, Derbyshire Collection, DC 9953

(Title page)

Hundred of Wirkesworth

Micha(elma)s 1670

John Wheeldon

Hearth money

1

Derb. Ashbourne

Wircksworth Wappentake

The number of Fyre Harths

one halfe years duty ended at

Michalmas 1670

Ashborne

Will. Osborne	4	
Henry Smith	2	
Mr Brookes for Robt Port	1	
Will. Collwich	1	
Susanna Hopwood	2	
Rich. Dutton	1	
Jahn Hawksworth	1	Ret
George Hasken	2	
Isaac Shipley	2	
Mr John Buxton	8	
Mathew Scrips	2	
John Jackson	3	
Mr John Heanes	1	Ret
John Holland	1	
Gervas Hollis	2	
George Woodward	2	
John Port	2	
Tho. Corden	1	Ret
Henry Wright	1	
John Walker	4	
Robt Allcocke	1	
Widd. Buxton	1	
Richard Peach	1	
Edward Manlove Esq.	5	
Tho. Allsopp	4	
Arthur Hollinworth	2	
Tho. Watson	4	
George Webster	1	
Mr Henry Kniveton	7	
Widd. Hunt	1	
Barnyby Hall	2	
Tho. Brassington	1	
John Cockayne	1	
Widd. Webster	3	
Will. Lewis	1	
Mr Edw. Pegg Esq.	10	

2

Mr Tho. Goodread	4
Widd. Hewson	2
Free Schoole	2
Tho. Smith	2
Humphrey smalpage	1
Widd. Drakfield	3
John Hollinworth	3
Will. Froggat	3
Will. Jones	1
Richard Titterton	1
Will. Bradshaw	1
Henry Adams	2
Sidney Soare	1
Will. Smith	2
Robt Watson	1
Francis Hall	3
Will. Hewson	1

Mr Antho. Eaton	4
Will. Yates	2
Mary Yates	1
Widd. Moult	3
Humphrey Manifold	3
Rich. Watson	2
Tho. James	3
Mary Allen	3
Robt Yates	3
Baswell Dixwell (?Dipwell)	1
John Askew	3
Tho. Watson	4
John Hall	3
Tho. Rollins	3
Mr Abram Cade	2
Mr Charles Holmes	4
Widd. Pegg	2
John Atkins	1
John Hurd	1
Will. Froggat mercer	2
Tho. Harrisson	1
George Birckcumshire	3
Michall Offley	1
Mr Ben. Talor	6

3

Widd. Parker	3
Will. Burgaine	3
Josephe sheldon	4
George Bowne	1
Tho. Bridgs	1
Will. Cantrell	1
Richard Bentley	3
Tho. Tomlinson	2
George Cowper	2
George Wood	5
Mrs Fowler	5
Tho. Allsopp	1
Will. Brunt	2
Tho. sheapey	6
Mrs Sleigh	6
Will. Bradshaw	1
Richard Morrise	3
Humphrey Wall	2
Daniell Morley	1
Mr Bagguley	2
Gilbert Swift	2
Will. Dikenson	1
Robt Sholto	4
Tho. Browne	1
Robt Buxton	2
Widd. Cundey	2
George Buxton	2
Widd. Cowper	2
Mathew Lancaster	1
Adam Hawksworth	1
Robt Wagg	1
Will. Stanfield	3
Mrs Taylors void house	3
Sammuell Hunt	2
Tho. Jeffrey	2
Will. Chadwicke	3
Mr Charles Holmes	2
Will. Titterton	3
Jonathan sheldon	1
Richard Adamson	3
John Barnes	2

4

Renold Mattisson	1
Will. Allsop	1
Tho. Hill	1
Thomas Moult	1
Samuell Moule	1
Widd. Marple	3
Tho. Kirtland	1
Tho. Brids	1 Ret

Balydon

Mr Rogger Hurt	4	
George Hambleton	1	
Richard Harvey	1	
Abram Hampson	1	
Stephen Dennis	1	
Tho. slacke	1	
Stephen Dennis sen.	1	
Robt Bagshaw	1	
Nicolas Smith	1	
Jo. Fearnehough	1	
Aurthur Dennis	1	
Henry Elts	1	
John Webster	1	
Will. Webster	1	
John Ward	1	
George Webster	1	
Will. Ensor & John Bateman for Jo. Taylor	1	
Ann Lane	1	
John Rooe	1	
Andrew Fearnehough	1	
John Bateman	1	

5

Brassington and Aldwarke

John Thacker	1	
George Tarr	1	
Robt Allsop	2	
Will. Wheeldon	1	
John Bacon	1	
Will. ?Laine	1	
Edw. Kircke	1	Ret
Robt Waine	1	
Edw. Knowles	2	
Tho. Lane	1	
Andrew Lane	1	
Will. Toplis	1	
Richard Knoles	2	
Will Rippond	1	
George Godbeheare	1	
George Lea	1	
Mr Rich. Buxton	5	
Henry Belfit	1	
German Buxton	4	
Ann Lane	4	
Henry Trevis	3	
John Allsop	1	
Robt Allsop	1	
Will. Charkon	1	
Mr Westerne	4	
Godfrey Haugh	1	
Henry Buxton	1	
Raphe Brunt	5	
Rich. Walton	1	
Daniell Bagshaw	1	
Rich. Gretton	1	
Tho. Johnson	1	
Will. Allsop	1	
Henry spenser	1	

6

Anthony Coates	1	
Robt Gretton	1	
Mr Blackwall	4	
Widd. Lane	2	Ret
Richard Goodwin	3	
John Madder	1	
John Briddon	1	
Francis Mosley	1	
George Hodkinson	1	
Gervas Buxton	1	
Joseph Caudale	1	
Andrew Wayne	1	
George Mosley	1	
John Caudale	1	
Will.Charton	1	
Richard Gretorax	1	

Will. Stone	1
John Hawsey	1
Will. Allcocke	1
James Shipley	1
George Stone	1

Fenny Bentley

Mrs Basford	8
Mr Will. Bott	2
Tho. Gretorax	1
John Keellinge	1
Rogger Wheeldon	1
Henry Elliot	2
Tho. Gilman	1
*John Wheeldon	1 ?nihill*
John Marple	1
Tho. Waterffall	5
John Keewood	3
Henry Elliot for Mr Dixwell (?Dipwell)	2
Richard Allen	2
James Harrison	1
Widd. Allsop	2

7

Widd. James	2
Richard Winckle	1
Tho. Ratclife	1
Widd. Frost	1
George Griffin	2

Calow & Ible

Mr Will. Keys	3
Michall Keys	2
John Gretorax	3
Antho. Gretorax	2
Robt Gretorax	2
John Riddyard	1
John Cowper	2
John Toplis	2
James Storrer	3
Anthony Gretorax	2
Mr George Hopkinson	3
Will. Younge	1
George Hopkinson Jnr	1
Edw. Butler	1
John Eginton	1
Tho. Lea	1
Tho. spencer	1
Grace White	1
Will. Langdon	1
Edmund Gretorax	1
Rich. Wigley	1
Dorothy Fearne	1 Ret

Hognoston

Robt Annable	1
John Allsop	2
Will. Elliot	1
Widd. Johnson	1

8

Godffrey Dethicke	1
Will Cockayne	5
Tho. Allsop	1
Tho. Bradley	1
Will. Jesop	3
Tho. Millington	1
Dorothy Allsopp	1
*Rich. ?Hand	1*
Will.Cockayne Jun.	1
Robt Jenney	1
Henry Buxton	3
Tho. Warrington	1
John Millington	1
Edw. Hurd	1
Row. Millington	1
Widd. Gilbert	1

Raphe Smith	1
Mr Allsop	1
Tho. Webster	1
Antho. Bradshaw	1
Row. Allsop	1
Tho. Langdon	1
Mr John Slator	3
Daniell Stone	2
Tho. Allsop	1

Midleton & Smerrill

Midleton Hall	1
Mr John Basford	4
Robt Bateman Gent.	6
Tho. Garret	2
Francis Garret	2
Nicolas Blackwall	1
George Ridiard	2
Will. Hall	1
Widd. Botham	1

9

Will. Melland	2
Will. Buxton	1
Widd. Marple	3
Humphrey Rowland	1
Widd. Riddiard	2
Gyles shingleton	1
Will. Ball	1
Widd. Botham	1
Hugh Bowme	1
John Brunt	1
Francis Smedley Jun.	1
Mathew Latham	1
Tho. Smedley	2
Christopher Daffin	1
Widd. Buxton	1
Will. Slator	1
Francis smedley sen.	1
Will. Parker	1
George Slator	1
Will. Frost	1
Will. Low	1
George Tomlinson	1
George Hardey	1
Henry Hardey	1
John Cottrell	1
John Sellars	1
George Wright	1
Tho. Hardey	1
Edw. Hollinworth	1
Robt Hardey	1

Midleton & Crumfford

10

Daniell Dale	1 Ret
Midleton Hall	6
Robert Spencer	1
Mary Spencer widd.	1
Tho. Bowre	1
Tho. spencer of the Ash	1
Tho. Spencer Jun.	1
Will. Spencer	1
Tho. Booth	1
Will. Adams	1
John spencer	1
Tho. Spencer slate house	1
John Tompson	1
Ann Hall	1
Edmund Spencer	1
Tho. Holehouse	1
Tho. Steere	1
Mathew Topham	1
Francis Spencer	1
Edmund Wigley	1
Ann spencer	1
Jo. spencer towne end	1

Jo. Spencer	1
Will. Wigley	1
Antho. Gell	1
Tho. Gell	1
Mr John Creswell	8
Tho. Summers	1
Adam Plats	1
Sisilla Godbeheare	1
George Smedley	1
George Hudson	2
Tho. Tumpson	1
John Lummas	1

<u>11</u>

Richard Rowse	1
Widd. Rowse	1
Tho Highton	1
Tho. Godbehere	1
Will. Roper	2
John Woodhouse	1
Tho. Wagstaffe Jun.	1
John Roper	1
Edward Banks	1
Widd. Bancks	1
Edw. Woollance	1
Widd. Cottrell	1
George Woodhouse	1
Antho. Godbeheare	2
Edw. Wort	1
George Killar	1
Jesper Holmes	1
Tho. Spencer	3
Anthony Weston	2
James Hall	1
Antho. Debancks	3
Tho. Godbehere	1
Will. Carmell	1
John Cates	2
John Toplis	1
Mary Schednes	1
Edward Roper	1
Anthony Highton	1
John Annable	3

<u>12</u>

<u>Dethicke Tansley & Lea</u>

John Statham	5
Sam. Houghe	5
Tho. Allen	2
Richard Marshall	5
Rich. Edges	1
Adam Knowles	1
Will. Roper	1
Nathaniell Bingham	1
Allexander Duffield	1
Natha. Whitington	1
Henry Statham	3
Will. Prime	1
Hughe Marshall	1
Robt Buntinge	2
Antho. Sowter	1
Tho. Heawood	2
Will. Johnson	1
Will. Marshall	1
John Clarke	1
Tho. Booth	3
Rich. Marshall	5
Tho. Slator	3
Francis Broockshaw	2
Robt Allen	2
Will. Wild	2
Robt Greensmith	1
John Buxton	1
John Nuttall	1
John Orme	1
George Flint	1
Tho. Allen of Lea	1

13

Widd. Bunton	1	
George Bolsover	1	
Francis Allen	1	
Elizabeth Burton	1	
George Flint of Howay	1	
Alice Allen	1	
John Coates	3	
Godfrey Eginton	1	
Henry Beardmore	1	
Tho. Edges	1	

Parwich

John Tomlinson	1	
John Allsop	1	Ret
Will. Beresford	3	
John Darrington	1	
Tho. Allsop	1	
Rich. Leeke	1	Ret
Josephe Basset	1	
Mr Will. Allsop	2	
*John Leake	1	C*
Edw. Creswell	1	
Tho. Creswell	1	
George Gould	1	
Henry Gibbon	1	
Tho. Gould Jun.	1	
Elizabeth Rowe	1	
Robert Ensor	2	
Will. Mellor for Hayes house	1	
Tho. Gould	1	
George Rooe	1	

14

Will. Needham	1	
?Maxim Watson	1	
Antho. Swindle	1	
John Tomlinson	1	
Tho. Gould	1	
George Brownson	2	
Thomas Eyley	1	
John Allsop	1	
Richard Sutton	1	
Tho. Dakin	2	
Elizabeth Gould	1	
Sam. Dakin	1	
Antho. Wright	1	
Will. Millington	1	
Tho. Millington	1	
John Basford	1	Ret
Tho Ball	1	
Ann Dakin	1	
Will. Tomlinson	2	
Mr Leeminge	6	
Mr Dale	4	
John Dakin	2	
Richard Swindle	1	

15

Bonsall

Mrs Dorothy Hopkinson	5
Mr Edw. Poole	5
Will. Killar	1
Will. Hardinge	1
Rich. Chadwicke	1
James Wooddise	1
Anthony Madder	1
Will. Gretorax	2
John Frost	1
John Abell	4
Widd. Strut	3
George Wood	1
George Renshaw	1
Nicolas Barker	1
Widd. Fearne	4
Raphe Marple	2
Mary Holehouse	1
Will. Shaw	1

Antho. Brunt	1
Henry Gretorax	2
Antho. Wooddise	1
Tho. Henstocke	1
Peter Rawlin	2
John Ragg	1
Robert Hall	1
Henry Elce	2
Will. shaw Jun.	3
Antho Gretorax	1
Edw. Harding	2
Tho. Marple	2

16

Will. Holehouse	1
Edward Wooddise	1
Widd. Greensmith	1
Widd. Wigley	1
Will. Wooddise	1
George Downes	2
German Greatorax	1
John Needham	1
John Marple	1
Robt Fearne	5
Henry Hill	3
John Dudley	1
Adam Holehouse	1 C
Henry Bowne	1
Will. Young	2
George Bowne	4
Henry Hardinge	1
Will. Hill	1
Will. Madder	1
Widd. Wooddise	1 C
Will. Cope	1
Robert Brittayne	4
Ellen Browne	1
John Elliot	1
Sam. Clarke	1

Rich Elce	1
Will. Reignes	1
Tho. Hasleam	2
Abram Browne	1
Tho. Greene	1
Edmund Killar	1
David Buckley	1
Wid. ?Flixon	1

17

Antho. Elliot	1
Tho. Downes	1
Henry Marple	1
Tho. Smedley	1
Robt Madder	1
Henry Massey	1
John Halehouse	1
Leanord Swallow	1
James Bollington	1
Will. ?Flixen	1
Francis Worthy	1
Tho. Chapman	1
Aurthur Hasleam	nothing
Widd. Marple	1
Adam Smedley	1
Elizabeth Beastoll	1
Edward Beastoll	1
Will. Beastoll	1
Tho. Worthy	1
George Madder	1
Antho. Simson	1
Edw. Needham	1
Nicolas Chadwicke	1
Edw. smedley Jun.	1
Will. Low	1
Raphe Kirtland	1
Mr Tho. Hardinge	3
Tho. Elce	2
Edw. smedley	1

Humphrey Chadwicke	1	
Henry Cooke	1	

18

Henry Wooddise	1	
Agnes Woodise	1	
Will. Massey	1	
Will. Gratton	1	
Widd. Prophet	1	
George Gratton	1	
Elizabeth Greensmith	1	
George White	2	
Tho. Eaton	1	

19

Hartington

Mr Bateman for his house at Pilsbury	1	
Tho. Harvey	2	
Nicolas Carder	1	
Mr John Bateman	8	
Mr Woodhouse	4	
Tho Milward	1	
Francis Hill	1	
Richard Bateman	1	
Widd. Ann Bateman	1	Ret
Tho. Brunley	1	
Raphe ?Croswaie	1	
Will. Lummas	1	
James Bateman	1	
Hugh Goodwin for Twycrose house	1	Ret
Tho. Stadon	1	
Richard Hardey	1	
Widd. Toplis	1	
Richard Ensor	2	
James Sleigh	2	
John Robinson	1	
Will. Ensor	1	
Edw. Longson	2	
Tho. Stearndale	1	
Phillip Wheeldon	1	
Henry Wheeldon	1	Ret
Widd. Goodwin	1	
Tho. Harrison	3	
Tho Stearndale	1	
Will. Goodwin	1	

20

Gervas Ward	1	
John Shoare	1	
Mr Nadin	1	
Tho. Bateman	2	
Richard Milward	1	
Widd. Grace Wood	1	
John Hardinge	1	
George Bullocke	1	
Will. Yate	1	
Sam. Howsley	1	
Richard Carr	1	
Rich. Ensor for Beach house	1	Ret
Will. Harrison	2	
Aurthur Heathcoate	1	
John Harrisson	1	
Henry Lummas	4	
Gervas Needham	1	
George Readfearne	1	
Will. Fletcher	1	
Will. Swindle	1	
John Fletcher	1	
Richard Swindle	1	
Tho. Stadon	1	
Tho. Roggers	1	
Edw. Goodwin	1	
John Roggers	1	
Will. Roggers	1	
Will. Wilson	1	
Will. Harrison	1	
Raphe Stearndale	1	

Humphrey Buxton	1	
Antho. Hyde	1	
Will. Melland	2	
Raphe Wayne	1	

<u>21</u>

Raphe Steveston	1	
George Wheeldon	2	
Raphe Steardale	3	
Robt Stearndale	1	
Robt Wheeldon	1	
Richard Wheeldon	1	
John White	2	
Will. Sleigh	1	
John Needham	2	
Widd. Bosley	1	
John Sleigh	1	Ret
Edw. Ensor	1	
Will. Melland	2	
Tho. Lummas	3	
Tho. Wooddis	1	
Mr Bruarton	5	
Joseph Goodwin	4	
John Froggat	2	
Humphrey Goodwin	2	
Richard Froggat	1	
Will. Brunt	1	
James Ball	1	
Raphe Newton	1	
Robt Needham	1	
Will. Goodwin	1	
*Humphrey ..	1	Ret*
Raphe Heathcoate	1	
Edw. Lummas	1	
Henrie Lummas	1	
George Lummas	1	
Humphrey Needham	2	
Aurthur Wardle	2	
Francis Heathcoate for John Fox	1	Ret
John Knowles	1	

<u>22</u>

Robt Cowper for Mr Dale	1	Ret
John Wheeldon	1	
Mr Rich. Peeters	4	
Robt Newton	1	
John Bradbury	1	
George Ouldfield	1	
George Needham sen.	1	
Edw. Needham	1	
Edw. Needham sen.	1	
Tho Knowles	1	
John Cleaton	1	
Robt Smith	2	
Tho. Knowles Jun.	1	
Tho Needham	1	
John Needham	1	
Nicolas Needham	1	
Will. Wright	1	Ret
Ann Knowles	1	
Huge Brockhurst	1	
Edw. Bennet	1	
Tho. Readfearne	1	
John Geskill	1	
Antho. Hallume	1	
Edw. Brockhurst	2	
Ann Moorewood	1	
Edw. Needham sen.	1	
Will. Wheeldon	2	
John Sellars	1	
Josephe Needham	1	
Anthony Wheeldon	1	

<u>23</u>

John Hudsfieild	1
Lawrence Wardlow	1
Francis Nadin	1
John Brownsart	1

Adam Wilson	1	
Will. Smith	1	Ret
John Nadin	2	
Tho. Lummas	1	
Lawrence Wardle Lee coate	1	
Rich. Readfearne	1	
George Nadin	1	
Tho. Heathcoate	1	
Row. Heathcoate	1	
Andrew Moorewood	1	
Tho. Roggers	3	
Sam. Howsley	1	
Mr Sleigh	7	
Widd. Higton	1	
Tho. Sheene	1	
Widd. Sheene	1	
George Bagshaw	1	
Will. Yate	1	
John Sutton	1	
Tho. Mellor	1	Ret
Tho. Buckley	1	
Tho. Bennet Coate	1	
John Bennet	1	
Will. Latham	1	
Widd. stanley	1	
Will. Allcocke	2	
Charles Fetherstone	1	

24

John Higton	2	
Will. Riddiard	2	
Peter Barker void house	1	
Will. Bonsall	1	
Tho. Latham	2	
Mr Bateman	3	
John Ball	3	
Mr Basford	2	
John Bemet	1	Ret
George Hynd	1	

George *Read*fearne	1	
*Rich. ?Readfearne	1*	
Mr Bateman for Stannige house	1	Ret
Humphrey Langdon	1	
Widd. Mort	2	Ret
Tho. Fearne	1	
Will. Bonsall	1	
Widd. Webster	1	
Tho. Webster	1	
Will. Wooley	1	
John Woolley	1	
Richard Hambleton	3	
Tho. Bagnall	1	
John Milward	1	
Tho. Bateman	1	
John Buxton	1	

25

John Hurd	1	
Will. Buxton	1	
John Carder	1	
Mr Sleigh for Handale	1	
Hugh Woolley	1	Ret

Matlock

Anthony Woolley gent.	10
and for the Milne	1
John Knowles	4
The Parsonage house	5
Mr Henrie Wigley	4
John Wigley	2
John Cockayne	5
John Woolley sen.	3
Adam Woolley	3
Will. steveson	4
George Addams	3
Henry Bowne	1
Widd. Joanes	1
Jo. Bowne Lin tree	2

Antho. Bowne	1	
Widd. Ward	2	
Henry Oxley	1	
Will. Bennet	1	
John Walker	4	
Will. Martin	1	

26

John Ward	3	
Robt Buntinge	1	
George Ogden	1	
John Taylor	1	
Widd. Granger	3	
Thomas Albot	1	
Tho. Ludlam	1	Ret
Henry Ragg	3	
Edw. Henstocke Jun.	1	
George Marshall	1	
Antho. Winfield	1	
James Stone	1	
Tho. Walker	1	
Edmund Walker	1	
Will. Wats	2	
Henry Graynore	1	
Will. Oates	1	
Will. Pidcocke sen.	1	
Will. Pidcocke Jun.	1	
Francis Brockshaw	1	
Tho. Wood	1	
John Oxley	1	
Luce Buntinge	2	
Will. Heath	1	
Anthony Woodward	1	
Robt Tipinge	1	Ret
Tho. Woodward	4	
John Badsley	3	

27

John Smith	2	
Tho. Flint	1	
Sam. Woolley	1	
Christopher Boadon	1	
John Bowden sen.	1	
John Bowden Jun.	2	
Anthony Bollington	2	
Henrie Wooddise	1	
Tho Knowles	1	
Edmund spencer	1	
Antho. Hasleam	1	
Edw. Henstocke sen.	1	
Robt Oates	2	
Will. Turner	2	
Henry Flint	1	
Row. Ragg	2	
Sam. Johnson	1	
Mrs Walker	3	Ret
Francis Columbell	2	
Francis Momford	2	
George Taylor	3	
John Knowles	1	
Henry Bowne Jun.	1	
Antho. Rawson	2	
Joane Oxley	1	
Will. Ash	1	
John Hasleam	2	
Tho. Steere	1	
Robt Cliffe	3	

28

Will. Millington	1	
Henry Allcroft	3	
Will. Addams	1	
John Martin	3	
Widd. Johnes	1	
John Becke	4	
Will. Wright	4	
Antho. Buntinge	2	
Edw. Bradwall	1	

Tho. Bowne	1
Adam Bowne	1
Antho. Taylor	1
Robt Ward	1
Henry Buntinge	1
Stephen Woodden	3
Mathew Prince	1
Rogger Ball	1
Edw. Hasleam	2
Raphe Bowne	3
John Ward	1
Tho. Ward	1
Adam Ragg	1
Henry Perkins	1
Tho. Taylor	1
Adam Thorpe	1
Tho. Marchant	1
Edmund Buntinge	1
Adam Younge	1
Antho. Johnson	1
Will. Buntinge	1

29

Henrie shepard	2
Will. Jackson	1
Tho. Carlile	1
Henrie Lacy	1
Tho. Parker	1
George Bradley	1
Edmund Rawson	3
Tho. Tomkinson	1
Widd. Whitackre	1
Henrie Knowles	1
Widd. Allsop	1
Robt Buntinge	1
Mr Wild	1 increase

Eaton & Allsop

Antho. Allsop Esq.	8
Henrie Mellor	5
George Milward	2
Will. Twycrose	1
Raphe Johnson	5
Tho. Hood	3
Henrie Grace	1
Antho. Johnson	1
Antho. Johnson sen.	1
Tho. Coates	1
George Cleaton	1
John Cleaton	nothinge

30

Wircksworth

Tho. Aspinall	2
Edw. Toplis & Will.	2
John Symes	1
John Moore	1
John Hitchcocke	1
Tho. Lockar	1
James Aspinall	1
Henrie Blunt	2
Robt Buntinge	1
Edward Collinson	1
Martin Tomson sen.	3
Thomas Tompson	2
Anthony Tompson	2
Edw. Smedley	1
Edw. Ragg	2
Anthony Ragg	1
Will. Madder	2
Widd. Whitefield	1
Antho. Higgot	1
George Tomson	2
Tho. Roggers	1
Martin Tomson Jun.	2
John Russell	2
Mr Winfield	2
Edw. Hasleam	3

Tho. Cleator	1
John Booth	2

31

John Topplis	1	
John Armefield	2	
Richard Allsop	1	
Henrie Buxton	1	Ret
Mr Edm. Ford	2	
Maximillian Pott	1	
John Prince	1	
John Brandricke	1	
George Vallance	1	
Widd. Haughton	1	
Anthony Cheadle	1	
John Wood	1	
James Guy	1	
Mrs Molanus	3	
Robt Toplis	2	
James Allen	1	
Will. Allen	1	
John Ashmore	1	
Mr Browne	8	
John Lees	4	
Antho. Allcroft	1	
Antho. Wall	2	
Mr Ballcoose	8	
Will. spencer	1	
Will. Wall	1	
Robt Wright	1	
Mercian Wheatley	1	
Mrs Buxton	1	
Mr Antho. Buntinge	3	
Francis Buntinge	1	

32

Tho. fletcher	2
John Booth	2
John Annable of Cromford voide house	1
Henrie Stone	1
Mr Sam. Clouse	1
John Hales	2
Mr Natha. Parker	1
Ann Botham	6
Mrs Alestry	1
James Wetton	1
Peter Colbourne	1
Richard Bradshaw	1
Antho. Storer	1
Will. Hemas	2
Edw. Alexander	1
Will. Heareinge	1
Henrie Adams	1
Will. Hellowby	2
John Cockayne	2
Edw. Hasleam	1
George Kempe	1
Tho. Richardson	2
Adam Soaresby	1
Francis Bradshaw	2
Robt Phillips	1
Tho. Brandricke	1

33

Tho. Vallance	1
Will. Higgot	2
Hughe Trige	1
John Wheatcroft	3
Tho. Brabrant	1
Tho. Spenser	1
Raphe Steeple	1
John Elloby	3
Robt Wright	1
Robt Sheldon	1
Richard Sheldon	1
Mr Tho. Beigton for his voide house	5
Mr Tho. Beighton	3

Ellen Vallance	1
James Sowter	1
Will. Bingham and Will. Glasebrooke	2
John Winfield	1
Henrie Winfield	1
Ann Clay	2
Tho. Madder	2
John Buxton	5
Edward Wooddise	1
Nicolas Smith	1
Richard Wheatcroft	1
Nicolas Stubs	1
Antho. fletcher	2
James Ragg	1

34

Will. Wheatcroft	1
Raphe Brasill	1
John Shoare	3
Francis Machin	1
Tho. Gregory	3
George Tompson sen.	1
Tho. Swindle	1
Richard Spalton	1
Tho. Brunt	2
Will. Toplis	1
John shawcrose	1
Mrs Henton	1
The Gate house	6
John Heaps	1
Abram Arthur	2
Widd. Crafts	2
Edw. Fogg	1
Tho. Jackson	2
John Greene	2
Sam Kempe	3
Widd. stanley	3
Tho. Holmes	1
Will. fletcher	2
Will. Blackwall	2
Ellen Allsop	1
Antho. Kemp	3
German Buxton	2
William Chrichlow	1

35

John fletcher	2
John Madder	1
Edw. Clay	3
Joseph Band	3
Widd. Higgot	4
Robt Spencer	3
Renold Kimber	1
Robt Ward	1
Tho. Woolley	1
Robt Hunt	4
Mr Creswell	4
Widd. Buxton	1
Richard Steere	4
George summers	1
Will. Greene	4
Henrie Wigley	4
Tho. Wigley	2
Tho. Wigley sen.	2
Miles Becke	1
George Lont	2
Robt North	1
Mr Blackburne void house	1
Mr Swetnam	1
Mr Blackburne	4
Tho Hunttington	1
Antho. Fogg	2
Mr John Botham	2
Tho. Hall	2
Antho. Bradshaw	3
Aurthur Bradshaw	2

36

Widd. Pidcocke	4	
Gervas Jackson	1	
Tho. Newden	1	
Will. fletcher	1	
George Pidcocke	1	
John Sadler	4	
John Ewdall	1	
Andrew Key	1	
James Winckfield	1	
Tho. French	1	
Francis Bealey	1	
Tho. Drakfield	2	
Francis Madder	1	
Will. Barnes	1	
Will. Cadman	1	
Peter Curtis	1	
Will. Sadler	1	Ret
Tho Toplis	1	
Antho. spadman	1	
Widd. Glasbrocke in Dale	2	
Richard Smith	1	
Edw. Vallance	1	Ret
Tho. Wild	2	
Gervas Woodhouse	1	
Francis Hardey	1	
Tho. Bradley sen.	1	
Widd. Glasebrooke	5	

37

Ellen Cunlove	1	
Henrie Hill	1	
Will. Hill	1	
Martin Tompson and Mr Heaps	6	
Francis Willimot	2	
Tho. Garner	1	
Will. Wall	1	
James spencer	2	
Mr Will. Hopkinson	6	
Mrs Focit	2	
George Tompson	4	
Robt Beardsley	2	
Antho. Eaton	5	
Edw. Milward	8	
Edw. Hodghkinson	1	
Law. Toplis	1	Ret
Rogger Sellars	1	
Elizabeth Wheatley	1	
Mrs Buxton Milne house	3	
John Higgot Jun.	1	
Michall Jowet	1	
Widd. fletcher	1	
Raphe Wigley	1	
Dennis Wetton and his Mother	3	
Will. Noton	2	
Edw. Worsley	1	
Mr Robt Carryer	4	
Mr Robt Toplis	3	

38

Toby Spenser	1
Will. Cragg	2
John Higgot sen.	1
George Summers house	1
Mr Manlove	6
Mrs Judith Wigley	1
William Blackwall	2
John Topliss of Blackwall & his brother	4
Ralph Spencer	1
Robert Wall	1
Steeple house	1
Mr Wigley of Wigwall	5
Nathaniel ?Waster	2
John Gregory	1
Ralph Wigley	2
John Wardlow	1

Kirk Ireton

Anthony Stone	4	
Mrs Catesby	4	
Richard Ward	2	
Christopher Sutton	1	
Robert Barlow	1	
Anthony Thacker	1	
Thomas Mellor	1	
Thomas Browne	1	

39

Paul Haughton	1	
John Harrison	1	
Thomas Harrison	2	
Peter Hutchinson	1	
John Blackwall	2	
Thomas Blackwall	4	
John Deane	1	
Mr Moore	4	
Richard Cowper	2	
Richard Cowper Jun.	2	
John Blackwall Jun.	2	
Edward Wambsley	3	
George Dakin	3	
William Smith	2	
William Storrer	4	
Thomas Toppliss	4	
William Mellor	4	
George Dakin	1	
John Toppliss	2	
John Stafford	1	
German Deane	1	
John Heane	2	
John Mellor	1	
George Dakin	2	Ret.
Ralph Higgot	3	
Thomas Blackwall	1	
Anne Beighton	1	
Anthony Blackwall	1	
Edw. Ellot	1	
George Crofts	1	
Thomas Hoone	1	
John Staddord	1	
Samuell Toppliss	2	
William Spencer	1	
John Thacker	1	Ret.
John Wiberley	2	

40

William Storrer	2	
Robert Higgot	2	
John Brunt	1	
Thomas Winfield	2	
John Davenney	1	
Anthony Rippond	1	
George Dakin for Edith Buxtons house	1	Ret.
Richard Thacker	1	

Hopton and Carsington

John Gell Esq.	13	
John Hews	1	
George Steeple	1	
John Hutcheson	3	
William Steeple	1	
John Wheeldon	1	
Ralph Gell	4	Ret.
Mr Stuffinge	4	
Anthony Ford	2	
John Hutcheson	3	
Robert Jackson	1	
Ralph Wood	3	
Mathew Bacon	1	
John Sladen	1	
William Gregory	1	
Edward Peate	2	
John Berisford	2	
William Smedley	1	

Thomas Parker	2
William Higgot	1
Francis Richardson	1
Richard Buxton	4
Abraham Hutcheson	1
Anthony Gell	1

41

Thomas Hutcheson	2
John Ford	1
Henry Ford	2
Anthony Rippond	1
Robert Stone	3
William Booth	3
Edmund Buxton	3
Henry Bealey	1
George Bealey	1
Henry Ashmoore	2
William Taylor	3
John Low	1
Mr Heward	4
Edward Hutcheson	2
Ralph Buxton	1
Wid. Vallance	1

Kniveton Offcoat & Underwood

Mr Josephe Whitehall	6
Mr Tho. Gaunt	4
Mr Sam. Hudson	3
Richard Lea	4
Will. Hurd	1
Robt Litton	2
Francis Barke	2
John Tomlinson	1
Robt Aulton	2
Bryne Bambrdge	1
Raphe Buxton	2
Francis Wibbersley	2
Tho. Frost	1
John Shipley	2

42

Edw. Frost	1
Will. Bagshaw	1
Mris Hurt	1
Robt Downes	4
Tho. Frost	1
Tho. Hood	1
Henrie Cantrell	1
Will. Haugh	1
Richard Lea	1
Henrie Fearne	5
Will. Bambridge	1
Will. Mellor	3
Tho. Johnson	1
Will. Hodghkinson	1
Will. Greenwood	4
George Burds	1
Ellen Burds	1
Richard Trevis	1
Sr Aston Cockayne	21
Mr John Heanes	6
Timothy Greenwood	6
Elizabeth Hancocke	3
George Wilcoxe	2
Water Buxton	2
Henry Taylor	1
Tho Yeomans	1 Ret
Humphrey Haugh	1
Robt Shorthouse	1
Dorothy Bowne	1 Ret
Robt Smith	1

43

Humphrey Sowter	1
Robt Mellor	1
Mode Grimes	1
Robt Hurd	1

Raphe Barnes	1	
John Jackson	1	
Mr Rogger Jackson	2	
Edw. Corden	1	
Humphrey Palmer	1	Ret
Richard Keelinge	1	
Tho. sheldon	1	

<u>Bradburne</u>

Mris Buxton	8	
& for the Milne	1	
The parsonge house	3	
George Hand	1	
Tho Cantrell	1	
Henrie Bradley	2	
Robt Allsop	1	
Francis Buxton	1	
Francis Burton	1	
John Stone	1	
Tho Buxton	1	
George Fearne	1	
James Bennet	1	
Will. Cheshire	1	
James Ouldfield	1	Ret
Tho. Willis	1	
Mathew Taylor	1	
Will. Orme	1	
Tho. Burton	1	Ret

<u>44</u>

Widd. Smedley	1
John Buxton	1

<u>Wensley & Snitterton</u>

John Henry Milward Esq.	14
John Clifton	2
Tho. Tomkinson	1
Agnis shoare	4
Ellen Kinge	2
Richard Burges	2
Tho. shoare	3
Henrie silkstone	1
John Fox	9
John Steere	6
John Adams	1
Nicolas Ward	2
George Low	1
Katherin Allsop	2
Will. Ragg	1
Henrie Walker	3
John Prime	3
Nicolas Eaton	nothinge
Will. Frost	1
Anthony Rushon	3
Robt Holmes sen.	3
Rowland Beastoll	1
James Beastoll	2
John Wall	1
Henrie Wall	1
Robt Reignes	3

<u>45</u>

Anthony Adams	2	
Tho. Adams Jun.	1	
Tho. Adams sen.	1	
John Turnner	1	
Will. Turnner	1	Ret
Rowland Hall	1	
Francis Ashmore	3	
Tho. Allen	1	
John Horton	1	
Will. Vicars	2	
John Stones	1	
George supper	1	
John Oxespringe	3	
Antho. Allsop	4	
Rogger Willimot	3	
George shore	3	

James Adams	1	
Josephe Hurd	1	
Mathew flint	1	
John Silkstone	1	Ret
Ann Adams	1	

Elton

Henry Newton	5	
Will. Ensor	2	
Will. staley	1	
Will. Baker	1	
John Robbinson	1	
Rogger Wallwine	1	
Raphe Haugh	1	

46

Richard Staley	1	
John Marshall	1	
Richard Wardlow	1	
Tho. Robinson	1	
Tho. staley	1	
Widd. Walker	1	
Edw. Botham	2	
Ales Patricke	1	
Francis shipman	1	
Will. Walline	1	
George Hawley	1	
Rogger Walker	1	
Will. Riddiard	1	
Robt Hawley	1	
George Abernathy	2	
John Adams	1	
Tho stone of Ashover a void house	1	Ret
Will. stone	1	
James Roose	1	
Will. stone of Hurst	1	
Tho Frost	1	
Tho. Burds	3	

John Stone	1	
Will. Stone	2	
George smedley	1	Ret
Will. Clarke	1	
Will. Salt	1	

47

Hughe Stone	1
Francis Evans	2
Will. Howson	2
Widd. staley	1
John steeples	3
Richard Stone sen.	1
Tho. Beard	2
Isacc Bridon	1

Tissington

Will. Fitzherbert Esq.	18
John Ensor	2
Will. Needham	1
John Baker	1
Sam. Smith	1
Francis Smith	1
Richard fletcher	1
Tho. Darbyshire	1
John Mellor	1
Robt fletcher	1
Antho. Goodwn sen.	1
Tho. Roggers	1
John Smith	1
Francis Tompson	1
John Bateman	1
John Allsop	1
Tho. Hand	1
John Hand	1
Edw. Fog	1
George Boadon	2
Tho. Johnson	1

48

Richard Readfearne	1
Henrie Woodise	1
Robt Davenney	1
Tho Degg	1
Richard Goodwin	1
Mr Orme	5
Tho. Stubs	1
Mr Wright	4
Will. Smith	1
Antho. Goodwin Jun.	1
John Goodale	1
Tho. Readfearne	2
Will. Pearson	1
Robt Smith	1
John Wheeldon sen.	2
John Wheeldon Jun.	2
Tho. Buxton	1
Nicolas Ball	3
Robt Ensor for the Lea	8
George Taylor	1
Will. Taylor	1

Thorpe & Mapleton.

Sr William Boothby	12
and att Hanson grang	6
Francis Ratcliffe	1
George Webster	1
John Bambridge	1
John Cocke	1
Thomas Clarke	1
Thomas Dakin	1
William Taylor	1
Mr Alex. Hambleton	3

49

William Dods	2
Thomas Greenesmith	2
Willm dods for Rich. Clarke	1
Thomas Stubs	2
Daniel Stubs	1
Tho. Stubs in the hole	1
Edw. Buxton	1
Thomas Bambridge	1
Willm Lees for dakins house	1
Willm Lees	1
Elizabeth Hambleton	2
John Goodwin	2
Henry Fletcher	1
William Salt	1
*Ralph Scoefield	1 Ret*
Richard Langford	1
Ralph Mellor	1
Thomas Plant	1
John Allcocke	1
Ferdinando Brimidgham	2
George Carter	2
*Wid. Bennet	2 Ret*
Richard Carter	1
*Wid. Pearson	1 Ret*
Phillip Tunicliffe	1
John Carter	1
John Maddocke	1
Robert Yates	1 *Ret*
Willm Allcocke	1
*Humphrey Peach	1 Ret*
Phillip Tunicliffe for Mr Trots house	6
Robert Phillips	1
*Robert Smith	2 Ret*
*Wid. Haucksworth	1 Ret*
*Willm Plant	1 Ret*
Wid. Gratton	1 *Ret*

50

Francis Bott	1
George Raworth	1
Rich. Carter webster	1

Newton Grange

Mr Francis Berisford	5
Richard Wagstaffe	1
Henry Marlidge	1

In toto 2453 hearthes

INDEX OF PLACES

INDEX OF PERSONS

Note: A figures in brackets after a page reference indicates the number of times that the name appears on that page.